NORTH UIST

ORKNEY

Stromness

Kirkwall

BENBECULA

Kingsburgh

Portree

SKYE

Rogart

Dornoch

Culloden

Inverness

IONA

Fort William

ARGYLL

SCOTLAND

Aberdeen

ISLAY

ISLE OF GIGHA

Lagavulin Bay

IN D

KINTYRE

ARRAN

Greenock

Glasgow

Renfrew

Kilmarnock

Tarbolton

Mauchline

GALLOWAY

Scone

Perth

Stirling

Bannockburn

Abroath

Dundee

Kirkcaldy

St. Andrews

Firth of Clyde

Mull of Kintyre

Campbelltown

rgus

Alloway

Lanark

Falkirk

Edinburgh

Auckinlech

Ettrick Valley

Abbotsford (Melrose)

Selkirk

Berwick-upon-Tweed

Dumfries

ISLE OF MAN

Ramsey

Douglas

astletown

ENGLAND

ES

N

CELTIC LIGHTNING

NON-FICTION BY KEN MCGOOGAN

50 Canadians Who Changed the World
How the Scots Invented Canada
Race to the Polar Sea
Lady Franklin's Revenge
Ancient Mariner
Fatal Passage
Canada's Undeclared War

CELTIC LIGHTNING

How the Scots and the Irish
Created a Canadian Nation

KEN MCGOOGAN

PATRICK CREAN EDITIONS
HarperCollins*PublishersLtd*

Published by Patrick Crean Editions, an imprint of HarperCollins Publishers Ltd

First edition

HarperCollins books may be purchased for educational, business,
or sales promotional use through our Special Markets Department.

HarperCollins Publishers Ltd
2 Bloor Street East, 20th Floor
Toronto, Ontario, Canada
M4W 1A8

www.harpercollins.ca

Library and Archives Canada Cataloguing in Publication
information is available upon request

ISBN 978-1-44342-550-6

Printed and bound in the United States of America
RRD 9 8 7 6 5 4 3 2 1

For Sheena
(Long may we run)

CONTENTS

CELTIC LIGHTNING

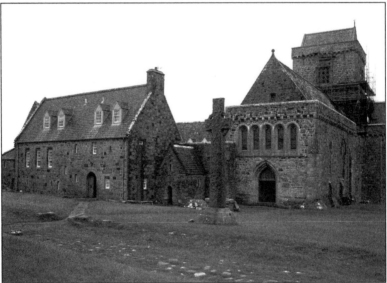

Top: A Celtic cross marks the birthplace of Saint Columba in County Donegal, Ireland. Bottom: In 563, Columba founded a monastery on the Scottish island of Iona, and from there promulgated a literate, Celtic-Christian culture that turned the Irish and the Scots into one people.

A Discovery of Ancestors

Not long ago, while driving with friends in Newfoundland, an Irishman heard a local man caution a third party against stepping out of a car into traffic: "Don't get out on the Ballyhack side." The Irish visitor, astounded, asked the Newfoundlander to explain. The man said the expression meant, "Don't get out on the right." But he had no idea why it meant that or where it came from.

The Irishman, who hailed from New Ross in County Wexford, told him that, for someone travelling the short distance south from his hometown to the coast, the village of Ballyhack lies to the right. Not only that, but the Irishman could account for how the expression had crossed the ocean: generations of fishermen had sailed from New Ross to fish for cod off the Grand Banks of Newfoundland.

The man who told me this anecdote, Patrick Grennan, shares an ancestor with former American president John F. Kennedy. Grennan has developed the original Kennedy Homestead, just outside New Ross, into a tourist attraction. The town itself is home to

8,200 people, and also to the Dunbrody Famine Ship, an authentic reproduction of one of the coffin ships that, in the late 1840s, carried at least 1 million immigrants—some say as many as 2.5 million—to North America.

We had gravitated to New Ross—my wife, Sheena, and I—during one of several rambles around Ireland and Scotland. Having tracked my Scottish Protestant forebears to the Isle of Gigha, and written about that in *How the Scots Invented Canada*, I was on the trail of my Irish Catholic ancestors. One of them, Michael Byrne, had been born in New Ross in 1825—two years after JFK's ancestor Patrick Kennedy. As boys, they must have known each other.

A week or so after visiting New Ross, north up the coast in County Mayo, we visited Westport House, a spectacular country estate built in the 1700s on the site of an ancient castle. We chatted with a staffer in his early twenties who asked if we had any ancestors from Ireland. I said yes: "A man named Byrne, born in New Ross in 1825."

He said, "My name is Byrne."

"My ancestor's first name was Michael."

"That's my name," he said. "Michael Byrne."

"The father of my immigrant ancestor was named Patrick."

"My father's name is Patrick."

I squinted at him: "You're too young to be my ancestor."

Who doesn't love a coincidence? On the other hand, Byrne is the sixth most common surname in Ireland. And a cursory glance at any database of emigrants reveals a jungle of Byrnes named Michael and Patrick. Still, this serendipity made me feel at home, and pointed up the enduring nature of Canada's connections with Ireland.

North Americans in search of their roots quickly realize that an ocean is an artificial barrier. Thanks to advances in digital technology, we cross the water and go back as far as we can: five generations, seven generations, nine. We trace our personal stories to people who lived centuries ago in County Kerry, Kintyre, the Aran Islands. As genealogists, we revel in these discoveries.

Canadian intellectuals tend to fail here. Instead of voyaging with genealogists, who navigate through time and space, they hunker down with geographers and sociologists. They assume geography's limitations and cease investigating our collective past at the edge of the Atlantic Ocean. The end result can only be one-dimensional, paper-thin—a survey of the present. For meaning, substance, depth, and a sense of direction, you need history . . . or what I think of as cultural genealogy. Despite our perpetual obsession with our collective identity, we Canadians have never investigated the demographic reality that informs this book—the fact that more than nine million Canadians claim Scottish or Irish ancestry. Did the ancestors of more than one-quarter of our population arrive without cultural baggage? No history, no values, no vision?

Surely the idea is ridiculous. Canada is not just a geographical land mass. It is a cultural, political, and economic entity. It is a complex web of interconnected governments, businesses, institutions, organizations, and individuals—an interweaving of social, cultural, and communications networks. Canada is a multi-dimensional creation. To the east, Canadian geography finishes at the Atlantic Ocean. But this nation's history crosses that ocean. And it does so more often to Scotland and Ireland than to anywhere else.

Look at the numbers. Canada's population recently exceeded 35 million. But in 2011, out of 32.8 million citizens, Statistics Canada reported 4.7 million Canadians (14.3 per cent) claiming Scottish ancestry, and 4.5 million (13.7 per cent) citing Irish. Those of Scottish and Irish heritage, taken together, constitute the largest minority of Canadians: 28 per cent. That compares with 19.8 per cent English and 15.2 per cent French. Even if a couple of million Scottish and Irish claims overlap, "Celtic" Canadians represent the largest cultural aggregation in the country. These numbers suggest that the Scots and the Irish, many of whom arrived relatively early, must have strongly influenced the shaping of multi-dimensional Canada.

Purists will argue that the two national narratives, the Scottish and the Irish, should properly remain separate. But fifteen hundred years ago, the Irish and the Scots constituted a single people. They were Gaelic-speaking Celts, citizens of the same maritime sphere. They plied regularly between Scotland and Ireland. The arrival of the Vikings, and their eventual integration, only enhanced the turbulent coherence of that seafaring world. By the 1100s, after three centuries of Scandinavian immigration and influence, that maritime culture had become Norse-Gaelic.

Not until the 1100s, when the Anglo-Normans invaded both countries, did the Scots and the Irish begin fighting separate battles for survival. Over the centuries, despite constant interaction, the two related peoples developed distinct national epics, different parades of warriors, scholars, adventurers, pirate queens, and revolutionaries.

But as a Canadian whose ancestors include both Scottish Protestants and Irish Catholics, I perceive in the two traditions more commonalities than differences. In fact, I see a single braided narrative celebrating the same bedrock values. In this book, to encompass that dual history, I use the word "Celtic" in its popular sense, to embrace all things Scottish and Irish. Lightning strikes when the two electrically charged traditions come into contact.

Returning to cultural genealogy, I would draw your attention to a work that surfaced on the *New York Times* list of the one hundred most significant books of 2014: *The Invisible History of the Human Race: How DNA and History Shape Our Identities and Our Futures.* Author Christine Kenneally argues that until recently, no one has "ever tried to systematically measure whether and how culture is transmitted from one generation to another and, if indeed it is, to determine for how many generations it is passed along."

Scientific studies, she adds, are now indicating "that the way we see the world and act in it . . . is significantly shaped by internal beliefs and norms that have been passed down in families and small communities. It seems that these norms are even taken with an individual when he moves to another country."

Kenneally is building on the work of Richard Dawkins. In *The Selfish Gene*, Dawkins coins the word "meme" to describe what Kenneally calls "beliefs and norms." While today the word can suggest a silly photo that has gone viral on the Internet, Dawkins was seeking "a noun that conveys the idea of a unit of cultural transmission, or a unit of imitation." He started with the Greek word *mimeme*, which means "that which is imitated" or copied, and then, wanting a monosyllable that sounds like "gene," he abbreviated that to "meme." These units of human cultural transmission, Dawkins argues, which range from fashions and catchphrases to ideas and values, propagate "by leaping from brain to brain" via written records or even word of mouth. "When you plant a fertile meme in my mind," he adds, you turn it "into a vehicle for the meme's propagation."

Some memes, such as popular songs, don't last long. But others, such as a belief in life after death, Dawkins writes, or "the Jewish religious laws, may continue to propagate themselves for thousands of years." These "idea memes" are subject to mutation and blending, and can also form a "meme complex," or "a co-adapted stable set of mutually assisting memes."

The religious meme complex, for example, includes ideas of God, hellfire, and faith. According to Dawkins, such meme complexes and cultural traits evolve independently of biological genes. Once human beings have "brains that are capable of rapid imitation, the memes will automatically take over . . . [and] exploit the capability to the full."

This book, *Celtic Lightning*, arises out of these ideas. It argues that in Canada's cultural DNA, Quebec excepted, the dominant strain is a double helix rooted in Scotland and Ireland. Why should this be so? Why would certain social, political, and cultural values, certain memes, carried forward by Robert the Bruce, Grace O'Malley, Jonathan Swift, or Flora MacDonald, make their way to Canada? The answer begins with the Double Diaspora, the two waves of emigration that arose as a result of Scotland's Highland Clearances and Ireland's Great Potato Famine.

The clearances happened first. After the Battle of Culloden in 1746, the victorious English sought to eradicate Gaelic culture by banning kilts and bagpipes. Working with Scottish landlords, they evicted tens of thousands of farmers from their ancient family crofts in the Highlands and the Western Isles. Best estimates suggest that some 150,000 people were cleared from their ancestral lands, or almost 60 per cent of the area's population. Many of these farming families emigrated to Canada.

In Ireland, the Great Potato Famine proved even more devastating. When potato blight laid waste to much of Europe in the mid-nineteenth century, the Irish suffered worst because they had been driven to rely mainly on the potato for food. Repeated crop failures spawned the famine. Best estimates are that one million people died of starvation and related diseases. Another million fled Ireland in the late 1840s, and a third million followed in the next decade. Many of these refugees came to Canada.

Yet the Double Diaspora tells just part of the story. Modern scholars have demonstrated that many and perhaps most Scottish and Irish immigrants came to Canada not as a result of the Highland Clearances or the Great Potato Famine, but simply because they sought better lives. Between the late 1700s and the early 1900s, some 2 million Scots left their homeland. Of those who came to Canada, the greatest number—between 370,000 and 400,000— arrived not during the clearances but in the first three decades of the twentieth century. Similarly, in the two decades that preceded the famine, 450,000 Irish moved to Canada. Of the 1.2 million Irish who came between 1825 and 1970, at least half did so in the decades either before or after that terrible watershed.

By global standards, Canada is a young country with a short written history. Within that context, the Scots and the Irish began arriving early enough, and in sufficient numbers, to exert a shaping influence. And they kept on coming through the twentieth century. *Celtic Lightning* argues that, regardless of why they left home, Scottish and Irish immigrants brought matching sets of "memes," or cultural, social, and political values. Those bedrock values, honed through centuries of difficult history, together created a vision of the country in which they wished to live. That country looks a lot like Canada at its best.

❈❈❈

Four decades ago, in *Survival: A Thematic Guide to Canadian Literature*, Margaret Atwood suggested that we Canadians developed a sense of ourselves in response to the vast wilderness around us. She built on the work of earlier scholars, among them Harold Innis and Donald Creighton, who argued that the fur trade made us who we are—that it opened up the country from east to west, scattering trading posts and company towns throughout the northwest.

For some Canadians, the French-English divide remains the defining characteristic of our national identity, the two solitudes having emerged from the duality of our colonial past. Hugh MacLennan gave voice to this view. Pierre Berton, MacLennan's slightly younger contemporary, contended that Canada was shaped by notions of "peace, order, and good government." Today, rejecting that theory, John Ralston Saul argues that Canada is a "Metis nation" that should put aboriginal peoples at the centre of its national narrative.

But wait: a number of academics are now suggesting that any such national approach to Canadian history is outdated and obsolete. In *Contesting Clio's Craft: New Directions and Debates in Canadian History*, emerging scholars argue that the very idea of a "national narrative" is a thing of the past. Personally, I think they are wrong. I believe in the continuing relevance of all those ideas cited above, even if none of them tells the whole story.

What is missing? Cultural genealogy. A sense of continuity. We have forgotten our ancestors, and that we derive from those who shaped our history and heritage. Canadian scholars have written reams about Scottish and Irish immigrants. Historians have explored why and how they sailed and how they fared after they arrived in Canada. But what of those who nurtured and shaped the emigrants before they left home? Did they contribute nothing? *Celtic Lightning* suggests that Scottish and Irish immigrants brought with them certain values and attitudes they had learned from their forebears.

A writer friend reminded me recently that, back in 1991, in a book called *Canada's Undeclared War: Fighting Words from the Literary Trenches*, I insisted that this country has "a culture—a way of thinking and being, a nation-wide set of values and preoccupations—worth defending." The present volume clarifies and advances this proposition. It suggests that, again with Quebec excepted, Canada itself is built upon values that arrived with the Scots and the Irish. And it highlights five of those as foundational: independence, democracy, pluralism, audacity, and perseverance.

How did I settle on these five values or meme complexes and not others? Short answer: a back-and-forth process of trial and error. I did not start with fixed ideas but proceeded inductively. In *The Invisible History of the Human Race*, Christine Kenneally cites recent rigorous scientific studies demonstrating cultural transmission of the values or memes of trust and anti-Semitism. While the latter has an ugly presence in Canadian history, neither of these can be regarded as foundational. Still, Kenneally's examples are illustrative.

Of course, my approach here is not scientific but narrative. One value suggested itself, for example, during our arrival at Inishbofin, a small island off Connemara. I should explain that, in addition to visiting Ireland and Scotland half a dozen times each, and exploring both by car, Sheena and I also circumnavigated both countries with Adventure Canada, a Canadian travel company. Any reference to our voyaging refers to them.

On this occasion, as we rode from our ship to the dock at Inishbofin, eight or nine people to a Zodiac, we passed Dun Grainne, the remains of a fortress used in the 1500s by the legendary Pirate Queen "Grainne" or Grace O'Malley. Born into a powerful west-coast family, O'Malley rejected the traditional roles available to females. She became a skilled sailor, gained control of a merchant fleet, and conducted trade as far away as Africa. Her enemies denounced her as "the most notorious sea captain in Ireland," and complained that she "overstepped the part of womanhood."

It occurred to me that, although contemporary Canada can boast few notorious female sea captains, the country abounds in audacious or "overstepping" women. My last book, *50 Canadians Who Changed the World*, featured more than twenty, among them Margaret Atwood, Naomi Klein, Alice Munro, Irshad Manji, Louise Arbour, Maude Barlow, Joy Kogawa, Deepa Mehta, Michaëlle Jean, Joni Mitchell, Sheila Watt-Cloutier, Samantha Nutt . . . and the list goes on.

But what dawned on me, while riding past Dun Grainne, was that all of these Canadian women, regardless of ethnic origin, could be seen as embodying the same bedrock boldness as the Irish Pirate Queen. And what of Scotland? Flora MacDonald sprang to mind. In 1746, after the Battle of Culloden, she risked her life to save Bonnie Prince Charlie. And what of those courageous women who fought to abolish slavery? As late as 1859, when she was eighty-eight years old, Mary Ann McCracken would stand on the dock at Belfast and hand out anti-slavery leaflets to Irish emigrants. Her Scottish contemporary, the outspoken Eliza Wigham, set aside her lifelong pacifism to support Abraham Lincoln in the American Civil War because he promised to free the slaves. As we piled out of the Zodiac, I knew I had it: O'Malley and MacDonald, McCracken and Wigham—these women were among audacity's ancestors.

Trial and error and narrative: could they produce anything of value? Yes, I decided, and continued casting about for bedrock values. Early on, I looked to Christianity. But a cursory glance at the historical record reminded me that in Canada, as in Scotland and Ireland, Christianity has proven far more divisive than unifying. Catholics versus Protestants? Louis Riel versus the Orange Order? Not foundational. But neither, on the other hand, could I make a compelling case for secularity. So it went, back and forth, round and round.

Of course I recognize that in Canada we can find racism, injustice, greed, misogyny, and systemic discrimination. We have mistreated our aboriginal peoples. We have disgraced ourselves environmentally. But these failures represent Canada at its worst. I was investigating the positive dimension of our collective work-in-progress: what enables us to carry on despite shortcomings, setbacks, and defeats. I sought the attitudes and principles that underlie Canada at its best.

I have suggested that this country is audacious. It is also independent, democratic, pluralistic, and persevering. We Canadians never tire of proclaiming that we act autonomously, regardless of any superpower in the neighbourhood. We react with outrage to any attack on symbols of Canadian democracy. We have written pluralism into our constitution in the form of multiculturalism and individual rights. And we still celebrate, as an iconic example of our never-say-die perseverance, a young man who, having lost a leg to cancer, undertook in 1980 to run across the country on his one remaining leg. This book argues that these Canadian realities can be traced back to Scotland and Ireland.

Celtic Lightning has five parts, one for each bedrock value. Each part focuses on half a dozen pivotal figures, Scottish and Irish role models who profoundly influenced those around them, and also those who came after. Cultural genealogy. Somerled of Argyll. Maria Edgeworth. Adam Smith. Charles Stewart Parnell. Many Canadians have never heard of these figures. Those who have tend to believe that they belong exclusively to Scotland or Ireland. This book argues that they belong also and equally to Canada.

Having shaped the Scots and the Irish, by word and by example, these extraordinary individuals, among them both revolutionaries and political conservatives, worked an even larger miracle. They influenced generations of Canadian immigrants, fostering attitudes, beliefs, and values deeper than any political orientation.

Even new nations do not spring from nothingness. The individuals who loom large in this book came out of Ireland and Scotland. They are new to most Canadians because we have never claimed them. We thought, wrongly, that our history stopped at the Atlantic Ocean. But no matter our individual backgrounds, these Irish and Scottish figures belong to us, because they shaped the bedrock values that Canada embodies.

Think of the early explorers who "discovered" North America. They planted flags and claimed territories on behalf of one monarch or another. The time has come to return the favour. *Celtic Lightning* stakes a claim to a collective heritage. The outstanding figures celebrated here belong to Canada. Having forgotten them for too long, we discover them at last to be our ancestors. They shaped the values on which we have built a Canadian nation.

PART ONE
INDEPENDENCE

Our discovery of Canada's Celtic ancestry begins in Dar es Salaam, Tanzania, where in 1976, for some months, I taught French, grades three to nine, at an international school. This was decades before the digital revolution turned the world into a global village. Twice a week, my wife, Sheena, and I would walk four kilometres each way through stultifying heat to the Canadian consulate to read wire-service stories from home.

The consulate had posters on its office walls, among them three spectacular views of the Rockies, one each of Mount Rundle, Lake Louise, and Emerald Lake. Ridiculous as it sounds, these posters of Banff National Park brought tears to my eyes. But I visited the consulate to read the latest news from home, especially about the rise of the Parti Québécois, which wanted to take Quebec out of Canada. As a Canadian I was feeling homesick and threatened.

And now I came up against an African activist-intellectual, Kofi Buenor Hadjor, who insisted that Canada was not an independent country and never would be. A political exile originally from Ghana, Kofi had been a leading figure in the revolutionary government of the late Kwame Nkrumah, and would go on to write hefty books with titles like *Africa in an Era of Crisis* and *On Transforming*

Africa. He knew a surprising amount about Canada because, in addition to having taken advanced degrees at Stanford and Oxford Universities, he had studied at McGill in Montreal.

This he revealed only later. First, he blindsided me, without intending malice, at the School of Journalism in front of about forty students. He was the school's founding director. I had applied to teach there, and qualified because I had taken a journalism degree at Ryerson and worked as a reporter at the *Toronto Star*. Kofi had invited me to give a trial lecture about journalism in Canada. The classroom was sweltering hot, despite the giant fans whirring overhead. My talk went wonderfully well and the students spontaneously applauded.

But then Kofi picked up a piece of chalk and said that if I had no objection, he would provide a little context. He explained to the class that Canada was not really an independent country. First, it remained subservient to Great Britain, which retained final approval over constitutional amendments. Second, Canada's economy was so closely intertwined with that of the United States that it could never act independently. He drew arrows on the blackboard as he spoke, highlighting American ownership of Canadian oil and gas.

When he was done, Kofi asked if I wished to add anything. I had taken a few Canadian history courses, and poked around on my own, and I managed to respond that British approval under the Statute of Westminster was a mere formality. So Canada was essentially independent of Britain. And as for the Americans, what about the Vietnam War? Canada had refused to participate, and instead welcomed thousands of draft dodgers—surely a gesture demonstrating that, despite our close economic ties to the United States, we could still act independently.

Heading home, I wasn't satisfied with my response. I had said nothing about how, during the American Revolution, when

Benjamin Franklin visited Montreal to seek support for the insur-rection, francophone Quebecers sent him packing. Thanks to the Quebec Act, they already enjoyed more freedom of language and religion than they would as Americans. I had said nothing about how, during the War of 1812, Canadians beat back an American invasion. Or how Confederation was designed specifically to defend against the American doctrine of manifest destiny.

I wasn't satisfied. But a few days later, Kofi offered me the job teaching journalism. I thought it might be more interesting than teaching French to children, and was about to accept when, back in Canada, the Parti Québécois won the provincial election and came to power in Quebec. Having been abroad for a year, suddenly I needed to get home. I declined Kofi's offer and, at the end of the school term, returned to Montreal.

All this came flooding back to me in Ottawa almost four decades later, in May 2012. I was visiting the capital and found myself with a free afternoon. Out for a walk, I passed the Parliament Buildings and realized that, although I was a month late, this was my chance to mark the thirtieth anniversary of Canadian independence: April 17, 1982. That was when Prime Minister Pierre Elliott Trudeau patriated the Canadian constitution, and so the date when Canada became formally independent from Britain.

The House of Commons was not in session. I rode an elevator up into the Peace Tower and made my way to a window looking out over Parliament Hill. Thirty years before, tens of thousands had gathered here to watch Trudeau and Queen Elizabeth sign the Constitution Act in an outdoor ceremony. They were on a stage that had been set up directly below where I now stood watching people come and go in the sunshine.

Before witnessing the queen's signature, Trudeau had given an incisive speech. He observed that Canada "became an indepen-dent country for all practical purposes in 1931, with the passage of the Statute of Westminster. But by our own choice, because of our inability to agree upon an amending formula at that time, we told the British Parliament that we were not ready to break this last colonial link."

With the proclamation of the Constitution Act, Canada not only became independent of Britain but also gained a Charter of Rights and Freedoms that, as Trudeau noted, "defines the kind of country in which we wish to live." That Charter, he added, reinforces minority language rights, upholds the equality of women and the rights of disabled persons, and "recognizes our multicultural character." That last clause, I reflected, announcing the pluralism inherent in the Constitution Act, marked Canada's emergence as the world's first postmodern nation.

As I gazed out over Parliament Hill, I remembered that sweltering afternoon in Dar es Salaam when Kofi Hadjor had insisted that Canada was not an independent country. By now, I thought, surely he would have amended this view. Unaware that he had recently passed after a long illness, I fantasized running into him down below, out front of the Parliament Buildings. I would take him for a beer; why not? Maybe hit the patio at the D'Arcy McGee Pub on Sparks Street.

I would tell him: look, see? Canada's evolutionary approach works. Three decades have passed since Trudeau snapped that last constitutional link with Britain. As for subservience to the United States, we not only went our own way during the Vietnam War, as I told you long ago, but we did so again more recently. In March of 2003, under Prime Minister Jean Chrétien, Canada refused to join an American-led "coalition of the willing" in invading Iraq. Later, looking back, Chrétien told the *Huffington Post*, "We're an independent country, and in fact it was a very good occasion to show our independence."

Quaffing a cold one in the D'Arcy McGee, I would tell Kofi,

yes, Canadians go along and go along. But eventually, we reach a point. This is an independent country, I would tell him. Pushed to the wall, Canadians just say no. We try to be polite about it. But no, we won't take orders from Britain. No, we won't go to war against Vietnam. No, we won't make war on Iraq. Sorry, no. Independence is a bedrock value, I would tell Kofi, maybe pounding the table a bit. A bedrock value we inherited from the Scots and the Irish, courtesy of such figures as Michael Collins, William Wallace, Theobald Wolfe Tone, and Robert the Bruce.

I.

Michael Collins

▨▨▨

We got lost in the dirt roads north of Clonakilty. We were looking, Sheena and I, for the spot where Michael Collins got killed in an ambush. According to historian Tim Pat Coogan, Collins was "the man who made Ireland." For my purposes, he was the man who most clearly embodies Celtic independence in a Canadian mode. Collins represents one of the five bedrock values. Culturally, politically, he is one of Canada's ancestors. I wanted to know more about him. I wanted detail and texture. But first I needed context.

Since 1801, when the Act of Union came into effect, uniting Ireland with Great Britain, the Irish had voted repeatedly to reverse that legislation and renew their independence. But in the British Parliament at Westminster, the Irish representatives were outnumbered five to one, and could make no headway. In the nineteenth century, major rebellions were quashed in 1848 and 1867. But then, in 1916, the Irish Republican Brotherhood organized what would come to be called the Easter Rising. Its objective: political independence.

The First World War had been raging for almost two years. With British forces heavily engaged in Europe, among them a good many Irish troops, roughly 1,200 nationalist volunteers seized key buildings in Dublin. They set up military headquarters in the General Post Office (GPO) in the heart of the city on what is now O'Connell Street. Michael Collins, age twenty-five, had got wind of the impending insurrection in London, where he worked in financial services: white collar, blue pinstriped suit. Having wangled a transfer to join in the uprising, he ended up serving as the aide-de-camp to Joseph Plunkett, one of the principal organizers.

Collins was present when, out front of the GPO, Patrick Pearse read the Proclamation of the Republic—a document now displayed in the front window of that edifice. In part, it says: "We declare the right of the people of Ireland to the ownership of Ireland, and to the unfettered control of Irish destinies, to be sovereign and indefeasible. The long usurpation of that right by a foreign people and government has not extinguished the right . . . In every generation the Irish people have asserted their right to national freedom and sovereignty . . . Standing on that fundamental right and again asserting it in arms in the face of the world, we hereby proclaim the Irish Republic as a Sovereign Independent State."

The document continues, noting that, six times in the last three centuries, the Irish had taken up arms to assert their independence. It declares that Ireland should be a republic, not a monarchy; that this republic would guarantee "religious and civil liberty, equal rights and equal opportunities to all its citizens"; that it would be committed to universal suffrage (women could vote); and that it would treat "all the children of the nation equally." For Collins and his fellow rebels, the reading of that proclamation was the highlight of the Easter Rising.

Initially caught off guard, the British authorities regrouped. Based at Dublin Castle on the other side of the River Liffey, they were less than one kilometre from the post office. Before long, they had more than sixteen thousand well-equipped soldiers in Dublin. The rebels fought fiercely but, partly because so many Irishmen were off fighting on the continent as part of the British army, they attracted few new followers. They inspired no general uprising. After six days of bloody fighting in the streets of the city, they surrendered. More than 450 people had died in the battle: 64 rebels, 132 government troops, and 254 civilians.

The visionary freedom fighter Michael Collins addresses a crowd in Cork on St. Patrick's Day, March 17, 1922. Three months before, on December 6, 1921, Collins had signed an Anglo-Irish treaty promising Ireland "the same constitutional status . . . as the Dominion of Canada." Five months later, he was dead.

Militarily, the Easter Rising was a debacle. The British brought two thousand Irish prisoners, Michael Collins among them, to a gymnasium in Richmond Barracks. By taking advantage of a momentary lapse, Collins managed to shuffle off and blend in among those to be treated leniently. The British then made the mistake of executing sixteen of the rebel leaders, among them the Scottish-born James Connolly, so badly wounded that he had to be tied upright in a chair to be shot. This ruthlessness made martyrs of the rebels and turned many otherwise undecided Irish against the English.

Collins was one of twenty-five hundred Irish prisoners deported to Great Britain. At Frongoch internment camp in Wales, where men slept thirty to a wooden hut, he got himself elected leader of a revolutionary cell. He orchestrated an effective campaign of passive resistance. Also, having seen what happened when rebels occupied buildings, and so became sitting ducks for better-armed forces, he began conducting workshops in guerrilla tactics. Biographer Tim Pat Coogan describes Collins as "the founder of modern guerrilla warfare."

The Irish nationalists had lost the battle of 1916, but the underground war was just beginning. As Frank O'Connor writes in *The Big Fellow*, the detectives had "left behind them the one really dangerous man, the man who in a few short years would kill off the craftiest of them and render the rest so impotent that he would be able to walk the streets of Dublin undisguised."

▩▩

Michael Collins was born in October 1890 at Sam's Cross, seven kilometres west of Clonakilty in southwestern Ireland. The youngest of eight children, he grew up on a ninety-acre farm at nearby Woodfield. When he was six, his staunchly republican father died of a heart attack. Legend has it that the man pointed at Michael from his deathbed: "He'll be a great man yet and will do things for Ireland."

At fifteen, Collins moved to Clonakilty to board with one of his sisters and her husband. He studied with a schoolmaster who belonged to the Irish Republican Brotherhood, a secret society dedicated to making Ireland an independent republic. From him, Collins learned to revere Theobald Wolfe Tone, the most articulate leader of Ireland's 1798 Rebellion. Also, he worked at a local newspaper, the *West Cork People*, founded by his sister's husband. Starting in 1906, after he passed the civil service examination in Cork, Collins spent four years with the Royal Mail.

Then he moved to London, where he boarded with another older sister while advancing through various banking jobs and studying at King's College. Always big, strong, and physically active, Collins joined the London branch of the Gaelic Athletic Association, and through that organization, the oath-bound Irish Republican Brotherhood. Collins spent six years in London, climbing the financial services ladder at the Board of Trade and then the Guaranty Trust Company. Within the secret Brotherhood, he emerged as a skilled organizer. Early in 1916, he returned to Ireland with an accountancy firm—though really he wished to be where political action was building to a crescendo. And so he was.

Collins emerged from Frongoch internment camp in December 1916, when a new British prime minister, David Lloyd George, declared an amnesty. Early the following year, he began working as secretary to the Irish National Aid Fund. During the next couple of years, while travelling extensively, Collins established two underground newspapers, set up a national loans program, developed an arms-smuggling route, and created both an intelligence network and an elite unit of hit men known as "the Squad."

In 1918, with the First World War requiring ever more troops, the British government sought to impose conscription in Ireland. The previous year, in Canada, a conscription crisis had erupted in Quebec as a result of a similar government initiative. In Ireland, the British move galvanized support for the Sinn Fein party, which was committed to Irish independence. In a December election, that party won 73 of the 105 seats accorded Ireland in the British

Parliament. Sinn Fein's platform included abstentionism, or refusal to occupy parliamentary seats in London.

In January 1919, the elected members—Collins among them, representing South Cork—convened their own parliament in Dublin. This revolutionary parliament, the Dáil Éireann, or "Assembly of Ireland," ratified the 1916 proclamation of the Easter Rising and, in the name of the Irish nation, issued a Declaration of Independence.

The assembly declared "foreign government in Ireland to be an invasion of our national right which we will never tolerate, and we demand the evacuation of our country by the English Garrison." They insisted that the Irish people had been battling "foreign usurpation" for seven hundred years, harking back to the Norman occupation that followed the invasion of 1169–1171. The Dáil declared that there was an "existing state of war, between Ireland and England." So began a series of political assassinations and reprisals.

In February 1919, Collins contrived to free Eamon de Valera, the leader of the Sinn Fein political party, from England's Lincoln Prison. Soon afterwards, de Valera set out for the United States to raise funds, leaving Collins, officially his minister of finance, to lead the war effort. By 1920, the British were offering ten thousand pounds—worth roughly half a million dollars today—for information leading to the capture of "the big fellow," as Collins was now being called.

That November, the British Parliament passed an act partitioning the country, dividing it into Northern and Southern Ireland: six majority-Protestant counties and twenty-six majority-Catholic. The following July, they offered a truce to the rebels and the Irish accepted. More than 2,000 people had died—550 on the Irish side, 714 on the British, and 750 non-aligned civilians.

The time had come to negotiate terms. Eamon de Valera, recently returned from the U.S., would logically lead the Irish delegation. But as Tim Pat Coogan observes, alluding to unruly British recruits called the Black and Tans: "The man who had felt his place was in America during most of the Tan war felt he must stay in Dublin during the coming diplomatic offensive in London." De Valera insisted on sending his leading soldier and military strategist.

Aware that his legend as a warrior would be undermined, Collins resisted furiously. But de Valera mustered just enough support to get his way. Early in October of 1921, at age twenty-nine, Michael Collins went to London to negotiate with a formidable British team that included Lord Birkenhead, Austen Chamberlain, and Winston Churchill. For two months, through seven plenary sessions, nine meetings of subcommittees, and twenty-four sub-conferences, Collins fought and argued to achieve an independent Irish republic that would encompass both north and south.

By December, he understood that Ireland could have the same status as Canada, Australia, or New Zealand, but nothing more, and that Northern Ireland would have to join the south of its own free will or not at all. He understood that the British would go no further, but that, as he wrote during negotiations, "The advantages of Dominion status to us as a stepping stone to independence are immeasurable." Collins suspected that de Valera and his allies had sent him here "to do their dirty work for them," and that they would repudiate any agreement. When Lord Birkenhead remarked, after signing the Anglo-Irish Treaty, "I may have signed my political death warrant tonight," Collins replied, "I may have signed my actual death warrant."

Back home in Dublin, as Collins had anticipated, the treaty sparked a firestorm. Most of the public was ready to accept it. But de Valera was outraged that Collins had signed the deal without consulting him. In the Dáil, he denounced the treaty as a betrayal. He found support among the more extreme politicians, who rejected any settlement that left Ireland linked with the British Empire.

Collins argued that the treaty ended a bloody, revolutionary war and offered, as he put it, "not freedom but the promise of freedom."

This long, legalistic document began by establishing Canada as a model. "Ireland shall have the same constitutional status in the Community of Nations known as the British Empire as the Dominion of Canada," it said, "with a Parliament having powers to make laws for the peace, order and good government of Ireland." As well, the relationship of the Irish Free State to the British Imperial Government "shall be that of the Dominion of Canada, and the law, practice and constitutional usage governing the relationship . . . to the Dominion of Canada shall govern their relationship to the Irish Free State." Third, "the representative of the Crown in Ireland shall be appointed in like manner as the Governor-General of Canada."

For Michael Collins and a majority of the Irish, the Dominion of Canada provided a workable model. The authoritative Coogan argues that Collins "did not like the Treaty he signed with England, but he and most of his closest friends and advisors regarded it as a stepping stone to full independence and a united Ireland." The emergence in the twentieth century of an independent Canada—the patriation of the Constitution, the nation's refusal to join wars against Vietnam and Iraq—would appear to vindicate his position. And Coogan observes that nobody who followed Collins "has been able to improve on the territory he won for a native Irish government in Dublin."

In 1921, while de Valera raged, Northern Ireland opted out of the Irish Free State, as expected. Michael Collins, having become leader of the Provisional Government, received the handover of Dublin Castle from the British, who had based their government at that site since 1171. The historic transfer happened on January 16, 1922. As Collins arrived for the ceremony, a British official observed tartly, "You're seven minutes late, Mr. Collins." Collins responded: "We've been waiting 700 years, you can have the seven minutes."

Back in the Dáil, after weeks of debate, Collins carried the day. But the vote was close, 64 to 57, and de Valera refused to recognize this democratic result. He stormed out of the Dáil and took his allies with him—many of them old friends of Michael Collins. This walkout spawned the Irish Civil War, which would prove more destructive than the just-ended War of Independence. In Dublin, where the anti-Treaty forces occupied the Four Courts, a majestic domed building on the banks of the River Liffey, an accidental explosion destroyed irreplaceable public records, including centuries' worth of genealogical information.

Eventually, after eleven months and the loss of several thousand lives, the pro-Treaty forces won the Civil War. Tragically, Michael Collins himself did not get to enjoy the victory. On the evening of August 22, 1922, in a hilly area not far from Clonakilty, he drove into an ambush. He refused to flee and insisted on returning fire. A sniper who had served with the British Army during the First World War, a man just about to retreat over the hills, paused to take one final shot. He hit Collins in the head and killed him instantly.

Today, famously, a Celtic cross marks the spot where Michael Collins died. With Sheena, during one of our visits to Ireland, I set out to see it. In "Clon" itself, as they call the bustling town of Clonakilty, we had visited the house where, in his teens, Collins lived with one of his sisters. Out front, we had admired the larger-than-life statue of the legendary freedom fighter. And we had followed the signs to nearby Woodfield and explored the site of the family homestead.

As evening fell we drove north towards the ambush site, Béal na mBláth, roughly along the route Collins followed in August 1922. The movie *Michael Collins* made that final journey look easy enough. We had no GPS, and no cellphone, and foolishly believed that a Google Maps printout would serve. This being Ireland, sign-posts were scarce. We ended up driving this way and that until we spotted another vehicle and hailed the driver, a middle-aged woman with a teenager beside her.

A Celtic cross marks the site at Béal na mBláth, thirty-two kilometres west of Cork, where Michael Collins was ambushed and killed by a sniper's bullet on August 22, 1922.

She started to give directions but then gave up and cried, "Never mind, follow me!" She led us along dirt roads, at scary-high speeds, to within one kilometre of the site and then pointed the way. Finally, we reached it: the stone cross at the side of the road. Standing there at the spot where Collins died, I could only shake my head sadly.

As Michael Collins had foreseen, the country he did so much to create became increasingly independent. The Dáil adopted a new constitution in 1937, and the Irish Free State became the sovereign and current state of Ireland. Eamon de Valera founded a new political party, Fianna Fáil. He would serve as head of government for three periods over more than twenty years. After he retired, de Valera said: "It is my considered opinion that in the fullness of time, history will record the greatness of Michael Collins, and it will be recorded at my expense."

Some historians claim that de Valera never spoke those words. But if he did not, then he should have. Michael Collins is one of the great champions of Irish independence. What makes him special to Canadians is that, when he negotiated the truce in London, he sought to achieve it along Canadian lines, and through evolution rather than revolution. That he was killed in his prime is a tragedy. But in the long history pertaining to Canadians, and arising out of our Irish and Scottish ancestry, Michael Collins is far from alone.

Glasnevin Cemetery, three kilometres north of Dublin city centre, contains monuments and the graves of many national figures. In the foreground, the grave of Michael Collins; behind it is a round tower marking the grave of Daniel O'Connell, known as the Liberator.

2.

Somerled of Argyll

Seven hundred and fifty years before Michael Collins embroiled himself in the Irish struggle for independence, Somerled of Argyll, an ambitious sea lord with Irish connections, gathered an invasion fleet at Lagavulin Bay on Islay—the largest fleet yet assembled in the Scottish isles. In 1164, bent on establishing an independent kingdom of his own, Somerled guided that fleet south around the Mull of Kintyre. He then swung north past Arran into the Firth of Clyde, a long narrow inlet that leads to the heart of mainland Scotland. In describing this invasion in his historical novel *Lord of the Isles*, Nigel Tranter writes that "Somerled could not restrain a surge of pride . . . as he counted no fewer than one hundred and sixty vessels, longships and galleys."

Tranter writes that "the great majority were his own, of course, but there were over thirty from [the Isle of Man] and almost as many from Ireland. And there was no subterfuge nor pretence here, all the ships were packed with fighting men, a vast army of nearly twenty thousand. All would be required no doubt—but it made a heartening sight for the only man who could have assembled such a force out of the Celtic lands." Somerled was bent on establishing an independent sea-kingdom.

The novelist exaggerates the number of fighting men. Informed estimates vary, but the total was probably ten or fifteen thousand—still an enormous fighting force for that era. Historian John Marsden writes that Dublin probably supplied about sixty of the ships, roughly one-third of the total. But Tranter is the one who brings the scene vividly to life, evoking the clanging gongs and flashing oars, and working the same magic with Somerled as he did with many other historical figures.

To recreate this twelfth-century sea lord, the novelist had less source material than usual, though the outline of the story is documented in the Annals of Ulster, the Chronicles of Holyrood, of Melrose, and of Mann, and the *Carmen de Morte Sumerledi.* In *Somerled and the Emergence of Gaelic Scotland*, the insightful Marsden suggests that the sea lord mounted his invasion as a preemptive strike against the advance of Anglo-Norman culture, which had gained a foothold on mainland Scotland.

In arguing that Somerled fought for autonomy, he follows an earlier historian, Colin Macdonald, who wrote that the sea lord was aiming not at the seizure of the Scottish crown, "but rather at the establishment of an independent Gaelic kingdom in Scotland, which . . . was far from having been welded at this time into a compact realm with a definite national consciousness." In his historical novel, Tranter takes a similar line, explaining, "If he could take Scotland and Man, Ireland also would not be beyond his ambitions, that was scarcely to be doubted. It behoved the Celtic peoples to unite against the threat."

Those Celtic peoples, as Marsden later clarified, had by this time absorbed three centuries of Scandinavian influence and immigration, and had become essentially Norse-Gaelic. Somerled dreamed of forging a unified kingdom composed of Gaelic-speakers from Scotland, Ireland, and the Isle of Man. Though for centuries he would be portrayed as a Celtic hero who drove the Vikings out of western Scotland, he himself was Norse-Gaelic. The name Somerled mac Gillebride combines a Norse given name with a Celtic patronymic meaning "son of." His mother was almost certainly Norse-Irish from Dublin or Limerick.

Scholars have long contended that his given name derives from the Norse *sumerlidi*, which means "summer voyager." They received corroboration in 2005, when a geneticist based at Oxford University discovered that Somerled's paternal DNA, traced through his descendants, pointed unmistakably to a Norse heritage. Bryan Sykes, whose bestselling books include *Saxons, Vikings, and Celts: The Genetic Roots of Britain and Ireland*, concluded that today, some five hundred thousand living males are descended from Somerled (a total exceeded only by Genghis Khan). They include between 25 and 45 per cent of MacDonalds, MacDougalls, and MacAllisters. Sykes repudiates traditional genealogies, which trace Somerled's ancestry to a long line of Celtic-Irish kings. "That's not what the Y-chromosome says," he declares. Somerled "is certainly of Norse Viking paternal origin."

Somerled was on my mind a few years ago as by sea we approached Islay, which is just thirty-five kilometres north of the Irish coast. This time, Sheena and I were circumnavigating Scotland in an eighty-passenger ship, the *Clipper Odyssey*. At least once a day, we would pile into Zodiacs and zoom ashore to explore a different location.

Islay is best known for its whisky distilleries: Lagavulin, Laphroaig, Ardbeg, Bowmore, Bruichladdich. We had investigated these during a previous visit, and this time, after landing at Port Askaig near Lagavulin Bay, we hiked a narrow road and then a pathway to Loch Finlaggan, once the heart of the Lordship of the Isles. From this location, the earliest Macdonalds had ruled a Gaelic-

Norse sea kingdom that, for three centuries, remained independent of both Scotland and Norway.

In western Scotland, as in Ireland, the Viking occupation dates
back to the early ninth century. Initially, thanks to their advanced
longboats, seafaring Scandinavians would "go a-viking." They
would plunder the monastic settlements situated near the coasts
and sail home to Norway or Denmark. Then they created a permanent settlement in Orkney, while in Ireland they established naval
bases at Dublin, Waterford, Limerick, and Linn Duachaill, near
Annagassan. Soon enough, the raiders settled and married, began
speaking Gaelic, and became nominally Christian. They integrated
with the Celts who had preceded them and so, in a process that
would be mirrored in Canada, created a more complex culture—in
that early case, a Norse-Gaelic fusion.

*In the northeast corner of the island of Islay, Finlaggan became the centre of a sea world
ruled from the thirteenth through the fifteenth centuries by the MacDonald Lords of the
Isles. They followed Somerled of Argyll, who created an independent kingdom from Islay.*

Not long ago, while exploring the stone ruins on tiny Council Island in the middle of Loch Finlaggan, we came face to face with the early parliamentary practices of Somerled's descendants, the Lords of the Isles. The MacDonald chieftains and their thanes or sub-lords would arrive from islands north and south, pulling their craft onto sandy beaches. Then they would meet on this tiny island while the less powerful stood on a larger island nearby, permitted only to watch and listen.

Both groups included the ancestors of countless Canadians, people with such surnames as MacNicol, MacEachern, MacKay, MacGillevray, MacMillan. For this voyager, at least, seeing the island arrangement drove home the extent of Norse influence on both Scottish and Canadian traditions: this business of meeting on a council island began with the Vikings. Judging from DNA testing and other genealogical research, some of my own ancestors, closely affiliated with the Clan MacNeill, probably shared in the decision-making at Finlaggan.

All this followed hard on a period known as the Age of Somerled. About the man himself, Somerled the son of Gillebride, certain facts remain uncontested. In 1156 or 1157, from Islay, he led a rebellion against Norwegian rule, then exercised authority from the Isle of Man. He married Ragnhild, daughter of Olaf Godredson, the Norse sea king of the Isle of Man. As his name suggests, this Olaf was the son of Godred Crovan, a Norseman who may well have been related to Somerled by more than marriage. Crovan, too, had come from Islay. He had seized control of the Isle of Man, and from there ruled the largest sea kingdom yet created. From 1091 to 1094, Crovan controlled not just the Scottish Hebrides, but also Dublin and key areas of Ireland.

Crovan's granddaughter Ragnhild gave Somerled three sons (Dugald, Ranald, and Angus) and one daughter, Bethoc. Somerled already had one son, and had named him after his own father,

Gillebride. In the 1300s, one of Somerled's grandsons, Donald of Islay, gave rise to Clan Donald and the dynasty of the Lords of the Isles (MacDonalds). Somerled's daughter, Bethoc, became the first prioress of a nunnery on Iona.

This stone, located just west of Ramsey on the Isle of Man, marks the spot where in 1079, Godred Crovan hid three hundred men before launching his forces towards victory at the Battle of Sky Hill.

Against this factual background, much requires piecing together. When was Somerled born? Estimates range from 1103 to 1117, and the best guess would appear to be 1113. Where was he born? Maybe in Ireland, maybe in Morvern, in Argyll. Both his father and grandfather had Gaelic names. Years before his birth, Norse invaders, led probably by the kilt-wearing Magnus Bareleg, had driven his grandfather from Argyll into exile in Ireland. His father, Gillebride, eventually raised an army of five hundred men and tried unsuccessfully to regain the family lands.

Legend has it that Somerled spent part of his youth in a cave, surviving by fishing and hunting. Around 1135, he cleared northern Argyll of the latest wave of Viking interlopers loyal to Norway, and so became Thane of Argyll. This won the tentative blessing of King David of Scotland, who hoped to gain control of the western islands.

In 1153, after the death of King David, Somerled joined an unsuccessful rebellion against Malcolm IV, the newly crowned twelve-year-old king. According to the *Carmen de Morte Sumerledi,* a narrative poem written in Latin by a Scottish churchman, he sacked Glasgow, its cathedral, and the surrounding area. Around the same time, Somerled's renowned father-in-law, King Olaf of Man, was murdered by his Dublin-based nephews. He was succeeded by one of his own sons, the tyrannical Godfrey the Black.

Already committed to achieving independence, Somerled assisted in overthrowing Godfrey and driving him back to Norway. Three years later, in January 1156, during the Christian feast of Epiphany, Godfrey invaded by sea to regain control of the southern Hebrides. During a fierce, night-long battle off the northern coast of Islay, Somerled defeated Godfrey and so gained undisputed control of the western islands. Two years later, according to the Chronicle of Mann, Somerled launched another assault on Godfrey and drove him from the region. So he became the undisputed ruler of an autonomous island kingdom.

Godfrey and his predecessors had owed allegiance to Norway. Somerled's kingdom of the isles was independent of both Norway and Scotland. The same was true of neighbouring Galloway in southwestern Scotland. This did not sit well with Malcolm IV of Scotland. In 1160, he invaded Galloway. Somerled fought alongside Fergus of Galloway, who lost the battle and withdrew to an abbey. Somerled secured a truce.

King Malcolm championed the expanding Anglo-Norman world, with its different culture, language, and laws. Over the next few years, as his followers sought to move westward, the Gaelic-speaking Somerled decided on his pre-emptive strike. In 1164, he gathered forces from Argyll, Kintyre, the Western Isles, and Dublin, and probably also from Galloway, Moray, and Orkney. His 160-vessel fleet was roughly the size of the one led in 1098 by Magnus Bareleg, when he had formally reasserted sovereignty over Scotland's western islands.

Now, sailing at the head of this massive fleet, Somerled landed on the mainland at Greenock. He then led the way into the Firth of Clyde and up the river to Renfrew, where the steward of Scotland had his headquarters. Somerled camped near the town and, though he brought an overwhelming force, that is where he lost his life. In one version of how this happened, he was betrayed by a kinsman or a servant. In his novel *Lord of the Isles*, Tranter follows that scenario, probably because it provides a vivid climactic scene.

In fact, the "betrayal thesis" did not arise until centuries later. And the earliest accounts indicate that Somerled was killed at the outset of what came to be called the Battle of Renfrew. A force hastily assembled by the bishop of Glasgow, seven miles from the town, had a stroke of luck. In the *Carmen de Morte Sumerledi*, the eyewitness churchman reports that Somerled was "wounded by a [thrown] spear and cut down by the sword." Such were the times that a priest then severed his head and brought it to the bishop.

Having lost their leader, the invaders retreated to their boats and sailed away. Somerled's body was eventually removed and reburied. Some say his remains were interred at Saddell Abbey in Kintyre, but the bulk of the evidence points to the Scottish holy island of Iona. What else is certain? As John Marsden writes, Somerled was neither Norseman nor Celt, but was "the one historical figure who reflects in his every aspect the same fusion of Norse and Gael which binds the deeper cultural roots of modern Gaelic Scotland." History would have taken a very different course, he adds, "had Somerled's great host of west Highlanders, Islemen and Dublin Norse not failed in the venture of 1164."

On the island of Islay, standing in the ruins of Loch Finlaggan, I realized that, of the estimated five hundred thousand living males who owe their existence to Somerled, thousands must be Canadians, and probably tens of thousands. In that concrete sense, this sea lord is one of Canada's ancestors. But more than that, 850 years ago, Somerled of Argyll sought to create a cultural, social, and political intertwining of Celtic peoples that would become a reality only in twentieth-century Canada. That precociousness makes him one of ours. Five centuries after Somerled, another wily, independence-minded warrior would arise—not among the Scots, but among the Irish: the Great O'Neill. He, too, was a man ahead of his times—one so influential that, as Canadians, we can claim him as one of our ancestors.

3.

The Great O'Neill

✳✳✳

The most moving memorial in Ireland can be found near a beach on Lough Swilly. Starting from Londonderry, you drive west to Letterkenny, and then north to Rathmullan, a total distance of roughly sixty kilometres. After parking the car, you cross a grassy area and there you have it: a complex sculpture commemorating the 1607 Flight of the Earls. It features two small groupings of stylized figures.

The first group consists of three enormous, elongated characters reaching skyward, their arms flung high over their heads. These are the three departing earls, the most powerful Gaelic lords in Ireland, the foremost among them being the Great O'Neill. The second group includes half a dozen nameless people, relatively tiny, in postures of pleading and supplication. These are the common folk piteously imploring the chieftains to remain: *Please, no, please don't leave us, please don't go.*

Behind this memorial, Lough Swilly is in fact not a lake but a large inlet that opens into the North Atlantic. From here at Rathmullan, on September 14, 1607, Hugh O'Neill and his two closest allies departed for Spain. With them, these three powerful earls brought their families, close friends and retainers, ninety-nine persons in all. Their departure changed Ireland so dramatically that, centuries later and an ocean away, the shock waves would still be felt in Canada.

The Flight of the Earls in 1607 gave rise to the Plantation of Ulster. This bronze memorial by John Behan, located near the pier in Rathmullan, evokes that watershed moment.

Born in County Tyrone around 1550, Hugh O'Neill had seen his family caught up in a struggle over who would inherit the chieftainship of the mighty Clan O'Neill, and with it the title Earl of Tyrone. After his father was killed by rivals, young O'Neill fled south under the protection of a family of English administrators, descendants of the Normans. He grew up in the Pale, an extensive area around Dublin and the only part of Ireland completely controlled by the English.

As a result of this upbringing, according to biographer Sean O'Faolain, O'Neill was "caught up in a dual loyalty—one of the very first, perhaps the first, modern Irishmen so divided by the impact of a complex and sophisticated civilization on the quiet certainties of a simpler way of life." At seventeen, O'Neill returned to Ulster (essentially the northern counties) under the protection of Sir Henry Sidney, the English-appointed lord deputy of Ireland. The English recognized him as the Gaelic chieftain of all the O'Neills, and also as Earl of Tyrone (one of the counties of Ulster). In 1580, he fought alongside the English in quelling a rebellion in western Ireland, and four years after that, he helped them in a battle against an uprising of Ulster Scots.

To undermine the power of the Gaelic clans, which tradition-ally controlled the distribution of lands, the English had devised a system of "surrender and regrant." In 1587, after visiting the court of Queen Elizabeth in London, O'Neill benefitted, becoming rightful owner of the lands of his grandfather. Eight years later, after compelling a rebellious cousin to renounce his counterclaim, O'Neill was crowned by his own people at an ancient ceremonial site in County Tyrone in the style of the ancient Gaelic kings. At age forty-five, he became "the O'Neill"—the most powerful chief-tain in Ulster. Over time, he would earn the adjective "Great."

But now he was raising suspicions among the English. All through the late 1500s, the Gaelic-Irish—influenced by Scandinavian settlement and culture, but never part of the Roman Empire—had battled the slow, steady encroachment of the English, who brought not just a foreign language but also a different strain of Christianity (Protestantism). While deferential to the authorities, O'Neill began forging alliances with other powerful Gaelic clans, among them the O'Donnells and the Maguires.

In 1590, after ordering the hanging of an English spy named Hugh Gaveloch, he was summoned to Dublin Castle to justify his action. Standing bare-headed before the board of the council, he claimed that Gaveloch was a traitor and a murderer, and that in executing him, he had merely acted according to ancient Irish Brehon laws.

After spending a few months in Dublin under house arrest, O'Neill was released with a reprimand and further orders. O'Faolain summarizes: "He must try to bring his people to adopt English habits, wear English dress, cut that long Gaelic *glibb*, or fringe of hair, through which they looked as through a visor. He must stop communicating with the Scots, and he must allow his land to be shired like any English county."

Within months of his return to County Tyrone, O'Neill made an enemy of a prominent English leader in Ulster by eloping with the man's sister. She died two years after they married, and O'Neill began more openly opposing the English authorities. He acquired armaments from Spain and Scotland. By 1594, he controlled an Irish army of over 17,500 men, among them 2,400 with horses. In addition, he commanded what O'Faolain describes as "an indeterminable number of Scots mercenaries." These elite Norse-Gaelic troops, who had begun to emerge in the days of Somerled, shared a language and culture with the Irish.

Reluctant to wage all-out war against England, O'Neill prevaricated. Early in 1595, he learned through his secret service that the English had decided to send two thousand veteran troops to subdue and arrest him. He responded by seizing Blackwater Fort, a few miles south of his headquarters at Dungannon. The English proclaimed him a traitor. And so it came into the open, the struggle that would later be called the Nine Years War. Acutely aware that England could muster an overwhelming force, O'Neill sent a message requesting help from the king of Spain, presenting himself and Hugh O'Donnell as champions of a Roman Catholic Church under siege. In 1596, Spain began promising to send forces, though none appeared.

By this time, O'Faolain tells us, O'Neill saw himself as leading an emergent Irish nation. His demands to the English constituted an assertion of independence, and included "liberty of conscience, full pardon, complete restoration of all his titles and patents, the return of his pledges, the restoration to his followers of all their ancient lands, the withdrawal of every garrison, and the making of Tyrone himself into a county palatine." Small wonder that one English official, faced with all this in writing, cried that he would not relay O'Neill's demands even as far as Dublin, but would throw this mad sheaf of papers into the fire in Dundalk.

In August 1598, O'Neill outmanoeuvred an English force at the Battle of the Yellow Ford, and won the most decisive Irish victory of the war. Yet he did not have enough men to move against Dublin, and he resumed his defensive posture. Eight months later, the English Earl of Essex landed in Ireland with seventeen thousand English troops, the largest force yet. O'Neill met him and negotiated a truce at a ford on the River Lagan. But when Essex relayed the terms to Queen Elizabeth, she rejected them furiously as outrageous in their generosity to the rebellious Irish.

Positioning himself increasingly as the champion of Roman Catholicism in Ireland, O'Neill received supplies from Spain and encouragement from the pope in Rome. According to O'Faolain, O'Neill was seeking "what later centuries called Home Rule." He demanded that Catholicism be openly practised throughout Ireland; that all churches and cathedrals now in the hands of the English be restored to Catholic churchmen; that a Catholic university be created; that all senior law-making officials be Irishmen; that the English crown have no sway over Irishmen; that he and his fellow earls enjoy all lands and privileges pertaining to their ancestors; that the Irish be able to travel freely in England; and that they be able to build and arm ships at their own discretion.

In 1600, the English established a position at Derry (later also known as Londonderry). They dispatched a dynamic new lord deputy, Sir Charles Blount, a.k.a. Baron Mountjoy. He ventured north with a considerable force and pushed O'Neill back to Armagh. Supported by an army of eighteen thousand soldiers, he also offered a considerable reward for the capture of the Great Earl, dead or alive. But as long as he remained in Ulster, surrounded by friends, O'Neill felt secure.

One shudders to imagine his dismay when, in October 1601, he learned that the Spanish had landed four thousand troops at the southern Irish town of Kinsale. For years, O'Neill had been imploring Roman Catholic Spain, the most powerful nation in Europe, to help him drive the Protestant English out of Ireland. But now, instead of landing in Ulster, which as Earl of Tyrone he controlled— and where, with the help of the Spanish, he could have created an unstoppable juggernaut and possibly taken control of all Ireland— the Spanish had landed on the southwest coast of the country. They were deep behind enemy lines and, from his home base at Dungannon, more than four hundred kilometres away. O'Neill was staggered by the strategic stupidity of it.

The Spanish quickly turned Kinsale into a fortress. But already, as O'Neill learned from spies, the Dublin-based English were preparing to besiege the town. Before long, Queen Elizabeth would send thousands more troops from England. O'Neill's closest ally, Red Hugh O'Donnell, wanted to set out immediately to join forces with the Spanish. But to do that, O'Neill would have to abandon his impregnable redoubt at Dungannon and make an almost impossible forced march across the country.

For the past seven years, while maintaining his independence in the face of a vastly more powerful adversary, he had drawn on an inherent wiliness, an almost Canadian savvy of the kind that would manifest centuries later at Vimy Ridge, when Canadians would use meticulous planning and tactical innovation to achieve what others could not. O'Neill had survived by weighing the consequences of every action, and he intended to do that now.

The Spanish would soon be surrounded by a huge English army. And he would have to undertake a long, difficult march through enemy territory to relieve the newcomers. Unbelievable. But finally he admitted that he had no choice. And so with winter coming on, he and O'Donnell led their armies south in two separate marches. They hoped to gather supporters as they went, but few men joined them. The two armies became one at Bandon, twenty kilometres northwest of Kinsale. By December 15, 1601, they had surrounded the English who were besieging the small town.

Now, according to O'Faolain, came the "decisive moment in Tyrone's life. It was one of the decisive moments in the history of Ireland, incomparably more important than the Battle of the Boyne or any other battle in the whole course of her history . . . Kinsale was to mean to Ireland, forever, a parting of the ways, a scission with everything that had gone before, an ending as absolute as death. Tyrone had the game in his hands, and he threw it away. He decided to attack. He should have hung on. He should have been faithful to time, which had never been unfaithful to him."

Instead of besieging the besiegers, as he was inclined to do, O'Neill listened to O'Donnell and attacked . . . and so wasted his advantage. In the cold and fog, he lost touch with O'Donnell and his forces. The Spanish troops, expected to sally forth, hunkered down where they were. When the English mounted a daring cavalry charge, O'Neill's exhausted men scattered. Soon enough, the Spanish in the town surrendered. The Battle of Kinsale ended in defeat soon after it began. And with that disaster went O'Neill's dream of forging an independent Ireland.

Back in County Tyrone with a diminished army, O'Neill defended his shrinking territory while seeking a truce and a pardon. The English army drove north under Mountjoy, destroying crops and livestock. In April 1603, as yet unaware of the death of Queen Elizabeth, his arch-enemy, O'Neill surrendered to Mountjoy. Had he waited, he might have secured better terms. In Dublin, he received confirmation of his title and core holdings, but most of his lands were placed under English law and distributed among his tenants. As freeholders with new legal rights, some began challenging his ancient prerogatives.

In 1607, when King James invited him to London to argue one of these cases, O'Neill realized that if he went, he would never see Ireland again. With Rory O'Donnell, who had succeeded his late brother as principal ally, Hugh O'Neill, the Great Earl of Tyrone, acted on his only other option. At midnight on September 14, from Rathmullan on the northern coast of Ireland, he and O'Donnell and a third earl, Cuchonnacht Maguire, sailed for Spain with their families and friends. Such was the Flight of the Earls.

As for the Great Earl himself, he spent the winter of 1607 in the Spanish Netherlands and proceeded to Rome the following spring. There, he received a warm welcome from the pope. He never stopped plotting to oust the English, but after nine years in Rome, in July 1616, he died of natural causes.

In the judgment of Sean O'Faolain, Hugh O'Neill has been underrated, faintly praised as a local patriot and a guerrilla chief. In fact, O'Faolain writes, "he associated his struggle for independence with the whole movement of the counter-reformation, and that was a European idea and a European link." Thanks to O'Neill, "something has persisted out of the old Gaelic world . . . which forms an attractive element in life wherever the unspoiled Irish nature strikes in the world of today some note from the far-off Hebrides."

In early seventeenth-century Ireland, with the Gaelic resistance broken, the English confiscated all the lands that had belonged to the O'Neills and their allies—more than two thousand square kilometres of territory—and launched the Plantation of Ulster. Wealthy Protestants had already undertaken, privately, to settle some Protestants in Ulster, notably in the counties of Antrim and Down. But now the English government introduced a systematic colonizing or "planting" of other traditional holdings.

By 1622, some 6,400 Protestant males resided in Ulster, with Scottish Presbyterians slightly more numerous than English Anglicans. Together with those who had already settled in Antrim and Down, and including extended families, the Protestant population of Ulster hovered around 19,000, representing almost half the total of the entire province. By 1720, Scottish Presbyterians had become a majority in Ulster. And in Ireland as a whole, a Great Divide had been born, one that would linger into the twenty-first century.

The town of Kinsale, roughly 285 kilometres southwest of Dublin, is today one of Ireland's most popular coastal resorts. It provides yachting, angling, golf, art galleries, and restaurants, and plays host to an annual gourmet festival. Because the town is hilly, with winding streets that dwindle unexpectedly to single lanes, most visitors who arrive by car park their vehicles as soon as possible.

A few kilometres outside town, however, if you are prepared to seek direction more than once, you will find a series of green-and-white signs marking locations related to the Battle of Kinsale. A locally produced pamphlet describes that battle, which took place on January 3, 1602, as the one in which "Ireland lost control of its destiny." After overwhelming the native Irish force led by Hugh O'Neill, the Elizabethan army had marched north and eventually destroyed a symbol of Irish authority: the chieftain's chair of the O'Neills, on which Ireland's leaders had long been crowned. In 2001, the people of Kinsale erected a new stone chair at a crossroads near the site of the ancient battle. Today, you can sit in it and, as the pamphlet suggests, perhaps "feel supported by the invisible heroes around you." When I tried the chair, just a few years ago, I felt sad to think that in Ireland, the Great Divide lingers still, though the battle that engendered it is more than four centuries old.

But then I thought of Canada, home to Irish immigrants from both north and south, and I realized that in this country we have bridged the Great Irish Divide. It took decades. The process included ugly episodes and even a political assassination. But in the second half of the twentieth century, as Canada became increasingly secular, and as tens of thousands of Canadians realized that our own ancestors include both Protestants and Catholics, the old enmities began to look ridiculous. Over time, they began to wither and fall away. Yet the lives of the freedom fighters continue to inspire. Among the Irish, we look to the Great O'Neill. Among the Scots, we discover the man known as Braveheart: William Wallace.

4.

William Wallace

✖✖✖

The Scottish Referendum of 2014, in which 45 per cent of Scots voted for independence, swept me back not only to both Quebec referendums, but also to the Quebec election of November 1976, when the Parti Québécois, which championed Quebec independence, was elected provincially for the first time. Who has not seen the cartoon by Aislin (Terry Mosher) that first appeared the next morning, featuring PQ leader René Lévesque, cigarette in hand, addressing the viewer: "O.K. Everybody take a Valium." The end of the world was not yet at hand

For Canadians, however, that election did mark a turning point. In Scotland, a similar moment came in 1997, when during a "devolution referendum," 74 per cent of the electorate voted to establish a separate Scottish parliament with taxing powers—a body something like a provincial legislature in Canada. In the present context, what interests me is that Scottish commentators were unanimous in suggesting that a Hollywood movie played an important role in attaining that result.

That movie, of course, was *Braveheart*, which still turns up on

Canadian television. Released two years before the referendum, and starring Mel Gibson, it celebrates William Wallace, a Scottish nationalist who was martyred by the king of England. Scholars have turned up falsities and fabrications in the movie, and insist that it can be viewed only as the roughest of guides to the life of an extraordinary figure. And the American who wrote the screenplay, Randall Wallace, is on record admitting that he fictionalized. "Historians agree on only a few facts about Wallace's life," he says, "and yet they cannot dispute that his life was epic. There were times when I tried to be a fair historian, but life is not all about balance, it's about passion, and this story raised my passions."

※※※

Seven centuries ago, on the morning of the day he would die, the Scottish warrior who would be remembered as Braveheart told his accusers: "I can not be a traitor to Edward, for I owe him no allegiance." Speaking at Westminster Hall in the heart of London, on August 23, 1305, William Wallace added: "He is not my sovereign. He never received my homage. And while life is in this persecuted body, he shall never receive it."

In this version of his final words, presented in *Lives of Scottish Worthies* (1831), Wallace freely admits that he had taken the towns and castles that King Edward I had illegally claimed as his own: "If I or my soldiers have plundered or done injury to the houses or ministers of religion, I repent me of my sin. But it is not of Edward of England I shall ask pardon."

This rendition of Wallace's rebuttal, written by Patrick Fraser Tytler (1791–1849), is too elaborate to be strictly factual. But it captures the thrust of Wallace's response to the charge of treason, which was probably more of a throttled cry: "I am no traitor! I never was *his* subject!"

The William Wallace Statue at Bemersyde near Melrose, erected in 1814, looks out over the River Tweed towards England, and is said to be watching for the next invasion.

William Wallace has come to symbolize the Scottish passion for independence. Historians agree that the man himself made some such statement as that quoted here. And they can point to documentary evidence not only of his "trial" and horrendous fate, but also that he led the Scots to an inspirational victory at Stirling in 1297, and suffered a devastating defeat near Falkirk the following year.

They have turned up many bits and pieces, but the oldest biographical source is a narrative poem written almost two hundred years after Wallace died. This work, by a poet called Blind Harry, served as the primary source for *Braveheart,* the fictionalized movie that turned Wallace into a legendary figure.

To separate truth from fiction may be impossible. But biographers—notably Andrew Fisher with *William Wallace*—have done some excellent sleuthing. Wallace was born around 1270 not far from Glasgow—either in Elderslie, Renfrewshire, twenty-three kilometres west, or in New Cumnock, Ayrshire, seventy-two kilometres south. Unlike Robert the Bruce, who would follow his lead, Wallace came of humble stock, though his father did own land. Because he would later demonstrate military genius and prove adept at both ambushes and fighting pitched battles, Wallace probably apprenticed as a soldier, fighting in either Wales or France. A powerful, strapping man, he knew how to handle sword, bow, and arrow, and he emerged as a leader of men.

Wallace does not enter history until 1297, when he avenges the murder of Marion Braidfute, the woman he loved. The movie *Braveheart* dramatizes this transformative moment. Picture Wallace as a lusty young outlaw in his late twenties, larger and more capable than most men, who has gathered a couple of dozen followers. At this point, the English have occupied Scotland.

One afternoon in May, while visiting Marion at her home, the outlaw Wallace is surprised by an English patrol. He fights his way clear and escapes. Marion and her friends take shelter in the house. When Sir William Heselrig, the High Sheriff of Lanark, arrives, he orders the house burned to the ground. He kills everyone in it, including Marion.

When he hears of this, Wallace vows to take revenge. He gathers his men, tracks Heselrig and his patrol into a woods, and falls on them at night. He kills Heselrig and cuts him into small pieces. "In an age of brutality," Fisher tells us, "he was brutal. He was no less cruel than those against whom he fought."

After this, there could be no turning back. But many young Scots, inspired, hurried now to follow William Wallace, who had dared to strike a blow against their English overlords. Wallace led a small army to join forces with the volatile Sir William Douglas in carrying out a lightning raid on Scone. During this surprise attack, Wallace narrowly missed capturing William Ormsby, a senior English administrator. He had to content himself with carrying off many valuables.

In July 1297, as rebellions erupted around the country, a number of Scottish nobles gathered to fight the English occupation at Irvine in Ayrshire. Some historians say that Wallace was there, others that he was not. Certainly, the nobles fell to arguing among themselves. This led to the Capitulation of Irvine, when without a fight the nobles submitted to King Edward. Wallace took no part in any such submission. He established a new base in the Ettrick Forest seventy-five kilometres south of Edinburgh, and then joined forces with Andrew Murray (Moray), a nobleman who was leading a rebellion in the north.

With Murray, early in September, Wallace laid siege to Dundee Castle. While there, he learned that the English were moving an army from Berwick, on the east coast, to Stirling, in the Scottish heartland. Clearly, they were bent on bringing the fractious country to its knees. But now came the battle that would make Wallace a legend.

With Murray, he quit Dundee and led 2,300 men to Stirling, among them 300 cavalry. Having a shorter distance to travel, and moving faster, they arrived before the English. They set up camp on

Abbey Craig, a ridge overlooking both the town and Stirling Bridge, where the invaders would have to cross the River Forth. There they waited.

The English arrived with ten thousand infantry and twenty-five hundred cavalry. Led by Hugh Cressingham, King Edward's treasurer in Scotland, they established themselves on the south side of the river. Cressingham sent two friars to demand surrender. Famously, Wallace responded: "Tell your commander that we are not here to make peace but to do battle to defend ourselves and liberate our kingdom. Let them come on, and we shall prove this in their very beards."

This response enraged Cressingham. One of his officers, a Scottish knight who had joined the English after the Capitulation at Irvine, suggested that the cavalry ride upriver and outflank the Scots by crossing fifty or sixty at a time at a broad natural ford. The furious Cressingham rejected this advice in favour of a direct attack. On the morning of September 11, 1297, he gave the order to advance. Stirling Bridge was so narrow that only three men could march abreast, or two could ride.

High on Abbey Craig, William Wallace watched and waited. When half the English army had crossed, he ordered an attack. Scottish spearmen seized the end of the bridge, trapping the cavalry. Wallace ordered his horsemen into the fray. English soldiers fell back into the river where, in their heavy armour, many drowned. Half the English army watched, helpless, as the Scots routed Cressingham and his forward guard. Then, they turned and fled.

According to the Lanercost Chronicle, written by friars from northern England, Cressingham's body was flayed and his skin cut into pieces. William Wallace took "a broad strip . . . from the head to the heel, to make therewith a baldrick [a belt worn over the shoulder] for his sword." Brutal age, brutal man.

The Battle of Stirling Bridge cost Wallace his ally Andrew Murray, who was wounded and soon died. But the victory galvanized the Scottish nation. By March 1298, Wallace had been knighted—possibly by Sir Robert the Bruce—and elected Guardian of Scotland. Having risen from some distance down the social ladder, Sir William Wallace assumed command of all Scottish forces. He led several raids into northern England, though certainly he did not attack the well-fortified city of York, as dramatized in the movie *Braveheart*.

Wallace did gather his forces for a looming battle. He well knew that King Edward, who styled himself "the Hammer of the Scots," would never accept Stirling Bridge as a final outcome. Sure enough, as soon as Edward arrived back in England from fighting in France, he began preparations for yet another invasion. At York, he gathered his most formidable army yet. Again estimates vary. But when Edward set out early in July 1298, he led at least fifteen thousand men, including an elite cavalry of twenty-five hundred. By this time, Wallace had put together an army of six thousand, including a thousand on horseback.

Given the disparity, he fell back, employing a scorched-earth policy as Edward led his massive force northwest through Roxburgh and past Edinburgh. The invaders found their supplies running low, and rioting broke out within the ranks. Eighty Welsh and Irish conscripts died battling their own English cavalry. The strategy was working. Wallace would wait until Edward turned back towards Edinburgh, and then conduct a series of devastating ambushes.

But in the woods outside Falkirk, on the morning of July 22, 1298, he learned that the English had got wind of his whereabouts, and had set out on a forced march through the night. Now, against impossible odds, Wallace could only stand and fight. He organized his army into four bristling, hedgehog-like "schiltrons," his men standing shoulder to shoulder in a thick circle, their spears pointing obliquely outwards.

These formations could do serious damage even to men on horses. But the expert Welsh archers, those who remained, thinned the Scottish ranks. Then came the rush of the English cavalry. Wallace ordered his own horsemen forward. But these mounted noblemen—they were led by John Comyn, the rival of Robert Bruce—saw that defeat lay ahead. They turned and fled.

The Scots were decimated. Wallace escaped with a remnant of his army. If the Battle of Stirling Bridge had created his reputation, that of Falkirk destroyed it. Not long after this defeat, he resigned as Guardian, yielding that office to two men: Robert Bruce and John Comyn.

At that point, for several years, William Wallace disappeared from public life. Historians agree that he sailed to France and requested military assistance from King Philip IV. In November 1300, that king also gave Wallace a letter to French envoys in Rome, ordering them to assist him in attracting Roman Catholic allies. That letter, ordering his French envoys to ask Pope Boniface VIII to support Wallace, went on display in Scotland in 2014, during the run-up to the seven hundredth anniversary of the Battle of Bannockburn. It suggests that, while looking for allies to battle the English, Wallace probably visited Norway as well as Italy.

By 1304, he was back in Scotland. But Wallace did not re-enter the historical record until the following year, when he was betrayed. On August 5, 1305, he was surprised and captured near Glasgow by Sir John Menteith, a Scottish knight who turned him over to the English. Wallace was carrying documents, including letters of safe conduct from John Balliol, the exiled king of Scotland, and from the kings of Norway and France. These availed nothing, though some commentators suggest that they may have contained mention of Robert Bruce, and so made King Edward doubt Bruce's loyalties—a suspicion that would inspire action and reaction and alter the course of Scottish history.

William Wallace, forced to ride south with his legs tied beneath his horse, reached London on August 22. The next morning, he was hauled before a kangaroo court at Westminster Hall, where he was given no opportunity of defence. Crowned with a garland of oak, he heard himself charged with committing atrocities against civilians and also with treason. He managed a few words before he was silenced, denying he was a traitor because he had never been Edward's subject.

Wallace then heard his sentence. He was to suffer the most gruesome death imaginable. He was to be drawn, hanged, and quartered. To the medieval mind, the quartering implied everlasting damnation, because on the Day of Judgment, the dead man would have no body in which to meet his maker. Immediately, Wallace was stripped naked, wrapped in an animal skin to preclude early death and, with his feet tied together at the ankles, dragged seven kilometres through the streets at the heels of a horse.

At Smithfield, a traditional site of executions, he was strung up by the neck but cut down before he died. He was then emasculated and eviscerated, and saw his entrails set ablaze. When the executioner tore out his heart—if not before as a result of shock—William Wallace died.

On the orders of King Edward I, the English cut off his head. They dipped it in a tar preservative, then mounted it for public viewing on a pike at London Bridge. They displayed the four quarters of the renegade's body at Newcastle, Berwick, Stirling, and Perth. Unlike most of the Scottish nobles, who had at some point pledged allegiance to King Edward, this man had never submitted. With his victory at Stirling Bridge, he had galvanized a nation. Down through the centuries, Wallace's story inspired countless poets, from Blind Harry through Robert Burns, who turns up later in this book. Burns wrote that Wallace moved him to explore "every den and dell where I could suppose my heroic countryman to have sheltered . . . My heart glowed with a wish to be able to make a song on him equal to his merits." In a letter to a friend, he added that "the story of Wallace poured a Scottish prejudice in my veins which will boil along there till the floodgates of life shut in eternal rest."

Wallace also inspired historical novels by such celebrated authors as Walter Scott and Nigel Tranter. Here in Canada, novelist Jack Whyte carries on the tradition. In 2010, that Scottish-born Canadian, who grew up in Wallace country, published a fictional tour de force entitled *The Forest Laird: A Tale of William Wallace*. Having lived in Canada for forty-odd years, Whyte returned to Scotland and spent five weeks on a fact-finding mission. He concluded that "the Scotland Wallace knew no longer exists, except in the loneliest, most inaccessible spots."

No matter. Novelists Walter Scott, Nigel Tranter, and Jack Whyte are well-respected leaders among those who, down through the centuries, have carried forward the idea or meme of William Wallace as the quintessential freedom fighter—as Braveheart. For many Canadians, as for most Scots, Wallace is the prototypical martyr to the cause of independence. Among the Irish, and of course among Irish Canadians, he is rivalled in this respect by an equally committed eighteenth-century figure—the doomed, courageous, and scapegoated Theobald Wolfe Tone.

5.

Theobald Wolfe Tone

✹✹✹

A t Rathmullan on Lough Swilly, near the north coast of Ireland, we crossed the sandy beach to water's edge. Having lingered at the memorial to the Flight of the Earls, I stood looking out across the expanse towards a town called Buncrana on the far shore. The afternoon was hazy and I could see little. But I knew that here in these salty waters, on November 3, 1798, British and French warships engaged in a fierce naval battle. The former carried the day.

Theobald Wolfe Tone, a leading Irish nationalist who had sought French assistance in the struggle for independence, donned his naval uniform, hoping to be treated as what he had become: an officer in the French navy. But as he marched off the ship, somebody recognized him. The British seized Wolfe Tone and, after keeping him briefly in Buncrana, transported him thirty kilometres south to Derry Jail, where they clapped him in irons as a common criminal. Wolfe Tone wrote a letter to the British general in charge, protesting that he should be treated as a prisoner of war. The general responded that he looked upon Wolfe Tone as "a traitor and rebel to your Sovereign and native country, and as such you shall be treated by me."

On the beach at Rathmullan, as I looked out over the water where the naval battle had raged, I did the arithmetic. Between the Flight of the Earls and the capture of Wolfe Tone, almost two centuries had elapsed. The technology of warfare had changed dramatically. The French had survived a violent revolution and were witnessing the rise of Napoleon. Across the ocean, surrounded by forested wilderness, Upper and Lower Canada were sorting out repercussions from the American Revolution. But here in Ireland, politically, not much had changed since the days of the Great O'Neill. That, certainly, was the view of Wolfe Tone.

Seven years before, he had written what would become one of the most famous passages in the history of the Irish struggle for independence: "To subvert the tyranny of our execrable government, to break the connection with England, the never-failing source of all our political evils, and to assert the independence of my country, these were my objects." He wanted "to unite the whole people of Ireland, to abolish the memory of past dissensions, and to substitute the common name of Irishman, in place of the denominations of Protestant, Catholic and Dissenter." His approach would have resonated in Canada, where just such alliances—French-English, Catholic-Protestant—would emerge in the next century.

Theobald Wolfe Tone, by his daughter-in-law Catherine Anne Tone. Taken from a miniature Tone had made for his wife in September 1798.

✂✂✂

Born in 1763, Theobald Wolfe Tone grew up as the oldest son of Peter Tone, a Protestant (Church of Ireland) coachmaker with a farm in County Kildare. But he was almost certainly the natural son of Theobald Wolfe, his godfather, a wealthy Protestant who would inherit the estate on which the Tones had their farm. His mother had worked in the big house there. Born and raised a Catholic, she converted to the Church of Ireland when Wolfe Tone was eight.

As a youth, Wolfe Tone got into the habit of cutting classes to watch military parades mounted by the British based at Dublin Castle in the heart of town. When his father found out and threatened to cut off his allowance, the young man said he wanted to quit school and join the army. His father refused. Back at school, Wolfe Tone did just enough work to get into Trinity College, where he studied law and the classics. He shone as a member of the Historical Society, and won two medals for oratory. He also got interested in theatre and did some acting.

In 1785, while still attending Trinity, Wolfe Tone eloped with a young woman who lived near the college. They would have four children, though only one, a son named William, survived into adulthood. For two years, starting in 1787, his wife lived at the family farm while Wolfe Tone attended the Inns of Court in London. He returned to Dublin after qualifying as a barrister.

Having honed his natural eloquence in London, Wolfe Tone began writing reviews, articles, and pamphlets about Irish politics. Like countless young men of his generation, he had been much taken with the American Revolution of 1776, and also embraced the principles of the 1789 French Revolution: liberty, equality, and fraternity. All around him, lingering inequalities fostered political unrest. In northern Ireland, Roman Catholics and Protestant dissenters, or "Whigs," began holding joint meetings to find common ground. Anglicans like Wolfe Tone made up one-tenth of the population, but owned five-sixths of the land.

Irish politician Henry Grattan had recently won concessions from England that made the separate Irish Parliament nominally independent. But in practice, England controlled this parliament through an appointed Lord Lieutenant. Roman Catholics, who made up three-quarters of the population, were barred from membership, and Presbyterians (of Scottish heritage), twice as numerous as Anglicans, were excluded from holding public or military office.

In August 1791, writing as "A Northern Whig," Wolfe Tone published the twenty-four-page pamphlet quoted above. In *An Argument on Behalf of the Catholics of Ireland*, he sought to convince Protestants and Catholics alike that "the depression and slavery of Ireland was produced and perpetuated by the divisions existing between them, and that consequently to assert the independence of their country, and their own individual liberties, it was necessary to forget all former feuds, to consolidate the entire strength of the whole nation, and to form for the future but one people." He might have been drawing up a blueprint for a future Canadian pluralism.

Wolfe Tone's pamphlet proved spectacularly successful. It sold six thousand copies within a few months, and thousands more afterwards. Soon after it appeared, Wolfe Tone accepted an invitation to Belfast to discuss the creation of a political organization—the Society of United Irishmen. He helped draft its manifesto, which aimed at parliamentary reform as outlined in his pamphlet. The British government, rightly worried that French revolutionary ideas might take hold, made overtures to Irish Catholics and drove the United Irishmen underground.

That organization became more radical and evolved into a secret society. To Wolfe Tone's chagrin, sectarian strife arose in the north. In September 1795, it culminated in a pitched battle in County Armagh between Protestant "Peep o' Day Boys" and Catholic "Defenders." The former routed the latter and, that evening, with a view to maintaining the Protestant Ascendancy, founded the Orange Order.

That fraternal organization would expand into Upper Canada (Ontario) in the early 1800s, and would influence Canadian politics for more than a century. Orangemen helped suppress the Upper Canada Rebellion of 1837, battled the American-based Irish Fenians in 1866, and lobbied in 1885 for the hanging of Louis Riel. By then, the Orange Order had become politically dominant in Toronto. Through the first half of the twentieth century, until 1954, every Toronto mayor would be an Orangeman.

Trouble was, where Wolfe Tone sought to transcend religious differences, the Orange Order put Protestants first. It represented everything he opposed, and would never have received his blessing. But three months before it emerged, Wolfe Tone was driven into exile in America. After winning concessions for the Catholic Committee, which sought removal of the legal restrictions against Catholics, Wolfe Tone was threatened with jail.

The United Irishmen had begun swearing revolutionary oaths. With France and Britain at war, several leading United Irishmen had already fled the country. Against this background, Wolfe Tone wrote an incendiary letter and was implicated in assisting a French spy—a man who was also an Irish clergyman. Wolfe Tone still had some influential friends, and British authorities agreed not to charge him if he wrote a detailed description of what had happened, and also left Ireland. In the summer of 1795, with his wife, his three children, and his sister, Wolfe Tone sailed to the United States. He arrived with seven hundred pounds to his name (around twenty thousand dollars today).

In Philadelphia, known as "the Athens of America," he met several United Irishmen in exile. They introduced him to a French foreign minister. France was at odds with England, as it so often was, and had expressed interest in the Irish situation. Wolfe Tone insisted that the landing of a powerful French force in Ireland would inspire a popular uprising that would overthrow the British government. Even so, he was arranging to buy a farm in New Jersey when he heard from Ireland that republicanism was rapidly gaining support. His friends urged him to go to France to seek help. He abandoned the farm idea, made arrangements to leave his family in the United States and, five months after he arrived, sailed for Paris, bent on securing French assistance for the cause of Irish independence.

▨▨▨

Less than one year later, on December 15, 1796, Theobald Wolfe Tone sailed aboard the flagship of a French fleet bound for Ireland. He had succeeded in his mission beyond the wildest imaginings of his allies. In Paris, he had badgered the War Office, urging the French to invade the Dublin area with twenty thousand men. Barring that, he said they should land at least five thousand troops in Ulster, where a massive rising would certainly follow. In July, he had been summoned to meet General Lazare Hoche, a rising star in the French army. He had made an impression and, one week later, was commissioned as a French officer.

By Christmas Eve, aboard the flagship of an invading fleet of sixteen ships, Wolfe Tone was beating back and forth off Bantry Bay on the west coast of Ireland, waiting for the howling wind to abate. Originally, the fleet had boasted forty-three vessels, including seventeen of the largest warships, and fourteen thousand four hundred and fifty French troops well supplied with artillery, arms, and ammunition. But collisions, gale-force winds, and stormy weather had reduced and scattered this powerful force.

Instead of waning on Christmas Day, the storm grew worse. As evening drew on, and with the gale still blowing, the admiral ordered all ships to cut cable and put out to sea. Wolfe Tone could hardly believe it. But the next morning brought thick fog, and in his journal he admitted that "dreadful stormy weather and beastly winds . . . have ruined us." As the French fleet withdrew, he added that "England has not had such an escape since the Spanish Armada, and that expedition, like ours, was defeated by the weather."

With this, Wolfe Tone anticipated the judgment of posterity. The Spanish Armada, defeated off the Netherlands in 1588, had represented the last great threat to England. And not since the Battle of Kinsale, part of that same, intermittent Anglo-Spanish War (1585–1604), had Irish independence so nearly become a reality. Not until the twentieth century would any uprising or rebellion come so close to setting Ireland free as when, in 1796, the French fleet departed in disappointment.

Over the next couple of years, Theodore Wolfe Tone soldiered on. He reunited with his wife and children, who arrived from the United States. With an Irish Catholic emissary, he met Napoleon, recently appointed to command a new army intended to defeat England. But that great general had already decided to fight his next war in Egypt, and soon left for the Mediterranean.

Meanwhile, during the spring of 1798, the English government went about arresting the remaining leaders of the United Irishmen. Wolfe Tone wrote that the arrested included "almost every man I know and esteem in Dublin." Among them was Lord Edward Fitzgerald, the chosen leader of a city-wide uprising planned for May 23.

Of all the leading United Irishmen, Fitzgerald alone had visited the territories that one day would form part of Canada. Nine years before, he had spent twenty-six days travelling with First Nations people from Fredericton to Quebec City. Now, four days before launching the insurrection, Fitzgerald was betrayed. Wounded while being captured, he died on June 4, age thirty-four. In Dublin, the ensuing uprising lasted just two days.

An insurrection in County Wexford, in the southwest, went on for almost a month. In June, there were smaller risings in Ulster, and in Counties Antrim and Down. The British authorities quashed all of these, and jailed or executed virtually all the leaders. On June 25, with most of the bad news yet to arrive in France, the French government—urged on by Wolfe Tone—created another plan to land troops in Ireland. This time, it would send three small expeditions to three ports.

These three in the end achieved nothing. The most successful foray, under General Jean Joseph Amable Humbert, landed a thousand men in County Mayo in the northwest. They registered one surprising victory over the larger English army, but survived as a fighting force for little more than two weeks. A brilliant novel by Thomas Flanagan, *The Year of the French*, vividly evokes how this unfolded. Theobald Wolfe Tone had sailed with the largest expedition, which numbered 2,300 men under General Jean Hardy. He was on the flagship *Hoche*: 74 guns, 640 men, 24 officers.

As this ten-vessel fleet approached Lough Swilly, that deep inlet on Ireland's northern coast, it encountered a powerful British force. The battle lasted hours, but finally, with the *Hoche* battered and sinking, the French had to raise a white flag. The English towed the *Hoche* to shore at Buncrana, which is directly across the bay from Rathmullan, where, more than two centuries later, I stood with Sheena, looking out across the water.

Theobald Wolfe Tone went ashore wearing his uniform, signalling his status as a French officer. He was seized and jailed as a common criminal. The French commanders interceded for him, but to no avail. He was brought to Dublin, charged with treason, and, on November 10, 1798, tried by a military court.

Wolfe Tone pleaded guilty, but asked leave to make a statement. "What I have done, I have done," he said, "and I am prepared to stand the consequences. The great object of my life has been the independence of my country; and for that I have sacrificed everything that is most dear to man . . . Whatever I have said, written, or thought on the subject of Ireland I now reiterate: looking upon the connection with England to have been her bane I have endeavoured by every means in my power to break that connection. I have laboured in consequence to create a people in Ireland by raising three millions of my countrymen to the rank of citizens."

Cautioned that his remarks were becoming inflammatory, Wolfe Tone omitted a warm tribute to the Catholics who had supported him. He regretted that atrocities had been committed by both sides in the struggle, and that the war had "degenerated into a system of assassination, massacre, and plunder." He summarized: "I have attempted to establish the independence of my country; I have failed in the attempt; my life is in consequence forfeited and I submit. The Court will do their duty and I shall endeavour to do mine."

Asked if he had anything more to say, Wolfe Tone requested the death of a soldier by firing squad. He wanted to be shot as a political prisoner, rather than hanged like a criminal. The court responded that the Lord Lieutenant of Ireland would make that decision.

Back in his cell, Wolfe Tone wrote last letters to friends, his father, and his wife, on whose behalf he also wrote to the French government. Then he learned that he was to be publicly hanged the next day at 1 p.m. This spectacle would be staged at Dublin's Newgate prison, near Christ Church Cathedral. That night, Theobald Wolfe Tone cut his own throat with a penknife. A doctor managed to close the wound, but warned that to move him would prove fatal.

The Theobald Wolfe Tone Memorial is in Dublin at St. Stephen's Green and Hume Street. Erected in 1967, it was bombed to smithereens four years later and then rebuilt in the same location.

Wolfe Tone lingered for a week and then, on November 19, 1798, having thwarted the British authorities in their yearning to make a spectacle of him, he passed away. Theobald Wolfe Tone would become an icon of the struggle for a pluralistic, inclusive independence, inspiring not just iconic leaders like Michael Collins, but also countless more average men and women who would make their way to Canada.

Case in point: Irish immigrant Michael McAteer. In July 2013, he challenged the requirement that to become a Canadian citizen he must pledge allegiance to the queen. In a story widely reported in the media, McAteer, who immigrated in the 1960s, told the Ontario Superior Court that he would happily swear an oath to Canada, but not to "a hereditary monarch who lives abroad."

His father had been persecuted in Ireland, he said, for supporting Irish independence. Taking an oath to the queen "would

violate my conscience and be a betrayal of my republican heritage."
That September, a Superior Court justice ruled against McAteer,
insisting that the Canadian oath is taken "to a domestic institution
that represents egalitarian governance and the rule of law." In so
saying, as we shall see in Part Two, the judge was echoing Thomas
D'Arcy McGee.

Here, on both sides of the argument, we see cultural genealogy
in action. McAteer was transmitting a meme complex or bedrock
value he had learned from his father, whose republican thinking owed much to Theobald Wolfe Tone. For many Irish, both in
Ireland and Canada, the example of Wolfe Tone lives on. His commitment to the cause of independence stands comparison with that
of the greatest of Scottish heroes: Robert the Bruce.

6.

Robert the Bruce

⬚⬚

The first time I heard "Flower of Scotland," that unofficial national anthem, I judged it dreary and droning—more boring, melodically, even than "O Canada." We were sailing around Scotland and, after a Scottish fellow staffer led passengers in singing the song, a few of us got into a discussion. I said: "You're familiar with 'La Marseillaise' and 'The Star-Spangled Banner.' Is there any comparison? There, we hear melodies well-suited to rousing a people to action. But 'Flower of Scotland'?"

My friends assured me that, at Scottish sporting events, this almost-anthem never fails to excite the crowd. The fans get to do a callback. I must have shaken my head, unconvinced, because someone handed me a lyric sheet and told me to check it out. A quick glance revealed what I had missed: Robert the Bruce.

"Flower of Scotland" recalls the 1314 Battle of Bannockburn, when "the Bruce," or the most celebrated leader of the Clan Bruce, drove "proud Edward's army" back to England. By defeating the English invaders, he achieved for Scotland an autonomy that lasted four centuries. The song is a paean to Scottish independence. The sudden comprehension must have shown in my face, because I vaguely recall a round of derisive applause.

As for the man who inspired the song, himself the "flower of Scotland," his complex biography is instructive. It explains why, in 2014, seven hundred years after Bannockburn, nationalist politician Alex Salmond found inspiration in Robert the Bruce while leading the latest charge for Scottish independence. According to the *Edinburgh Evening News*, Salmond said: "Bruce came into my mind quite a bit during the referendum campaign." In fact, Bannockburn and the Bruce were top of mind as far away as Toronto, where the local St. Andrew's Society organized both a day-long symposium and a blazing-fiddles evening concert.

Born into Scottish nobility in Ayrshire in 1274, Robert Bruce was the eldest son of the Lord of Annandale and the Countess of Carrick. As a child of nobility, he received a superior education, even learning three languages: Anglo-Norman, Gaelic, and Scots. Bruce was also a great-grandson of King David I, who had brought Anglo-Norman feudalism to Scotland during the previous century. This royal lineage gave him a claim to the Scottish crown.

The kingship had been contested since 1286, when King Alexander III died without a male heir. His three-year-old granddaughter—Margaret, the Maid of Norway—was next in line. The Guardians of Scotland helped arrange a marriage contract between her and the five-year-old heir to the English throne, the future Edward II, stipulating that Scotland would remain "separate, apart and free in itself without subjection to the English kingdom." But in 1290, while en route to be married, the child-queen died in Orkney.

To decide among various competitors for the Scottish throne, the Guardians sought the help of King Edward I of England. This was a mistake, as Edward would prove to be one of the most ruthless rulers in British history. The two strongest Scottish claimants were John Balliol, Lord of Galloway, and Robert Bruce's grand-father, known to history as Bruce the Competitor. In November 1292, by which time Robert Bruce was an eighteen-year-old knight, Edward awarded the Scottish crown to Balliol. Naturally, the Bruces denounced Balliol as a usurper.

When tensions arose between King John Balliol and the over-bearing King Edward, the Bruces, still bent on attaining the Scottish crown, supported Edward. They withdrew in 1295 to their English estates, and Balliol awarded their Scottish lands to John Comyn, the Earl of Buchan. The following March, Comyn led a surprise attack on the Bruces, who fought them off from the walled city of Carlisle in northern England.

Balliol then refused to support an English war against France, giving King Edward an excuse to invade Scotland. He sacked Berwick, a coastal town southeast of Edinburgh, and then crushed Scottish resistance at the Battle of Dunbar. Edward deposed King John Balliol, imprisoned him in the Tower of London, and restored the Bruces to their Scottish estates. In August 1296, the Bruces were among fifteen hundred Scots who swore an oath of fealty to King Edward.

But less than one year later, in July 1297, the twenty-two-year-old Robert Bruce broke with his father to join a Scottish revolt led by friends of his late grandfather. These included Robert Wishart, bishop of Glasgow, and James Stewart, the high stew-ard of Scotland. This revolt culminated in a collective submission called the Capitulation of Irvine, which found most Scottish lords swearing allegiance to the English king.

In September of that year, as narrated above, the recalcitrant William Wallace defeated an English army at the Battle of Stirling Bridge. Wallace became a Guardian of Scotland, but served in the name of the imprisoned usurper, King John Balliol. So Bruce did not participate in the Battle of Falkirk, when in 1298 Wallace was defeated and resigned as Guardian. The Scottish nobles replaced Wallace with two men: Robert Bruce and his archrival, John Comyn.

The following year, to reconcile these two ambitious men, they appointed a neutral third Guardian—William Lamberton, bishop of St. Andrews. Lamberton failed in the impossible task of uniting Bruce and Comyn, and in 1300, Bruce resigned. His first wife had died and in 1302 he married Elizabeth de Burgh, a daughter of the Earl of Ulster. Within two years, he and all other Scottish nobles—including John Comyn, now the sole Guardian of Scotland—had submitted to King Edward. In 1304, with the death of his father, the thirty-year-old Bruce became his family's claimant to the Scottish throne.

For the past couple of years, Bruce had been playing a dangerous game. While ostensibly supporting the English king in his efforts to bring Scotland under control, he had secretly done everything he could to undermine that campaign. Ordered to conduct a mounted raid on Selkirk forest, Bruce had somehow failed to capture the targeted rebel, William Wallace. Soon after that, instructed to forward English siege engines for an attack on Stirling Castle, Bruce had complied. But he had somehow neglected to send a crucial part, so the machines could not function.

In October 1305, when an ailing King Edward, now sixty-six, appeared to be on his deathbed, Bruce entered into a secret agreement with John Comyn, his only serious rival for the Scottish crown. In *Robert the Bruce: King of Scots*, biographer Ronald McNair Scott summarizes their deal succinctly: "Help me be King and I will give you my estates or give me your estates and I will help you."

Not long afterwards, Bruce realized that King Edward had begun to suspect his intentions. Perhaps, when William Wallace had been captured in August, he was carrying incriminating letters and documents. In any event, without stating a reason, the king, having recovered from his illness, withdrew a gift of lands.

Yet he allowed Bruce to remain on the Scottish advisory council. This meant that, in January 1306, as Earl of Carrick, he would be expected to attend King Edward at his court. No less wily than the king, Robert Bruce arranged for a trusted ally to warn him should he detect any sign of a threat.

Sure enough, late one night in London, not long after he arrived, Robert Bruce received a peculiar gift from the Earl of Gloucester, an old family friend who had access to the king's inner circle. Ostensibly a message of thanks, it consisted of twelve pence and a pair of spurs. Clearly, the spurs meant make haste, and the number of the pence probably reinforced this, indicating the degree of certainty: not five or six, but twelve. On receiving this gift, whose meaning he instantly understood, Bruce slipped away into the night. With his squire, he rode north, travelling non-stop.

As he approached the Scottish border, he chanced to meet a fellow Scot riding south. Suspicious, Bruce seized and searched the man. He found a letter to King Edward from John Comyn—and with it, the agreement he and his rival had signed. King Edward would certainly have viewed this document as evidence of treason, and would have dealt with Bruce as he had dealt with William Wallace. Bruce killed the unlucky messenger. With the agreement in his possession, hell-bent on vengeance, he resumed racing northward.

Five days after leaving London, Bruce reached his castle at Lochmaben, northeast of Dumfries. He consulted with his younger brothers. As it happened, King Edward's magistrates were about to hold court at Dumfries. Bruce saw an opportunity. He sent a friendly invitation to John "Red" Comyn, his betrayer, who was at his castle twenty-five kilometres northwest of the town. He asked that they meet before sessions at Greyfriars Church. The unsuspecting Comyn agreed and turned up.

In the church, the two men moved to the high altar to speak privately, and there Bruce produced the agreement he had taken from Comyn's messenger. The men exchanged words. Both drew their daggers and lunged, but few could cross weapons with Robert Bruce. Comyn fell wounded onto the altar steps. His uncle rushed forward and attacked Bruce, but was struck down by a blow from the young earl's brother-in-law.

Rattled by having committed a sacrilegious act in the church, Bruce rushed outside. In answer to a question from another of his men, Roger Kirkpatrick, Bruce said, "I doubt that I have slain Red Comyn."

"Do you doubt?" Kirkpatrick replied. "Then I'll make sure."

With another man, he rushed back into the church and finished Comyn.

Bruce and his men made short work of those who had accompanied his rival. Then they rode so quickly to Dumfries Castle, three kilometres away, that they arrived before the news spread, and surprised the English garrison. The magistrates barricaded the heavy doors of the great hall, and Bruce gave them a choice: burn to death in the castle or accept free passage back to England. They deliberated, preferred the latter option, and hurried home to tell King Edward what had transpired.

Robert Bruce rode north to Glasgow. There, having confessed his sacrilege, he received absolution from Bishop Robert Wishart. Bruce would be excommunicated by the pope in Rome, but the Scottish clergy, always secretly supportive of Scottish independence, never wavered. Six weeks after the events at Dumfries, on March 25, 1306, Bishop William Lamberton crowned Robert Bruce King of Scots. Resistance had become outright rebellion.

Over the next eight years, Robert Bruce would lead his people through one of the most tumultuous periods in Scottish history. The killing of John Comyn and the assertion of Scottish independence enraged King Edward, who styled himself "the Hammer of the Scots." Swearing vengeance and vowing that Robert Bruce would suffer the same fate as William Wallace, he sent an army north under the Earl of Pembroke to invade Scotland. Bruce had raised 4,500 men, but on June 18, ambushed and outnumbered at Methven near Perth, he suffered a shattering defeat and lost many of his finest warriors.

With the English army rampaging, Bruce could do nothing but retreat into the mountainous north. King Edward proclaimed that the wives of his enemies were outlaws, and could be robbed, raped, or murdered with impunity. With five hundred men at his command, and England's Earl of Pembroke on his heels, Bruce took the women with him and made for the Western Isles, where he had allies among the descendants of Somerled of Argyll.

Robert the Bruce led Scotland in the Wars of Scottish Independence and served as King of Scots from 1306 to 1329.

After a second defeat in the mountains, however, Bruce grew worried about the women, among them his wife and sisters. As a safeguard, he decided to send them north towards Orkney, accompanied by his brother Nigel and a small group of knights. Not long afterwards, this party was captured, and killed or imprisoned. The women—except for his wife, protected as a daughter of the Earl of Ulster—were kept in wooden cages open for public viewing. But Bruce did not learn of this until later. With his few remaining followers, armed only with swords, daggers, and bows, he trekked south through the wooded hills, sheltering in caves and surviving on roots and berries while making for the Firth of Clyde, waterway to the Western Isles.

At last he reached friends who provided a few small galleys. In the south of Kintyre, he was welcomed at Dunaverty Castle by Angus Og Macdonald of Islay, descended from Somerled and known as Lord of the Isles. After three days, with his enemies still giving chase, Bruce withdrew southwards another twenty kilometres, to tiny Rathlin Island, nearer to Ireland than Kintyre. From there, he directed his younger brothers to gather forces from among friends and relations in northern Ireland.

Bruce himself sailed north to Garmoran, west of Fort William, accepting the hospitality of the powerful Christina of the Isles, a widowed sister-in-law and yet another descendant of Somerled. According to one fourteenth-century source, John of Fordun, "it was by her help and power and goodwill that Bruce was able to return to Carrick." In February 1307, with thirty-three galleys, and expecting another eighteen from Ireland, Bruce landed at Carrick on the south coast of Ayrshire. He learned that his brothers had been ambushed and defeated, and that the English were thick on the ground. He ransacked the village beneath Turnberry Castle, where he had probably been born, and then slipped away into the hills.

While camped in the woods with sixty men, he received a visit from Christina, generally believed to have been his mistress. She brought fifteen men and horses . . . and also the grim news about his wife and sisters, now in captivity, and his brother Nigel, who had been beheaded. At this lowest point, or so the story goes, while sheltering in a cave, Robert Bruce noticed a spider hanging by a thread from the rocks overhead. It was swinging from side to side, trying to reach the wall. Six times it swung and fell short, but then, on the seventh try, it achieved its objective. Bruce admired the spider's perseverance, and resolved that the King of the Scots could show no less.

Some sources situate this episode on Rathlin Island, while others wonder if it ever happened. But about the resolve and tenacity of Robert Bruce there is no doubt. Bruce had been raised in a tradition of chivalric combat. He had become famous as a mailed warrior who, on horseback, armed with lance and sword, could defeat the hardiest fellow knights. But now, taking stock of his circumstances, and observing that most of his followers were lightly armed with swords and daggers, he decided to develop a new approach—one pioneered by William Wallace.

Robert Bruce would specialize in forest ambush and nighttime raid. Against the thousands of soldiers Edward sent into Scotland, he waged guerrilla warfare. And again, he proved dauntless. At one point, tracked into some woods by three would-be traitors, a father and two sons, he told his young page to hand him his bow and arrow and stand aside. When the three men refused to withdraw, Bruce fired an arrow through the father's eye. With his broadsword, he cut down one charging son with a single blow, and then grabbed and snapped the spear of the other and dispatched him as well. To his joyful page, while wiping his sword, Bruce pronounced them "good fighting men until they were ruined by their treachery."

Over the next few years, more than once, Bruce accomplished similar feats in single combat. And in May 1307, he led his men to a notable victory at Loudoun Hill, not far from Kilmarnock. Two months later, good news: King Edward I, having taken personal charge of a mission to destroy Robert the Bruce, had died at sixty-eight of natural causes. Of course, English forces still held much of Scotland. But Bruce now attracted more followers. He turned them into a fighting machine and began systematically destroying the power of the Comyn family, seizing lands and castles they had controlled for 150 years.

In 1309, Robert the Bruce held his first parliament at St. Andrews. And the following year, at a general council, the Scottish clergy disregarded his long-standing excommunication and reaffirmed him as King of the Scots. When England's new king, Edward II, prepared yet another invasion from Berwick, Bruce sent him a letter as one monarch to another, offering peace on condition that he recognize Scotland's independence. This king prevaricated. In 1311, he withdrew to London to resolve problems with France and recalcitrant English nobles.

Robert the Bruce consolidated his gains. He captured castles held by the English, including Edinburgh and Castle Rushen on the Isle of Man, strategically situated between Ireland and England. Early in 1314, his brother Edward laid siege to Stirling Castle, whose governor agreed to capitulate if not relieved before June 24. This set the stage for one of the most celebrated events in Scottish history: the Battle of Bannockburn.

Drawing on a population five times that of Scotland, King Edward II came north with an army of twenty thousand men, the largest yet gathered by an English king. Designed not just to relieve Stirling Castle, but also to put an end to all assertions of Scottish independence, this mighty force included twenty-five hundred cavalry and three thousand archers. Scotland had suffered through eighteen years of warfare, but Robert the Bruce managed to muster between five and seven thousand fighting men, among them two hundred archers.

As well, Bruce knew the Scottish countryside. He split his men into three divisions, and positioned them strategically to force the invaders onto the "carse" of Stirling, an area wet in winter and hard in summer. He then dug numerous pits in that only possible main route of attack and covered them with brush. These, together with

three nearby "burns" or streams, would force the English into a con-
stricted area. And now came an episode that would cap the legend
of Robert the Bruce. With his men hidden in the trees above him,
the Scottish king, armed with nothing but a battle-axe, rode a small
horse along the side of the hill, checking positions and preparations.

Hearing the thunderous hooves of an approaching warhorse,
Bruce turned and saw an English knight, Henry de Bohun, charging
towards him with his lance lowered. The king faced his adversary,
waited until the last possible second, then avoided the lance by
turning aside his agile mount. As the knight passed, Bruce rose in
his stirrups and slammed down his axe with such force that he split
the knight's helmet and head in two.

This moment would come to symbolize the David-and-Goliath
nature of the ensuing battle. At Bannockburn, intelligence and
agility routed brute force. Bruce had made an offensive weapon of
Wallace's "schiltron," the hedgehog of tightly packed men armed
with spears. With these, and by bringing in his five-hundred-man
cavalry at a crucial time, he smashed the English army and sent
Edward home, as the unofficial Scottish anthem would later have
it, "to think again."

Bannockburn marked a final turning point in the war of
independence. Over the next few years, Robert Bruce repeatedly
raided northern English towns for money and provisions, and in
1318, he recaptured Berwick. He also turned his attention to
Ireland. This initiative is especially noteworthy from a Canadian
perspective, because Bruce sought to create an Irish-Scottish alliance that prefigures what, centuries later, would finally become a
reality in Canada. Bruce's undertaking is the subject of a two-part
documentary, *The Quest for Bannockburn*, which the BBC was creating as this book was written.

After Bannockburn, Bruce wished to prevent the English from
using Ireland as a staging point, and also hoped to create a pan-

Gaelic alliance ruled by himself and his heirs. In approaching the Irish with this idea, essentially a version of Somerled's dream, he highlighted his personal links with Ireland. He had married a daughter of the Earl of Ulster, which encompassed most of northern Ireland; and on his mother's side, he could trace his royal ancestry to the legendary Brian Boru.

Bruce sent envoys to Ireland with a letter addressed to the Irish kings, prelates, and people: "Whereas we and you and our people and your people, free since ancient times, share the same national ancestry and are urged to come together more eagerly and joyfully in friendship by a common language and by common custom, we have sent you our beloved kinsmen, the bearers of this letter, to negotiate with you in our name about permanently strengthening and maintaining inviolate the special friendship between us and you, so that with God's will our nation . . . may be able to recover her ancient liberty."

In the north of Ireland, this approach earned the desired response. The Earl of Tyrone, Donal O'Neil, asked Bruce to send military aid to expel the English. Later, he would explain to a pope that "the Kings of Lesser Scotia [Scotland] all trace their blood to our Greater Scotia [Ireland] and retain to some degree our language and customs."

Robert Bruce sent his brother Edward into Ireland with six thousand troops. He won victories against the Anglo-Irish and their allies, and in 1316, at Dundalk, Edward Bruce was recognized by some as High King of Ireland. But in the south of the country, though at one point Robert Bruce arrived to assist his brother, clan feuds overrode all other concerns. These were famine years in Ireland, and some of the Irish viewed the arriving Scots as indistinguishable from the English.

In 1318, after his brother Edward was killed at the Battle of Faughart, near Dundalk, Robert Bruce abandoned his goal of uniting the Scots and the Irish. Michael Penman, a historian featured in the BBC docudrama, says the defeat at Faughart was "so categorical Bruce must have thought, 'I cannot throw another 6,000 men at this.'" According to a report in the *Scotsman*, Penman believes that the Irish campaign may have been downplayed because "it doesn't fit with the image of a patriot king defying English imperialism if he, in turn, invades another country."

Robert Bruce undoubtedly saw his initiative rather as an attempt to reunite two Celtic peoples. That objective would be met centuries later in what, to Bruce, would have been an inconceivable manner. Here in Canada, the reuniting of the Scots and the Irish would take the form of an intertwining, and a recognition that the two peoples share certain foundational values—not least among them, a commitment to independence.

Situated on a hill near the Alberta College of Art and Design in Calgary, this equestrian statue of King Robert the Bruce is a duplicate of the one at Bannockburn, Scotland. Canadian philanthropist Eric L. Harvie funded the creation of both in 1964. The Calgary Burns Club added a new plaque in 2014 to mark the three-hundredth anniversary of the Battle of Bannockburn.

PART TWO
DEMOCRACY

In October 2014, Canadians were outraged by the cowardly, cold-blooded murder of a soldier standing on ceremonial duty in Ottawa. We were angry that the gunman had then been able to race into the Centre Block, the main building of Canada's Parliamentary complex, and wound several guards before dying in a hail of bullets. We were glad that this despicable fanatic was cut down before he could do any more damage. And the next day, we felt proud when our elected representatives returned to Parliament Hill and, after a brief but emotional display of solidarity, went back to work. We expected no less. Canadian democracy is alive and well.

Less than one month later, an Ontario judge sent a former Conservative Party staffer to jail for violating the Canada Elections Act. Michael Sona got nine months for "an affront to the electoral process." He was convicted in the "robocalls" scandal for preventing or trying to prevent electors from voting. Twenty-two years old at the time, Sona sent out 6,700 automated phone calls with misleading information about how to vote.

The judge described this as "a deliberate and considered course of criminal conduct designed to subvert the inherent fairness of the electoral process." The federal election was not "some Grade

8 election campaign for student council," he said, but was held "to elect representatives who form the governing body of our nation." The bottom line? In this country, democracy is held dear.

Canada's parliamentary variation, in which the prime minister is responsible to the legislature, derives from the Westminster model of Great Britain. The same is true of the way we conduct elections: first-past-the-post, winner-take-all. This voting system frequently creates governments that a majority of Canadians do not want, which is why we should probably introduce a measure of proportional representation. But to abandon the egalitarian principle of democracy itself: one citizen, one vote—for Canadians, that is unthinkable. Democracy is so deeply rooted in Canada as to be inseparable from the country's existence.

Why should this be so? Cultural genealogy. Consider the ancient Celts, whose legal system of Brehon laws, administered by judges or Brehons, is generally regarded as the most democratic of the fifth and sixth centuries. Saint Patrick is credited with codifying many of these laws in the five-volume Senchus Mor. To originate or abolish a law required nine representatives: chief, poet, historian, landowner, bishop, professor of literature, professor of law, noble, and lay vicar. The laws applied equally to the king and the tradesman, though for the same offence, a wealthy clergyman might be fined twice as much as a poor layman.

Under Brehon law, nearly everyone in Gaelic Ireland and Gaelic Scotland could participate in choosing their own tribal leaders or kings. Well into the Middle Ages, each of the five provinces in Ireland had an elected king. And until the end of the twelfth century, even the High King was elected under Brehon law.

As for women, they had as much right as men to education and property. They could be druidesses (priests), poets, physicians, sages, and lawgivers. Elected queens would often lead armies into battle. The legendary Cuchulainn learned his warrior trade from a woman named Aoife and fought his greatest battles against Queen Maeve. Women were exempted from warfare in 697, under the influence of Christianity, but the female-warrior tradition lived on and gave rise, much later, to the likes of Grace O'Malley.

In the early 800s, Scandinavian Vikings arrived and ransacked monastic settlements in both Ireland and the Scottish isles. Then, over the next three centuries, the raiders became settlers. They integrated and joined the Celts in creating a Norse-Gaelic culture. And they reinforced the prevailing democratic tendencies. Since around 600, Vikings had used assemblies called Tings (Things) to settle disputes, pass laws, and elect kings, who then swore allegiance to the Ting. These assemblies gave rise to a parliamentary "Tynwald," which in Old Norse meant "meeting place" or "field of the Thing." It was situated on the Isle of Man, south of Scotland between Ireland and northern England.

From here, late in the eleventh century, the sea lord Godred Crovan created a uniquely extensive, quasi-democratic Norse-Gaelic kingdom. It encompassed western Scotland, Wales, Ireland, parts of England, and the Isle of Man. Some scholars say Crovan was born in Islay, while others claim he was Norse-Gaelic from Ireland. Either way, from 1079 to 1095, Crovan used the Norse system of government, Tynwald, to govern his far-reaching maritime kingdom. Kings and chieftains came annually to the Isle of Man from Dublin, Islay, and beyond to participate in what today is recognized as the world's oldest continuous parliament.

Such was the historical background against which, in 1320, the Scots produced the Declaration of Arbroath, often cited as a precursor to the American Declaration of Independence. This document, produced soon after Robert the Bruce won independence for Scotland, took the form of a letter to Pope John XXII. Written to signal that Scotland was a sovereign state, and signed by eight Scottish earls and thirty-one barons, it contained the democratic assertion that independence was the prerogative not of the King of Scots but of the Scottish people. And it added that, if Robert the Bruce proved unable to maintain Scotland's independence, the nobles could choose someone else to be king.

After Arbroath, democracy in Scotland waited more than two centuries for another major advance. Finally, in the 1500s, it arrived through the unlikely agency of a firebrand preacher named John Knox. Almost despite himself, Knox engineered a literacy revolution that would cross the Atlantic Ocean. In Canada, democratic principles arrived with such figures as Lord Elgin, the Scottish Governor General who faced down an insurrection in the name of responsible government; and Robert Baldwin, a Canadian of Anglo-Irish heritage who forged an alliance with a Roman Catholic Quebecer to create a democratic government answering to the people it governed. We will enter our story deeper still, with the birth of Canadian Confederation, before we flash back to shuttle again between Scottish and Irish ancestors.

7.

Sir John A. Macdonald

I t is easy enough to reach the chief Canadian site dedicated to Sir John A. Macdonald, the foremost father of Confederation. From City Hall in Kingston, you make your way west along King Street for two kilometres. Walk, drive, ride a bus. At Centre Street, turn right and proceed half a block to number 35. There it sits: Bellevue House, where in the 1840s, Macdonald lived with his wife and infant son. You can poke around the house and gardens, study exhibits celebrating Macdonald's career, and interact with interpreters in period costume.

The main Scottish memorial, harder to reach, is much more fun—not the historical plaque in downtown Glasgow, marking the neighbourhood where Macdonald was born, but the cairn at the site of his grandfather's croft. From Inverness, you drive north for an hour before swinging west off the highway. For ten minutes, you follow a secondary road, the A839, and then, at a hamlet called Pittentrail, you turn north. After passing through Rogart, you spot a small sign and veer onto a rutted dirt road that winds away into the trees.

This cairn in Rogart, Sutherland, is built of stones from the croft of Sir John A. Macdonald's grandfather, ousted during the Highland Clearances. It was dedicated to Sir John in 1968 by Canadian prime minister John Diefenbaker, whose mother, Mary Bannerman, descended from a Red River colonist.

Follow that track, rattling along through the woods. Go under the trestle and around a sharp corner. Shake off the idea that you have missed it. Eventually, you come over a rise and there it stands on the left: a cairn with a bench and a Canadian flag. The cairn is built of stones from the croft that belonged to Macdonald's grandfather, ousted during the Highland Clearances. It bears a plaque inscribed to Sir John A.: "His monument is a nation. This cairn is but a footnote to his greatness."

In recent years, Macdonald has been called a racist by those who would condemn a nineteenth-century figure by twenty-first-century standards. But were it not for Sir John A., as biographer Richard Gwyn has demonstrated, those critics would not be around to carp because Canada itself would not exist. Macdonald led the way to the invention of a democratic country in which freedom of expression allows for fierce criticism. As a corollary accomplishment, he engineered the creation of the Canadian Pacific Railway, which gave rise to a country extending from the Atlantic to the Pacific. And he instituted the North West Mounted Police, so engendering Canadian attitudes about guns and gun control that are profoundly different from those found in the United States.

John A. Macdonald was far from perfect. He did not transcend his era in every attitude. As Gwyn demonstrates, the man was not an ideologue but a pragmatist: a man who could get things done. He committed bad mistakes. He made hurtful comments about Asian immigrants, giving voice to Canadian prejudices which were then near-universal. But he also intervened to stifle a racist protest against a black postal worker. Today, many Canadians are justifiably appalled by the treatment accorded First Nations peoples, both then and now. Of the latter, he declared: "We must remember they are the original owners of the soil of which they have been dispossessed by the covetousness or ambition of our ancestors."

Macdonald was not a visionary. When he introduced the Indian Act of 1876, he did not foresee that it would lead to the mistreatment and sexual abuse of native students in residential schools. He did worry that building the railway was having a negative impact. But he warned that "we cannot as Christians, and as men with hearts in our bosoms, allow the vagabond Indian to die before us." Later, he insisted "We must prevent them from starving, in consequence of the extinction of the buffalo and their not yet (having) betaken themselves to raising crops."

John A. Macdonald sought to broaden Canadian democracy by extending the vote to both women and First Nations peoples. Historian Donald B. Smith has argued that, "if judged by the standards of his age, not ours, [Macdonald] emerges as a complex and relatively tolerant individual." True, in 1885, he suppressed the Northwest Rebellion. "Yet, in the same year," Smith writes,

"Canada's first prime minister worked to give all those adult male Indians in Central and Eastern Canada, who had the necessary property qualifications, the federal franchise—without the loss of their Indian status." This singular politician, Gwyn argues, was indispensable in hammering disparate dreams and aspirations into a shared vision of an independent, continent-wide democracy.

❧❧❧

John A. Macdonald (1815–1891) grew up Scottish Presbyterian in Kingston, Ontario. In the late 1700s, his grandfather, also named John, was one of the tens of thousands of crofters driven off their small farms by landlords bent on turning their holdings to more profitable sheep farming. He moved his family to Dornoch, twenty kilometres south, and in that bustling town became "the merchant Macdonald." His son, Hugh, grew up, married well, and moved south to Glasgow, where he tried and failed to break into the textile business.

In 1820, the ambitious Hugh, unwilling to admit defeat, pulled up stakes and crossed the Atlantic to start a new life in Kingston, a bustling market town of four thousand people. With him he brought his wife and four children, among them a five-year-old son named John Alexander Macdonald. In Kingston, dominated by Scottish immigrants, Hugh Macdonald operated a series of shops and businesses. He flourished. By 1829, he had become a local magistrate.

His son, the future prime minister, proved an insatiable reader. According to biographer Donald Creighton, "He would sit for hours deep in a book, almost oblivious to what was going on." He attended private schools as a boy, switching at fourteen to a co-educational school founded by a Presbyterian minister recently arrived from Scotland, and brimming with Scottish values and attitudes. The following year, because the law profession demanded experience rather than specialized education, Macdonald went to work as an apprentice in the office of a Kingston lawyer, George Mackenzie.

At twenty, in August 1835, he opened his own Kingston law office. After serving (without firing a shot) in the militia that quelled the Upper Canada Rebellion of 1837, Macdonald nevertheless defended a rebel leader named Nils von Schoultz. That man rejected the young lawyer's advice, pleaded guilty to treason, and so, to Macdonald's lasting regret, got himself hanged. Welcome to the real world.

By this time, Macdonald had become active politically with the Celtic Society, the Young Men's Society, and the St. Andrew's Society. In March 1843, at twenty-eight, he won election as a Kingston alderman. The following year, after a campaign championing the maintenance of close ties with Britain, he was elected as a Conservative to the legislative assembly of the united Province of Canada. That province had been created in 1841, when Upper and Lower Canada, renamed Canada West and Canada East, were brought into a single legislature affording each of them forty-two seats.

Over the next thirty years, based in Kingston, Macdonald would win ten consecutive elections—seven to that legislature and three, beginning in 1867, to the confederated Parliament. He proved wonderfully witty. During one campaign, while serving as Member of Parliament for Kingston, Macdonald turned to a colleague and asked: "Do I have your support?"

"You always have my support," the man said, "when you're right."

"That I can get from anyone," Macdonald answered. "I need people who will support me when I'm wrong."

During his first decade as an elected politician, Macdonald remained a staunch Conservative. He opposed any initiative that might weaken ties with Great Britain or undercut the propertied interests he represented. This meant resisting any extension of the right to vote to men without property, and opposing even responsible government—the notion that the prime minister and his cabinet were responsible not to the Governor General (who represented the British monarch) but to the legislative assembly elected by the people.

In 1854, Macdonald became Attorney General for Canada West in a French-English coalition government that emerged, according to historian John Charles Dent, from negotiations in which "his was the hand that shaped the course." For thirteen years, except for brief periods when the Conservatives lost power, he retained that office. Early on, he pushed through a controversial bill on private schools that formed the basis for the existing system in Ontario, defending the right of Roman Catholics "to educate their children according to their own principles."

After some deft political infighting, Macdonald became co-premier of the united Province of Canada, representing Canada West. The following November, when George-Étienne Cartier gained control of Canada East, he acquired a long-standing French Canadian partner. He controlled the Conservative Party tightly, intervening even at the riding level, and sought allies among the leaders of large blocks of voters, including the Methodist and Catholic Churches and the Orange Order.

Socially, Macdonald's instincts were progressive—prototypically "Red Tory." Already, as leader of the government, he had laid the foundations for Canada's social welfare system, setting standards for asylums, reformatories, and correctional institutions. He had reformed the judicial system, improved roads and transportation, and created a department of finance. As a strategic pragmatist, Macdonald had no rivals. During the onset of the American Civil War, he held together a fragile coalition of Conservatives and moderate Reformers—mainly by developing and controlling a patronage system.

Along the way, famously, Macdonald drank heavily. His bingeing became a serious public problem in spring 1862, when he had "one of his old attacks," as the *Globe* reported, during an extended debate over expanding the militia. Defeated on the Militia Bill, the government resigned. Macdonald would spend the next two years in opposition.

At his best, Macdonald was inspirational. Picture him in 1864 during the run-up to Confederation, addressing his fellow political delegates at a dinner in Halifax. "I thought there was no end, nothing worthy of ambition," he declared. "But now I see something which is worthy of all I have suffered in the cause of my little country." Macdonald, age forty-nine, was lauding Confederation as the first step in creating a new democracy, the Dominion of Canada, which would stand as a unified bastion against the expansionism of the United States.

The preceding conference, held in Charlottetown on Prince Edward Island, had originally been set to consider a legislative union of Britain's three maritime colonies: P.E.I., Nova Scotia, and New Brunswick. These three had agreed to welcome delegates from the Province of Canada, which included present-day Quebec and Ontario, and to hear proposals for a larger union.

Not everybody was happy with the end result. One New Brunswick newspaper complained that smooth-talking Canadian delegates, notably Macdonald and his Irish ally Thomas D'Arcy McGee, "had it all their own way." They entertained delegates with fancy, alcohol-fueled lunches. At these they put forward cogent, well-rehearsed arguments, leavening them with anecdotes and sparkling wit. It hardly seemed fair.

A few weeks after the Charlottetown meeting, delegates gathered in Quebec City. Once again, Macdonald took the lead. Drawing attention to American expressions of manifest destiny, the idea that the United States was destined to control all of North America, he argued in favour of retaining close ties with Great Britain. He stressed that a larger, more comprehensive union would prove stronger and more sustainable. Why not unite the two Canadas, East and West, with the maritime colonies? Why not then incorporate British Columbia and Vancouver Island to create a British North America that extended from sea to sea?

Sir John A. Macdonald, photographed by Mathew Brady between 1860 and 1875, drew on his legal background to draft the constitutional framework for an emerging nation. Macdonald drafted fifty of the seventy-two resolutions passed at the Quebec Conference of 1864.

Macdonald gained traction with these ideas as tensions increased with the United States. During the American Civil War, which began in 1861, an Underground Railway carried tens of thousands of runaway slaves into the northern colonies. In 1793, Upper Canada (Ontario) had passed the Anti-Slavery Act, and so achieved gradual abolition: slaves already in the province remained enslaved until death, but no new slaves could be brought into the province, and children born to female slaves were freed at age twenty-five. Then, in 1833, the Emancipation Act had abolished slavery throughout Britain and its colonies. In the 1860s, given this background, Macdonald refused to extradite former slaves or to allow "slave hunters" to return them to the owners.

Meanwhile, in 1857, some Irish Americans had initiated the Fenian movement to secure Irish independence from Britain. Some of these Fenians wanted to invade "British North America" to exert pressure on the British government—a desire that would give rise to five Fenian raids, ultimately unsuccessful, between 1866 and 1871.

The crisis atmosphere engendered by the American Civil War and the rise of the Fenians led opposition leader George Brown, urged on by Thomas D'Arcy McGee, to call for a coalition government that would look at creating a more flexible, federal union of Canada East and Canada West. Already, Alexander Tilloch Galt, son of the Scottish colonizer John Galt, had developed a plan to unite the two Canadas and the Maritimes. And in 1864, drawing on his legal background, John A. Macdonald began drafting a constitutional framework to create a still more extensive nation, one reaching from the Atlantic to the Pacific. Later, McGee would report that Macdonald wrote fifty of the seventy-two resolutions passed at the Quebec Conference.

Given a free hand, Macdonald would have established a stronger central government. But as he told a friend, "of course it does not do to adopt that point of view in discussing the subject in Lower Canada." *Plus ça change.* To the federal government, Macdonald reserved control over national defence, finance, trade and commerce, taxation, currency, and banking. He believed the provincial governments so weak they would wither and die.

Nor was that his only miscalculation. Macdonald failed to provide a mechanism for amending the Constitution—an omission that would haunt the country even after 1982, giving rise to more than one failed accord. He gave no thought to the importance of natural resources or to providing for cities, and he rode roughshod over the rights of aboriginal peoples—all of which would lead to major challenges in the twentieth and twenty-first centuries.

Yet, in December 1866, when Macdonald went to London to lead one final Confederation conference, and to shepherd the British North America Act through the British Parliament, he knew enough to bring representatives from all the colonies involved. With American officials arguing, outrageously, that Britain should cede Vancouver Island and British Columbia to the United States for damages sustained during the American Civil War, the British hailed Macdonald as "the ruling genius" of Confederation.

By March 29, when Queen Victoria gave royal assent to the British North America Act, stipulating July 1 as its effective date, Macdonald was back in Canada. The BNA Act signalled the beginning of a new era. On July 1, 1867, three British colonies became four provinces within the Dominion of Canada, as Quebec and Ontario (derived from the united Province of Canada) combined with New Brunswick and Nova Scotia. British Columbia joined Confederation in 1871, and Prince Edward Island did so two years later. Over time, the other provinces and territories became part of the emerging nation. For having led Confederation, Macdonald received a knight-hood from Queen Victoria. He became "Sir John A."

From the vantage point of the twenty-first century, we can see that, more than once, Macdonald stood on the wrong side of history. In 1885, Macdonald refused to commute the death sentence of Louis Riel, who was convicted of high treason after the Northwest Rebellion (but hanged for the execution of immigrant Orangeman Thomas Scott). One cannot help but think that if Thomas D'Arcy McGee had still been with him, Macdonald would have dealt dif-ferently with Riel. Also in 1885, Macdonald made racist remarks while denying Chinese immigrants the right to vote in federal elec-tions. On the other hand, three years before, he had intervened crucially in support of the escaped ex-slave Albert Jackson, whose appointment as Toronto's first black postal worker had sparked a racist backlash.

Macdonald also became the world's first national leader to advocate expanding democracy to include women. Early in 1885, while proposing legislation to allow women to vote, Macdonald suggested that Canada "should have the honour of first placing woman in the position that she is certain, after centuries of oppression, to obtain." This meant "completely establishing her equality as a human being and as a member of society with man." The change would come, Macdonald insisted: it was "merely a matter of time." His argument fell on deaf ears. In 1893, New Zealand became the first nation to grant women the vote. Canada did not follow suit until 1918—thirty-three years after Macdonald championed the idea.

Were it not for Sir John A. Macdonald, who absorbed Celtic values and philosophical memes from his Scottish Highlander par-ents, teachers, and peers, Canada as we know it would not exist. Since his day, Canadian democracy—one citizen, one vote—has brought Canadians to the point where we struggle, at least, to

eradicate the racist attitudes that prevailed in the nineteenth century, and to turn this country into a beacon of inclusion. According
to Richard Gwyn, Macdonald was "the one irreplaceable man." I
would say, rather, that he was "one irreplaceable man." To my mind,
and from the perspective of today, there was one other . . .

8.

Thomas D'Arcy McGee

⬚⬚⬚

Picture a cloud-dark night in September 1848, when, on the north coast of Ireland near Rathmullan, a few sympathetic souls embarked to row a brilliant young journalist out to a passing American ship whose captain had agreed to carry him to Philadelphia. Thomas D'Arcy McGee, charged with treason and running for his life as a too-articulate leader of the Young Ireland Rebellion, had narrowly escaped his pursuers. He could not know it, but his flight would lead eventually to Canada, to an alliance with John A. Macdonald—already serving as a Member of Parliament— and to his own emergence as one of the country's leading fathers of Confederation.

When he sailed on the *Shamrock*, though still just twenty-three, McGee had already spent three years in America. The precocious young man had served as the editor of a Boston weekly journal aimed at Irish Americans. He had also published two books—one a novella about a heroine of the 1798 Rebellion, the other celebrating Daniel O'Connell and his allies. After returning to Ireland in 1845, he had gone to work for the nationalist *Nation* newspaper, and had emerged as an especially effective Young Irelander.

By 1848, the Potato Famine was wreaking havoc in much of Ireland. With revolutions arising throughout continental Europe, Young Ireland broke away from Daniel O'Connell's gradualist Repeal Association to demand independence and an autonomous national parliament. Late in July, in south Tipperary, a Young Ireland militia had exchanged gunfire with four dozen Irish police during a standoff at the Widow McCormack's House. Reinforcements arrived, the rebels scattered, and the authorities began rounding up Young Irelanders.

In his definitive, two-volume biography, *Thomas D'Arcy McGee*, author David A. Wilson argues convincingly that, when McGee boarded the *Shamrock* for Philadelphia, his mind "contained the seeds for both Canadian Confederation and Irish American Fenianism." His early Irish nationalism, Wilson explains, resembled the platform he advocated at Confederation. Both sets of scaffolding involved "legislative autonomy within the British Empire, pluralism and minority rights, cultural and economic nationalism, railway development, and an overarching sense of destiny."

❈❈

Thomas D'Arcy McGee was born in Carlingford on April 13, 1825. His mother was the daughter of a Dublin bookseller, and taught him early to value history and literature. He spent his childhood at Cushendall on the north coast, where his father worked for the Coast Guard Service. When he was eight, his father was transferred to Wexford, where his mother's family had been active in the 1798 Rebellion. She died soon afterwards, and McGee attended a "pay school" run by an outstanding teacher whose father had been hanged at New Ross after one of the bloodiest battles of 1798.

At age fourteen, inspired by a nationwide temperance movement, McGee published two poems in the local newspaper, both paeans to sobriety. Around this time, his father remarried. McGee and his siblings disliked their stepmother, and when a sister of their late mother invited them to move to America, he and one sister quickly accepted. In 1842, at seventeen, McGee became one of almost 93,000 Irishmen to cross the Atlantic that year. He sailed from Wexford on a timber ship to Quebec. He went south, deposited his sister with his aunt in Providence, Rhode Island, and then proceeded back north, to Boston, to seek work.

McGee was already a wordsmith. On the ship, he had written poetry about Irish independence. And on the Fourth of July, American Independence Day, he gave a rousing speech to the Boston Friends of Ireland, blaming "a heartless, bigoted, despotic government," British of course, for the sufferings of the Irish. Ireland's "people are born slaves," he declared, "and bred in slavery from the cradle; they know not what freedom is."

This went over well and won him a job at the weekly *Boston Pilot*, an Irish Catholic newspaper. For two years, he travelled around New England building circulation by giving speeches about Daniel O'Connell and his campaign to repeal the Act of Union that tied Ireland to Britain. Meanwhile, believing that Irish literature provided an argument for independence, he wrote and, in the *Pilot*, published profiles of forty Irish authors. By March 1844, tiring of travel, McGee was planning to study law when he accepted an invitation to move beyond reporting and become editor of the *Pilot*.

Over the next year, he wrote editorials urging the Irish in America to support the independence movement in Ireland. He led a campaign to establish evening schools for immigrants. Looking north, McGee initially backed the Anglo-Irish Canadian Robert Baldwin in his drive for responsible government. But according to Robin B. Burns in the *Dictionary of Canadian Biography*, the 1845 Oregon boundary dispute between the British and the Americans led him to support the doctrine of manifest destiny: "Either by purchase, conquest, or stipulation," McGee wrote, "Canada must be yielded by Great Britain to this Republic."

On this subject, he would later reverse his position. But in May 1845, after a year at the helm of the *Pilot*, McGee sailed home to Dublin to work for the *Freeman's Journal*. A few months before, Daniel O'Connell had been transported through the streets of Dublin in an elaborate chariot after his release from jail. Now, when he saw O'Connell walk onto the stage at a meeting of the Repeal Association, McGee felt as if "an electric wire were pouring in its flood at every pore of my body . . . I had never seen a man with so great a load of history on his back, and the proximity of so much self-achieved greatness made the air hot about me, and immersed me in a kind of intoxicating delirium."

Early in 1846, McGee crossed the Irish Sea to London to cover parliamentary proceedings. Still just twenty years old, he felt drawn to Young Ireland, a group of young Irish intellectuals who were increasingly critical of O'Connell's gradualist approach to independence. McGee contributed two short volumes to their Library of Ireland series of books and also began writing for their newspaper, the *Nation*. This was too much for the *Freeman's Journal*, which fired him. As he turned twenty-one, he began writing regularly for the *Nation*. At the British Museum, he delved into Irish history. He produced a book on Irish writers of the seventeenth century, and did research that would fuel his 1852 book on the Protestant Reformation in Ireland.

In the summer of 1846, he returned from England to Ireland. When O'Connell announced an alliance with the British Whig government, McGee backed Young Ireland in breaking with O'Connell to form the more confrontational Irish Confederation. He became a main speaker at its public meetings, and in June 1847, he was elected secretary. He married Mary Caffrey the following month, and with her would have six children.

Thomas D'Arcy McGee, photographed on December 31, 1867, was the most eloquent democrat of the Irish diaspora. Roughly three months after William Notman created this image, McGee was ambushed and shot dead at his own front door.

The previous November, increasingly aware of the worsening potato famine, McGee had worried that "the famine which is fast making one wide graveyard of this island" was being overshadowed by O'Connell's attacks on Young Ireland. As the famine worsened, public works failed. More than three million people were surviving on soup. Some people advocated mass emigration to Canada, but McGee argued that the government should instead ban grain exports and spend money on improving the economy. He denounced wholesale emigration as a "swindling speculation" concocted by the landlords, who to save their own skins were ready to see "2,000,000 Irishmen . . . banished into the Canadian backwoods."

At one point, McGee gave a powerful speech declaring that the towns of Ireland had "become one universal poorhouse and fever-shed, the country one great grave-yard." The survivors of famine and pestilence had "fled to the sea-coast and embarked for America . . . and the ships that bore them have become sailing coffins, and carried them to a new world, indeed; not to America, but to eternity." His allusion to "sailing coffins" would spawn the term "coffin ships."

In February 1848, after a revolution in France overthrew a monarchy, the Irish Confederation began advocating armed rebellion. In July, McGee was arrested for sedition, but then released. The Irish Confederation sought to rally support throughout the country, and sent McGee to Scotland to gather sympathizers. In Edinburgh, he read in the *Times* that authorities were describing him and Thomas Meagher—later a hero of the American Civil War—as "the two most dangerous men now abroad."

After making arrangements for a small army of Scots to follow, he returned to northern Ireland to rally more support. He found that in his absence, and following the debacle at the Widow McCormack's House, the resistance had fallen apart. The government was rounding up and jailing Young Irelanders, most of whom would soon be transported in chains to Van Diemen's Land (Tasmania). With the authorities in hot pursuit, actively seeking to arrest him for treason, McGee made his way to the northern coast. On September 1, 1848, he boarded the *Shamrock,* and so sailed to Philadelphia.

Now began the long, slow transformation of Thomas D'Arcy McGee from Irish revolutionary into passionate Canadian democrat and father of Confederation. Even before he fled Ireland, as David A. Wilson shows in his tour-de-force biography, McGee had been taken with the thinking of the Scottish intellectual David Urquhart, who led a small pro-Repeal group in the British House of Commons.

He regarded Urquhart as "one of the most remarkable men of the age," and took from him a new appreciation of decentralized organization, or federalism, and the concept of the British crown as a powerful symbol of liberty. Over the next two decades, McGee would build on this foundation to create a vision of a new Canadian nation—a British North American democracy extending from sea to sea.

But in 1848, soon after arriving in Philadelphia, he moved to New York City and launched his own newspaper, the *Nation*. In his editorials, he supported nationalist revolutions in Europe and called, as before, for the American annexation of Canada. By the end of 1849, he had created enemies by backing an Irish reform movement that opposed violence and advocated working within the existing constitution. McGee described one revolutionary hothead, later a Fenian leader, as "a man who asserts as truth, what he knows not to be true." When the man challenged him to a duel, he brushed him off.

Early in 1850, McGee returned to Boston and started *The American Celt and Adopted Citizen*. He moved this newspaper to Buffalo and then, in 1853, back to New York. Meanwhile, between 1851 and 1857, he published five books. He wrote about the history of Irish settlement, revolutionary liberalism, the Protestant

Reformation in Ireland, Catholics in North America, and the Catholic priest Edward Maginn.

Also, and most significantly, he became critical of the American state, seeing it as discriminating against Roman Catholics. By 1855, he was urging Irish Catholics to leave the cities of the east to establish a colony in the American west. When that idea failed to gain traction, McGee looked north with fresh eyes.

Now came the sea change. McGee realized that in Canada East (Quebec), Roman Catholics constituted a majority, and had enjoyed legal protection since 1774. The united Province of Canada provided them far greater security than the United States. McGee looked again at manifest destiny, the doctrine that the United States would one day govern all of North America. This time, he judged it pernicious. It was an extension of the approach that, in the 1830s, had seen forty-six thousand native Americans forcibly removed from their homelands to open twenty-five million acres of land to white settlement.

In the spring of 1857, in response to an invitation from leading Irish Catholics, McGee moved north to Montreal. He had already visited twice. And for two years, he had been urging Irish emigrants to choose Canada over the United States. McGee had barely got off the train from Boston in 1857, historian Christopher Moore writes, "when he began advocating federal union, westward expansion, and the nurturing of a national literature for Canada." In Montreal, while thinking to enter politics, he launched the *New Era* newspaper. From this editorial perch, he began articulating a program for "a new nationality" involving railway development, immigration, and "a federal compact" among provinces.

McGee had become an ardent democrat. Building on the strategies and ideas of Daniel O'Connell and David Urquhart, he championed the development of a North American alternative to the United States. This sovereign "kingdom of the St. Lawrence" would retain a connection with Great Britain. Drawing on the nationalist theories he had developed within Young Ireland, he highlighted the importance of creating a distinctive Canadian literature, and urged tariff protection for Canadian publishers.

In December 1857, backed by the St. Patrick's Society of Montreal, McGee was elected to Canada's legislative assembly. Now began a decade of political wrangling. McGee organized Irish Catholics in Canada West (Ontario). He issued a manifesto endorsing a federal union of the two Canadas. A sparkling orator, McGee became increasingly prominent through the early 1860s: "I see in the not remote distance," he declared, "one great nationality bound, like the shield of Achilles, by the blue rim of ocean . . . I see within the ground of that shield the peaks of the western mountains and the crests of the eastern waves."

In 1863, McGee published letters and articles outlining his vision of a British North America. He argued, as Wilson notes, that by retaining their links with the crown under a constitutional monarchy, Canadians had achieved a better balance between freedom and order than the U.S. had. And he insisted that "a man can state his private, social, political and religious opinions with more freedom here than in New York or New England. There is, besides, far more liberty and toleration enjoyed by minorities in Canada than in the United States."

To advance Roman Catholicism within Canada, McGee had taken to championing minority rights. That meant embracing pragmatism and pluralism. Having begun his career as an independent, he had survived several different alliances. By the early 1860s, he found himself increasingly aligned with Conservative leader John A. Macdonald.

This Celtic alliance, Irish Catholic and Scottish Protestant, augmented by the Quebec Roman Catholic George-Étienne Cartier, built on the democratic foundations inspired by earlier Scottish and

Irish figures, some of whom turn up in this book. Together, McGee and Macdonald would orchestrate Confederation into existence, unifying four separate British colonies into one country, Canada. At the same time, they imbued this new country with values they brought from their Celtic homelands.

Nobody knew better than McGee how much the Irish shared with the Scots. In his *Popular History of Ireland: From the Earliest Period to the Emancipation of the Catholics,* for example, McGee invokes the Age of Somerled: "On the eve of the Norman invasion," he writes, "we saw how heartily the Irish were with Somerled and the men of Moray in resisting the feudal polity of the successors of [King Malcom III of Scotland]." He turns then, in this astonishing two-volume work, to Robert the Bruce and his links to Ireland. Most Canadians think of McGee as a politician who died a martyr to the rejection of revolution in favour of democracy, but this history shows him to be also, and perhaps primarily, a towering intellectual.

Sure enough, biographer David A. Wilson tells us that this *Popular History*, later overlooked by both Canadian and Irish scholars, "was the crowning achievement of McGee's literary career." It fulfilled a boyhood ambition, influenced subsequent histories of Ireland, and at times echoed "his oft-delivered lecture on the historical connection between the Irish and the Scots."

In the 1860s, McGee told an Irish American journalist that, at present, "it would be little short of madness to expect" that Ireland would now be able to wrest political independence from England. Wilson summarizes McGee's thinking: "Far better, then, to focus on practical changes within the Act of Union, such as tenant rights and the disestablishment of the Church of Ireland, using Canada as a guide and a model. If Canada demonstrated that Irish Catholics were loyal when they were treated fairly, what better example could be set for British policy in Ireland?"

And so we come to the launching of Confederation. For years, Thomas D'Arcy McGee had been warning against the doctrine of manifest destiny then popular among Americans: "They coveted Florida, and seized it; they coveted Louisiana, and purchased it; they coveted Texas, and stole it, and then picked a quarrel with Mexico, which ended by their getting California . . . Had we not had the strong arm of England over us, we should not now have had a separate existence."

At the same time, and as a corollary, McGee advocated that the projected intercolonial railway should extend not just from central Canada to the Pacific Ocean but also to the Atlantic—a position that won him friends in the east. In 1864, when the maritime colonies organized a conference in Charlottetown to discuss forming a political union among themselves, he was ideally positioned to lead a Canadian delegation promoting the idea of a larger federation.

He convinced maritime boards of trade to invite him and a number of prominent businessmen on a goodwill tour of the eastern colonies. As Wilson writes, "Playing on civic pride, dispensing drinks, co-opting journalists, claiming to be nonpolitical, and pretending they had not invited themselves, McGee and his entourage privately and publicly pressed the case for Confederation and the new nationality." He debated naysayers, arguing that a common market would open up opportunities while an east-to-west railway would foster a national consciousness.

Maritime newspapers published paeans to the "brilliant D'Arcy," who could be "joyous and grave, comic and refined, all in the same sentence." Charles Tupper, soon to become premier of Nova Scotia, observed "that Mr. McGee has done more to promote the social, commercial and political union of British North America than any other public man in these provinces."

Having cleared the way, McGee relinquished the spotlight when the Charlottetown Conference began, and allowed Macdonald to hammer out the details of a federal arrangement dividing powers between national and provincial governments. As Wilson writes, McGee's main contribution to the conference lay not in working out details, but in the whirl of related social events. In *The Life and Times of Confederation 1864–1867*, P. B. Waite explains that the Canadian delegates "were suspect: their good faith was not something that Maritimers were prepared to take for granted. The removal of this miasma of hostility and suspicion was not to be the work of three halcyon weeks in August, 1864."

Opponents of Confederation, among them politician Joseph Howe, had reason to take aim at McGee. The Fredericton *Head Quarters* complained that the Canadian delegates, "what with their arguments and what with their blandishments, (they gave a champagne lunch on board the *Victoria* where Mr. McGee's wit sparkled brightly as the wine) . . . carried the Lower Province delegates a little off their feet." The conference moved from Charlottetown to Halifax, and delegates agreed to meet in Quebec to finalize the terms of political union.

At the Quebec Conference, McGee intervened only to protect minority rights in education, moving an amendment to guarantee "the rights and privileges which the Protestant or Catholic minority in both Canadas may profess as to their denominational schools." That conference adopted seventy-two resolutions to go before provincial legislatures. After a few further amendments, a final conference was held in London in 1866. And on July 1, 1867, the British North America Act created the Dominion of Canada.

Meanwhile, during an 1865 visit to Ireland, where former Irish rebels like himself had been pardoned, Thomas D'Arcy McGee spoke in Wexford and again urged emigrants to choose Canada over the United States. As a forty-year-old democrat who believed in the ballot box and constitutional change, he repudiated the American-based Fenian Brotherhood, which advocated attacking Canada as a way of pressuring Great Britain to vacate Ireland. And he disavowed his own revolutionary days as "the follies of one and twenty."

This speech created an extraordinary backlash, not just in Ireland and the U.S., but also in Canada. In September 1867, denounced as a traitor, and having been expelled from the St. Patrick's Society, McGee nevertheless won election to the House of Commons. But as a politician, he had become a lightning rod for criticism. McGee decided: enough. He would wash his hands of politics and devote himself to writing literature and history. The prime minister, Sir John A. Macdonald, promised to give him a civil service position that would enable him to do so.

But on April 7, 1868, after participating in a late-running session in the House of Commons, the most eloquent democrat ever to emerge from the Irish diaspora was ambushed on the steps of his Ottawa rooming house. Thomas D'Arcy McGee was shot to death by a Fenian sympathizer.

One cannot help wondering how different Canadian history might have been if McGee had escaped assassination. Historian Christopher Moore reminds us that McGee had outlined a plan "for a separate province to be set aside for the native nations on the plains of the far North West. He had begun to imagine a new country where none existed." How would McGee have responded to the Indian Act of 1876, which aimed to assimilate indigenous peoples? He did have the ear of Macdonald. And given that he was a champion of minority rights, and had envisioned the emergence of a separate province for First Nations peoples, he might well have sought to subvert that Act. Also, McGee was staunchly Roman Catholic. He had led the battle against Orange Order intolerance. How would he have responded to the judgment against Louis Riel? Would he have been able to prevent the hanging?

Richard Gwyn has described John A. Macdonald as "the one irreplaceable man" of Confederation. I would suggest, again, that he was "one irreplaceable man." To my mind, and from the perspective of today, there was one other. In retrospect, we can see that Macdonald needed Thomas D'Arcy McGee. One of the great tragedies of Canadian history is that a Fenian assassin removed the Irish statesman before he had finished his work. The assassin was caught and hanged. McGee has been recognized and celebrated, though perhaps not sufficiently, as a martyr to the cause of Canadian democracy—a cause that, ironically, could trace certain of its roots to the man who launched the Protestant Reformation in Scotland.

A plaque at the door of this mausoleum in Notre-Dame-des-Neiges Cemetery, Montreal, reads: "In Memory of Thomas D'Arcy McGee, the Most Eloquent Voice of the Fathers of Confederation." McGee remains the foremost Irish Catholic figure in Canadian history.

9.

John Knox

⌗⌗⌗

A few years ago, while out striding along the Royal Mile in the heart of Edinburgh, so thrilled to be there that the skirling bagpipes and blaring tourist-shop signs started me down the path to spending money on a kilt, I deked into St. Giles' Cathedral. This magnificent edifice, Scotland's answer to Westminster Abbey, is filled with statues and other memorials. While strolling around among the portraits, marble busts, and stained-glass windows, I came face to face with a life-sized statue of John Knox. And I found myself thinking that this "graven image" would have made that earliest dour Presbyterian spin in his grave.

Not long before, on the east coast of Scotland at St. Andrews, Sheena and I had visited the ruins of the cathedral where, in the mid-1500s, Knox emerged as the fiercest of prophets. We had also explored the ruins of the castle from which he was seized and taken to France to serve as a galley slave. In the castle museum, we had listened, bemused, while a talking effigy of Knox railed against "idolatry" and "hawkers of papistry"—a hokey exhibition that, even so, evokes the revolutionary spirit of the man.

For many years, Knox sermonized at St. Giles'. And here we encounter an irony greater than that of the life-sized statue. While preaching fire and brimstone, railing against Roman Catholicism, and battling the equality of women, John Knox launched a transformation that not only laid the foundations of the Scottish Enlightenment, but also eventually gave rise, in Canada, to a democracy notable, at least officially, for its pluralism and religious tolerance. John Knox sparked a literacy revolution. This he did, inadvertently, by pursuing a premise to its logical conclusion. His premise? That the Bible contained the word of God.

The story begins one freezing-cold afternoon in December 1545, when a thirty-one-year-old schoolmaster declined to relinquish his two-handed broadsword to the preacher he had been protecting. They argued about it on a roadway fifteen kilometres east of Edinburgh. For five weeks, the sturdy bearded swordsman, John Knox, had been travelling in eastern Scotland with the cleric George Wishart. Their audiences had dwindled as rumours multiplied that the Cambridge-educated parson would soon be seized, condemned, and burned at the stake for heresy.

Eighteen years before, as leading churchmen had sought to demonstrate that distant, wild, and lawless Scotland was just as orthodox as any heretic-burning nation in Europe, a well-educated young man named Patrick Hamilton had suffered that unhappy fate. Now, on the outskirts of Haddington, where he tutored the children of a gentleman, John Knox, a notary-priest educated at the University of St. Andrews, urged the itinerant preacher to let him remain as a guardsman.

According to a history Knox wrote later, Wishart said: "Nay, return to your bairns, and God bless you. One is sufficient for a sacrifice." Finally, Knox relinquished his broadsword. The two men parted. Nine hours later, in a town called Ormiston, Wishart was captured at midnight. On March 1, 1546, after a show trial orchestrated by Roman Catholic cardinal David Beaton, Wishart was brought to the stake outside St. Andrews Castle. Then, as Knox related, "he was put upon the gibbet, and hanged, and there burnt to powder." Today, the location is marked in the sidewalk by a rough stone etched with the initials *G.W.*

Although less barbaric than similar proceedings in England or France, where Protestant reformers were sometimes burned alive, the martyrdom of George Wishart launched the transformation of John Knox. It would turn this provincial schoolmaster into a figure of destiny, a man who would influence the history of Scotland and that, most notably, of a distant nation as yet unborn, and indeed unimagined.

Like Martin Luther and John Calvin in continental Europe, Knox would break with the Roman Catholic Church, the fount of all authority in sixteenth-century Europe. He would insist that Christian faith should be based not on church teachings as relayed through a hierarchy, but on the word of God as quoted in the Bible. To hear that word, and to establish the necessary personal relationship with God, people needed to read the Bible for themselves. To do that, they needed to know how to read and write. And so John Knox took up the cause of literacy for all.

Knox's rebellious vaunting of individual conscience would inspire some scholars to hail him as the father of democracy. Less controversially, his radical insistence on the necessity of literacy would lead Scotland to introduce a system of universal education in 1696, more than 170 years before England did so. That system would lead directly to the Scottish Enlightenment of the 1700s.

But we are getting ahead of our story. The second step in the transformation of John Knox arose out of the first. He was not among the sixteen men who, three months after the burning of George Wishart, slipped into the castle at St. Andrews, bent on avenging the death of that gentle preacher. But later he would describe what happened in detail. After convincing about 150 workers and servants to flee for their lives, the armed contingent broke into the private quarters of Cardinal Beaton.

Knox wrote that Beaton pleaded for his life: "I am a priest, I am a priest, you will not kill me." The intruders invoked the name of George Wishart—"who although he was consumed by the flame of the fire before men, yet asks for a vengeance upon you"—and stabbed the cardinal to death. John Knox could detail this scene, and the subsequent hanging of Beaton's dead body over the wall of the castle, because after being sought for questioning as a heretic schoolmaster, he joined the 120 Protestants who had emerged to occupy St. Andrews Castle. They were attempting a *coup d'état* against the Roman Catholic Church, which owned half the land in Scotland, and which Knox and others had taken to denouncing as the Antichrist.

The governor of Scotland—James Hamilton, Earl of Arran—proved slow to react. This was probably because the Castilians, as the uninvited guest came to be called, held his son hostage in the castle. Arran marched an army to St. Andrews three months after Beaton died, then quarrelled over who would pay for the operation and did not actively besiege the castle until the end of November.

Christmas brought a singular truce. Castilians were allowed to come and go as they pleased while Protestant and Catholic powers in England, France, and Rome weighed their options. Knox joined the occupation in April 1547. Within the walls, while instructing students, he caught the attention of Sir Henry Balnaves, a leading Protestant who had previously served as secretary of state. Encouraged by Balnaves, the congregation at St. Andrews called on Knox to become a preacher. This meant accepting a mission as public and dangerous as that of the martyred George Wishart. After soberly reflecting, Knox accepted the challenge.

Looking through the ruins of St. Andrews Cathedral, from one end to the other. Founded in the twelfth century, the cathedral was completed during the reign of King Robert the Bruce. In 1547, the French bombarded the nearby St. Andrews Castle from its roof.

Late in June 1547, the French government, irrevocably wedded to Roman Catholicism, sent a fleet of twenty galleys to Scotland. After bombarding St. Andrews Castle without success, the attackers breached the walls by mounting cannons on the roof of the nearby cathedral. The French forced a surrender after a five-day siege and a six-hour bombardment, and then transported 120 Castilians to France. John Knox was one of them.

So began the final stage in his transformation. After reaching Rouen, the French took the gentlemen prisoners to various strongholds. But they condemned Knox, the son of a farmer, and other rank-and-file prisoners to serve as galley slaves. At age thirty-three, Knox found himself barefoot, chained to a bench alongside five other men, and obliged for hours on end to haul on a forty-foot oar. Thirty feet wide, six feet high, and between a hundred and a hundred and fifty feet long, these French galleys were hellholes. The work was brutish, the food scarce and barely edible. The guards enforced discipline by applying whips to bare backs.

For nineteen months, with respite from rowing only in winter, John Knox laboured as a galley slave. Also, despite periods of fever and illness, he served his fellow prisoners as a spiritual adviser, and edited and summarized a theological treatise by Balnaves. At the end of that period, when in March 1549, as part of a prisoner exchange, Knox was released to go to England, he emerged as a firebrand preacher: he had been called, he had been tested by adversity, and nothing but death could prevent him from doing the work of the one God.

This sense of vocation, this certainty that he was following the only right, true path to salvation, turned the eloquent and tireless Knox into a mesmerizing orator: magnetic, charismatic. It made him a leader. But his unshakable conviction that he was always right also clouded his perception and judgment. If he was indeed a prophet called by God, then his opinions were not those of a mere mortal, but came from God, who was expressing His views through Knox. Impervious to counter-argument, the once reluctant preacher became a demagogue.

To effect change, the times required no less. Like other far-flung parts of continental Europe, Scotland had yet to emerge from medieval feudalism. Wealthy nobles or lords owned vast estates and controlled the lives of illiterate tenant farmers—vassals or serfs who paid tithes or rents to work their modest plots and were compelled to take up arms on command.

The nobles ruled in alliance with the Catholic Church, which, with an annual income of three hundred thousand pounds, compared with a mere seventeen thousand for the Scottish crown, had long since become corrupted. While preaching obedience, poverty, and chastity, priests, bishops, and cardinals lived in luxury and some, like Beaton, did not shrink from keeping mistresses or "borrowing" the wives and daughters of their parishioners. In a world where few people could read English, never mind Latin or Greek, the Church controlled the pulpits, the only means of reaching a mass audience.

In continental Europe, a similar situation had given rise to the Protestant Reformation. It had begun in Wittenberg, Germany, in 1517, when theologian Martin Luther is said to have nailed ninety-five criticisms of the Catholic Church to the wooden doors of All Saints' Church. Luther challenged the authority of the papacy, asserted that the Bible was the only source of religious authority, and argued that baptized Christians formed a universal priesthood.

Since then, John Calvin, a French Protestant trained as a lawyer, had built a reformist community in Geneva on the teachings of Martin Luther. Where Patrick Hamilton, the first Protestant martyr in Scotland, had studied theology in Luther's Wittenberg, George Wishart, the second, had trained in Geneva and adopted the more systematic approach of Calvin. Soon enough, John Knox would follow the path blazed by Wishart.

But first he spent four years in England, where he gained a reputation as a galvanizing preacher. He became royal chaplain to the Protestant King Edward VI and took a leading role in doctrinal debates in the Church of England—refusing to kneel, for example, while taking communion. But in 1553, when Mary Tudor, daughter of King Henry VIII, became queen of England and restored Roman Catholicism, Knox could not help recalling the fate of William Tyndale. Sixteen years before, for having translated most of the Bible into English, that devout scholar had been strangled to death and burned at the stake at the behest of the Church and the king.

Knox fled to continental Europe. For the next five years, except for a test visit to Scotland—during which he was condemned as a heretic—there he remained. In Frankfurt, he served as pastor to an English congregation, though eventually, over doctrinal nice-ties, he broke with that church. In Geneva, besides exploring theological questions, every week he preached three two-hour sermons. Meanwhile, he married and fathered two sons.

In 1558, Knox wrote and published a pamphlet that would damage his reputation forever: *The First Blast of the Trumpet against the Monstrous Regiment of Women*. Targeting the Roman Catholic Mary Stuart, nominally queen of Scotland, he argued that women, whom he viewed as naturally inferior to men, could not rightly become heads of state. Knox published *First Blast* anonymously because he knew it was seditious. Even Calvin would distance himself, deploring the "thoughtless arrogance of one individual" in writing such a pamphlet.

In 1560, with the Protestant Queen Elizabeth on the throne of England, and so dominating Scotland, John Knox returned to his native land. Able now to preach openly at St. Andrews, he advanced to the forefront of a burgeoning congregation. In laying out rules and regulations for a newly reformed Church, Knox made church attendance compulsory: householders had to hand in tickets to prove they had attended his Sunday sermon. With fellow elders, Knox sat weekly to adjudicate complaints of fornication, adultery, and other wickedness. The panel would dispense Calvinist justice in various degrees—ultimately excommunication, which meant banishment and exile, but more often the public humiliation of being denounced and shamed in the church while standing on a stool of repentance. This practice would one day give rise to the poetical rebellion of Robert Burns.

But now, in 1561, the Catholic Mary Stuart, a flighty eighteen-year-old who had been raised at the French court, arrived in Edinburgh to rule as Mary, Queen of Scots. This incensed John Knox, whose denunciatory sermons—dancing! frivolity! shameless flirtation!—managed to rouse even the Scottish nobility. The young queen attempted to bring Knox onside, even inviting him to become her personal adviser.

But self-appointed prophets are not amenable to compromise. Bent on ridding Scotland of Queen Mary, Knox needed to rationalize a more encompassing revolution. In a world that recognized the divine right of kings, he had to justify the overthrow of a monarch. Even William Tyndale, that English Protestant martyr, had accepted that an obedient Christian owed allegiance to the anointed king or queen, no matter how evil.

The puritanical John Knox would be scandalized to discover a statue of himself at St. Giles' Cathedral in Edinburgh and, at St. Andrews, an effigy on rollers which preaches a sermon.

John Knox took a different tack. He argued that if the sovereign was a Roman Catholic, then subjects were entitled—indeed, were morally obligated—to resist and ultimately overthrow that monarch. Why so? Because Catholicism was intrinsically evil, and the

Roman Church was the Antichrist of prophecy. How did he know this? The Bible told him so.

Yet surely the Bible was open to differing interpretations? Young Queen Mary, who had obviously been counselled, made this argument in the first of several meetings she had with Knox. She observed that the Catholic Church interpreted the Bible differently than he did, and who could say who was right? Knox answered that it was not a question of how he interpreted the Bible, or how Catholics interpreted it, but of what in fact it said.

So there it was, the position that would drive Knox to make his singular contribution. Backed into a corner, forced to identify his final authority, Knox put his hand on the Bible, in which God "plainly speaketh His Word." Because the Bible communicated the Word of God, it had to be distributed as widely as possible. By 1560, leading members of Knox's Geneva congregation had produced a new English translation: the Geneva Bible. Ironically, given Knox's literal-mindedness, it included interpretive notes running to three hundred thousand words.

Knox recognized that disseminating the Bible would accomplish nothing unless people could read it for themselves. And now he acted on that recognition. In the *First Book of Discipline*, which he wrote and supervised, Knox laid out an array of regulations to govern the newly reformed Scottish church. He stipulated that congregations could choose their own pastors, for example, and that bishops should be replaced by "superintendents."

But most significantly of all, this *First Book of Discipline* laid out a system of universal education. In addition to stipulating that every child should go to school, and so learn to read, write, and reason, it specified a detailed syllabus for universities, including such modern subjects as dialectics, mathematics, physics, and economics.

The nobles who controlled Parliament did not much like this scheme because they realized they would have to pay for it. In fact, this ambitious plan, which called for a parish-by-parish approach to education, would not be adopted during Knox's lifetime. But Scotland's introduction of universal education in 1696, almost two centuries before England did likewise, can be traced to Knox and his *First Book of Discipline*.

By 1750, 75 per cent of Scots could read—a level of literacy unprecedented in Europe. This skyrocketing literacy rate also fostered liberal attitudes that would have disturbed Knox. When parishioners are encouraged to read a complex holy book, and then to dispute its meanings with their religious leaders, they begin to think that people are created equal. This egalitarianism, transported to the wilds of British North America, made Scottish immigrants, as a group, more able than others to forge alliances with the native peoples, who proved invaluable allies.

Some suggest that Knox made other contributions of equal or greater significance. He is often called the father of Presbyterianism, for example—though that term emerged only later. Certainly, Presbyterianism helped to shape nineteenth-century Canada, making it disciplined and hard-working, though also more austere, self-righteous, and joyless than it needed to be. Yet Presbyterianism is not, like independence or democracy, a bedrock Canadian value.

And democracy is what Knox fostered with his emphasis on literacy and education. *Why* he acted is secondary. If he viewed education as subsidiary to religion, the end result, the slow-motion explosion of literacy and analytical thinking, is what signifies. A theological education develops the ability to handle abstractions and clarify arguments. Soon enough, Scottish farmers were disputing the fine points of scripture and winning arguments by quoting the Bible chapter and verse. From there they moved to philosophy, literature, and science.

And so we arrive at one of the paradoxes of Scottish history: John Knox's emphasis on literacy and education, born of his revolutionary Christianity, led directly to the Scottish Enlightenment—to figures like David Hume, that prince among godless skeptics, and Robert Burns, who would use poems like "Holy Willie's Prayer" to satirize the bigotry and hypocrisy of the church Knox created. Burns, in particular, would find an enduring audience in Canada, an eventuality whose magical culmination would earn the everlasting gratitude of two lucky Canadians.

10.

Robert Burns

■■■

I n January 2009, to mark the 250th anniversary of the birth of
Robert Burns, the Toronto St. Andrew's Society held a banquet at the top of the CN Tower. From Edinburgh, Kenny
MacAskill, Scotland's cabinet secretary for justice, came to deliver
the "Immortal Memory," a ritual ode to the country's national poet.
Not only that: MacAskill came bearing gifts. More specifically, the
Scottish government was going to award someone in attendance
a free trip for two to Scotland. This would include return flights
and a one-week stay at the five-star Cameron House, a magnificent
baronial mansion on Loch Lomond.

Sheena and I had visited Scotland the previous year, and had
investigated several sites pertaining to Burns. Still, we yearned to
go again. As we arrived for the banquet, we deposited our business
cards in the designated box, as instructed. "You might want to bring
your business cards," Sheena had told the friends who came with
us, "but I am going to win." The draw for the trip to Scotland came
late in the evening, after the "Immortal Memory," the "Toast to the
Lassies," and the "Reply to the Laddies."

Somebody held a jar filled with business cards high in the air, and Douglas Gibson, then society president, reached up and pulled out the card belonging to the lucky winner. "And the winner is," he said, "Donald Jenkins." A collective groan greeted this announcement. "Donald Jenkins, are you here?" Nobody answered. People looked around. "Donald Jenkins?" After a couple of moments, Gibson said, "What should I do?" The response was instant, loud and unanimous: "Draw again!"

Gibson again reached high overhead. He fished around for a while, without looking, then pulled out a card and read it. "And the winner is," he said, taking a beat, clearly incredulous: "The winner is Sheena Fraser McGoogan."

※※※

This explains why I have yet to see the Robert Burns Birthplace Museum. It opened in Alloway, one hour south of Glasgow, in 2011—two years after we won that free trip and made our second visit to the main sites related to Burns. Magnificent as the new museum is, I am told that it takes nothing away from those things I most vividly remember. These include the Alloway cottage in which, on January 25, 1759, Robert Burns first opened his eyes. Nearby, you can visit the Brig o' Doon, the bridge over the River Doon, where Burns's fictional Tam o' Shanter narrowly escapes from furious witches.

From Alloway, on that second trip, Sheena and I drove to Dumfries and took turns sitting in the chair in the pub where, in his later years, Burns himself often sat reading newspapers. We visited the upstairs bedroom where sometimes he slept. Down the street, in the humble home where he lived for three years, we visited his study and the bedroom in which he died. This was the house where, two weeks before he passed, according to a BBC documentary by

Andrew O'Hagan, Burns was driven to write a begging letter to a cousin, asking for a few pounds to keep him out of debtor's prison.

Burns Cottage in Alloway was the first home of Robert Burns. Built in 1757, the two-room, clay-and-thatch cottage is now part of the Robert Burns Birthplace Museum.

But for us, the Burnsian highlight of both visits came at the National Memorial in Mauchline, twenty kilometres east of Alloway. That is because Sheena's grandfather, an architect born in Lochgilphead, Argyllshire, designed it as a young man, before he emigrated to Canada. Constructed of red sandstone in 1896, the monument grows wider as it increases in height, and rises to more than twenty metres. It incorporates odd angles and circular substructures, diverse window treatments, unexpected balconies, and a curious turret. Taken together, these features render it remarkably evocative of the wild and original spirit of Robert Burns: unforgettable.

William Fraser, a young Glasgow-based architect, designed the evocative National Burns Memorial at Mauchline in the 1890s, before he emigrated to Canada.

The poet himself never set foot in Canada, never dreamed of it. Yet today, statues of Burns can be found in Halifax, Fredericton, Montreal, Toronto, Windsor, Winnipeg, Edmonton, Vancouver, and Victoria. And I doubt that this list is exhaustive. No other poet, and in fact no other writer, period, has inspired anything approaching this level of commemoration in Canada.

For many Canadians, Scotland is synonymous with Robert Burns. That is why, every January, tens of thousands of us celebrate the poet at convivial suppers across the country. All those who wish to wax nostalgic about Old Scotia, even if they've never visited, need only raise a glass to that country's national poet, or sing along with "Auld Lang Syne," his most famous song. In *How the Scots Invented Canada*, I suggested that some Canadian Burnsians probably enjoy the rebellious naughtiness of the "bad boy" poet, who flouted Church teachings and had more than his share of luck with the lassies. From this perspective, Robert Burns stands as the archetypal anti-Presbyterian, the subversive rejoinder to the professedly faithful.

Yet I have come to think that this analysis omits one crucial element: the political. Burns is frequently described as a Scottish nationalist, and that he was. He often wrote in the Scots language or Lallans, and his famous poem "Scots Wha Hae," which has become the party song of the Scottish National Party, runs (in standard English) as follows: "Who for Scotland's King and Law / Freedom's sword will strongly draw, / Freeman stand or freeman fall, / Let him follow me." Burns is called a republican, and certainly he believed that a country's head of state should be appointed by means unrelated to heredity. But above all, Burns was an egalitarian. And politically, that means one person, one vote. He disdained rank and privilege while insisting that "a man's a man for a' that." He gave voice to the common man and woman.

Thanks to the Presbyterian heritage that he resisted, Scotland's national poet became the quintessential democrat. He greatly admired his slightly younger contemporary, the political reformer Thomas Muir the Younger of Huntershill (1765–1799). This Muir made common cause with the United Irishmen during the rise of Theobald Wolfe Tone, and became sufficiently irksome that he got himself transported to Australia. After escaping to Vancouver Island and then Europe, Muir became a hero to Burns.

The poet came naturally by his rebellious egalitarianism. The cottage in which he was born had been built by his father. When he was seven, his father sold that house and became a tenant farmer nearby. Burns, the oldest of seven children, grew up doing hard manual labour on that seventy-acre farm. He learned how to read and write from his Presbyterian, education-oriented father. Then he studied Latin, French, grammar, and mathematics with a schoolmaster who boarded in the area.

Burns wrote his first poem, "Handsome Nell," at age fifteen, to a girl helping him with the harvest. The following summer, while finishing his education with a second tutor, he wrote two songs to another young woman, so confirming a pattern of seduction and commemoration that would endure for the rest of his life.

When Robert was eighteen, his father moved his large family to a hundred-and-thirty-acre farm near Tarbolton, about sixteen kilometres northeast. Here Robert began to assert his independence, joining a country dancing school over his father's objections and founding a Bachelors' Club. He became a Freemason, wrote poems and songs, and, rejected in love, moved a few miles north, to the town of Irvine to learn the difficult trade of flax dressing.

In 1782, a New Year's Eve party culminated in a fire that burned the flax shop to the ground, and the poet returned to the farm. Two years later, after the death of his father, Robert moved with the family to yet another farm, this one near Mauchline. When his first illegitimate child was born, to his mother's servant, Burns was compelled to stand penance on a stool in front of the local congregation—a ritual humiliation that did nothing to ease his feelings towards Presbyterian orthodoxy.

Burns endured this rite a second time when Jean Armour, the daughter of a local stonemason, bore him twins. But here the situation grew complex, as her parents, judging him to be a rake without prospects, contrived to thwart his efforts to marry the young woman—at least temporarily.

During this period, 1784 to 1786, Burns found his voice as a poet. He produced such works as "Address to the Deil," "The Holy Fair," "The Cotter's Saturday Night," and the satirical "Holy Willie's Prayer." This last, a hilarious attack on Presbyterian hypocrisy, finds the poet holding forth in the unctuous, prayerful tones of a church elder. The poem remains consistently within the voice of a hypocrite revelling in his supposed moral superiority while revealing (and justifying) various depravities:

> Besides, I farther maun allow,
> Wi' Leezie's lass, three times I trow—
> But Lord, that Friday I was fou [drunk],
> When I cam near her;
> Or else, Thou kens, Thy servant true
> Wad never steer her.

True to his "common man" affiliations, Burns wrote much of his work in this Scots-inflected English, the Lallans of the Scottish Lowlands. In this subtly political decision, he followed the poet Robert Fergusson (1750–1774)—a debt he acknowledged during his first visit to Edinburgh, when he erected a memorial stone at his forerunner's grave. Burns undertook that visit after he published *Poems, Chiefly in the Scottish Dialect*, a short book that became a literary sensation. Known now as the Kilmarnock edition, after the location of its publisher, the collection sold out its initial print run of 612 copies within a month. More important, influential critics lauded the work.

Critical acclaim culminated in an invitation to Edinburgh to oversee a revised edition of the book. There the widely read Burns, hailed as a "heaven-taught ploughman" of innocent genius, proved a singular success in intellectual and aristocratic circles. At one gathering, he made an impression on a sixteen-year-old Walter Scott, who later remembered him vividly: "His person was strong and robust; his manners rustic, not clownish, a sort of dignified plainness and simplicity which received part of its effect perhaps from knowledge of his extraordinary talents."

Burns used the voice of an uneducated ploughman as a literary strategy, a mask. Yet he was rightly perceived to be an enemy of class constraints and economic injustice, and a champion of free speech, individual freedom, and republican egalitarianism. During those few months in Edinburgh, Burns conducted a doomed, heart-rending love affair with "Clarinda," an educated, sensitive woman who remained agonizingly out of reach both socially and because she was married, albeit unhappily. Between December and April, the two traded eighty-two love letters. The affair ended in sadness, but it inspired Burns to compose "Ae Fond Kiss," surely one of the greatest love songs ever written.

At this period, the class structure of Scotland was so rigid that, despite concerted efforts, Burns could find no way to translate his extraordinary talents into a professional appointment. By 1788, with his wife, Jean Armour, he had moved to a farm near Dumfries. Desperate to find another way of making a living, he trained as an exciseman and, in 1789, began working as a travelling tax collector. As a writer, over the next few years, while earning his daily bread as a taxman, he produced some of his finest works.

Among them we count "Tam o' Shanter," a surrealistic flight of fancy which is by turns funny, sad, and insightful. It offers up some of the poet's most evocative images: "But pleasures are like poppies spread, / You seize the flower, its bloom is shed; / Or like the snow falls in the river, / A moment white—then melts for ever." Two centuries after Burns wrote that poem, Irish Catholic poet Seamus Heaney—a winner of the Nobel Prize for Literature—would cite the work in "A Birl for Burns," an homage that hails the Scottish poet for keeping language alive.

⬚⬚⬚

In the late 1700s, with the French aristocracy having grown increasingly decadent, the common people in France launched the French Revolution. The summer of 1789 brought both the assault on the Bastille and the Declaration of the Rights of Man and of the Citizen. The egalitarian Burns, steeped in Freemasonry and emerging Enlightenment notions of secular and religious equality, identified completely. Certain of his contemporaries knew him to be a republican. In 2008, biographer Robert Crawford noted that "it was dangerous to be called that then."

The British aristocracy, worried, had taken to deporting men such as Thomas Muir, the Scottish reformer, to penal colonies in Australia. Burns would die of a heart condition in 1796, at age thirty-seven. "Particularly towards the end of his life in the 1790s," Crawford later observed, "democracy was a dirty word. It was a word associated with terrorism, a word which had just come into the English language; it was associated with the *terreur* in France."

Robert Burns was no terrorist. But a radical democrat he certainly was. In poem after poem and song after song he celebrated the Scottish struggle not just against the English, but also against privilege and inequality. What begins with paeans to the Scottish Jacobites, such "Charlie, He's My Darling" and "The White Cockade," culminates in "A Man's a Man for A' That." And that explains why in downtown Toronto, near the northeast corner of Allan Gardens, a statue of Robert Burns was unveiled on July 21, 1902—the 106th anniversary of the poet's death. According to reports in the Toronto *Mail and Empire*, the unveiling of the statue, "which is of heroic size," featured the singing, by the male chorus of the 48th Highlanders' Pipes and Drums, of several of Burns's lyrics—among them, "Ae Fond Kiss."

This is the chair at the Globe Inn in Dumfries where, between 1791 and 1796, Robert Burns would often sit writing or reading. A Burns Supper was held at the Globe in 1819.

Six decades later, that statue of Burns remained a potent symbol. In the early 1960s, it stood as the symbolic heart of a well-publicized battle for free speech. A tempestuous workingman poet, Milton Acorn, rallied followers at the statue of Robert Burns while successfully challenging a Toronto city bylaw prohibiting public speaking in a park without a permit unless for a religious sermon. In the name of Burns, Acorn was striking a blow not just for free speech, but also for democracy.

Today, that Toronto statue, like many of its fellows across the country, continues to serve as a rallying point for Scots and Scottish Canadians. Each year, members of the St. Andrew's Society of Toronto gather in Allan Gardens on Robert Burns Day, often despite freezing winds and blowing snow, to honour the poet while the bagpipes play, and then to adjourn for a suitable libation. In one of his greatest poems, written towards the end of his life, Burns speaks in the voice of the common man, illustrating the sentiment that inspires this affection:

> *Ye see yon birkie ca'd a lord,*
> *Wha struts, and stares, and a' that,*
> *Though hundreds worship at his word,*
> *He's but a coof for a' that.*
> *For a' that, and a' that,*
> *His ribband, star and a' that,*
> *The man of independent mind,*
> *He looks and laughs at a' that.*

Decades before Canada came into existence, the egalitarian irreverence of Robert Burns caught the ear of his near contemporaries in Ireland. From the 1780s onward, the Scottish bard loomed large in the Irish imagination. The United Irishmen of Theobald Wolfe Tone admired Burns for his republican principles. And in the late eighteenth and early nineteenth centuries, he figured prominently in cross-Channel cultural exchange.

In a journal article entitled "'No Dumb Ireland': Robert Burns and Irish Cultural Nationalism in the Nineteenth Century," James Kelly writes that, for later Irish nationalists, the Protestant Burns and the Catholic Daniel O'Connell "represented different discourses of the nation—one cultural, and therefore sentimental, reassuring, and unifying; the other political and therefore potentially polarizing and partisan." Where Burns perfectly embodied the Scottish nation, Ireland's representative man "was too closely tied to a particular political and sectarian position," he writes, "to ever act as a unifying symbol of the whole nation."

Yet the even-handed O'Connell, born sixteen years after Burns, built a stupendous reputation internationally while spearheading a transformation in Ireland. Burns would certainly have applauded how, under O'Connell's leadership, the Irish developed the first mass popular movement in representative politics in the world.

Daniel O'Connell

If you visit Ireland today, at the south end of Dublin's grandest boulevard, overlooking a busy intersection and the River Liffey, you will find a larger-than-life statue of Daniel O'Connell. In Glasnevin Cemetery, on the city's outskirts, the man is remembered with a round tower that dominates the graveyard. And at Derrynane, the estate he inherited in southwest Ireland, you can see the magnificent chariot in which O'Connell rode through Dublin, waving to the cheering throngs who, in 1844, gathered to celebrate his release from prison. O'Connell had been jailed because his non-violent "monster meetings" proved too effective: the British authorities felt threatened.

O'Connell became known as the Liberator, and planted a flag for the democratic process that could be seen far beyond his native land. His commitment to non-violent change would inspire such twentieth-century figures as Mahatma Gandhi and Martin Luther King, who would adapt his approach to freedom struggles in India and the United States. At home, O'Connell cleared the way for Charles Stewart Parnell, who would lead the forces of constitutional change later in the century, and also for Thomas D'Arcy McGee, that youthful revolutionary who, as we have already seen, later became a fierce democrat and a father of Canadian Confederation.

In 1844, recently freed from jail, Daniel O'Connell rode through Dublin in this horse-drawn chariot. Today, it can be seen at Derrynane, his estate in southwest Ireland.

Along the way, O'Connell struck a blow for abolition, a profoundly democratic cause. When the escaped American slave Frederick Douglass undertook a lecture tour in Ireland, O'Connell shared the stage with him, denouncing slavery as an abuse of human rights. In sum, this man, the Liberator, is widely regarded as the greatest statesman Ireland ever produced. As Owen Dudley Edwards writes, "His genius gave Irish nationalism a universalism, a humanitarianism, a liberalism, an enmity to violence and a joy which too few later generations honoured."

DANIEL O'CONNELL

THE CHAMPION OF LIBERTY

Pub.ᵈ Sep.ᵗ 1847, by HOFFY, at N.° 20, South 5.ᵗʰ S.ᵗ Philadelphia.

Daniel O'Connell was renowned internationally. This poster, called Daniel O'Connell:
The Champion of Liberty, *by Alfred M. Hoffy, was published in Pennsylvania in 1847.*

Daniel O'Connell was born in 1775 in a stone farmhouse whose ruins can still be seen from a hilly side road at Cahersiveen in County Kerry, 350 kilometres southwest of Dublin. When he showed signs of being precocious, an uncle who owned an estate (Derrynane) stepped in to educate him. After studying in France, and narrowly escaping the violence of the French Revolution, O'Connell spent three years in London, where he trained as a lawyer.

At age twenty, he attended a debate on the fate of the British nation, and marvelled at the oratory of Prime Minister William Pitt. He admired Pitt's "majestic march of language"—the way he used lower tones to end sentences, threw his voice to make himself heard at a distance, and chose his words precisely. Inspired, O'Connell joined a debating society and began training himself as a speaker.

Meanwhile, he read voraciously. He plowed through books recognized as classics of the Enlightenment: *Rights of Man* (Thomas Paine), *A Vindication of the Rights of Woman* (Mary Wollstonecraft), *Wealth of Nations* (Adam Smith), and *The Life of Samuel Johnson* (James Boswell). O'Connell was twenty-one when, in December 1796, Theobald Wolfe Tone failed in his attempt to land a French fleet at Bantry Bay. He was intrigued but dubious about that endeavour, and feared that, as in France, sudden freedom would bring chaos, thievery, and murder. Early in the new year, with the vast majority of other young Irish barristers, he joined the lawyers' artillery, created to defend the country against armed rebellion.

Even so, he felt attracted to the ideals and objectives of the United Irishmen. In 1797, while out walking near Trinity College in Dublin, he spotted Lord Edward Fitzgerald, at thirty-four the most dashing of the rebel leaders. Fitzgerald had fought on the British side during the American Revolution, and narrowly survived a serious wound. He had also explored parts of what would become eastern Canada, travelling through forests with native peoples. The young O'Connell trotted ahead, biographer Patrick Geoghegan tells us, then turned and walked back "to enjoy a good stare at him." The following year, on May 19, 1798, O'Connell was called to the bar. That same day, while preparing a full-scale rebellion, the charismatic Fitzgerald was betrayed, arrested for treason, and fatally wounded.

O'Connell began his slow, steady climb to prominence. As a lawyer, he proved witty, incisive, erudite, theatrical, fluent in English and Irish, creative, and, soon enough, unrivalled. His forte, according to biographer Charles Chenevix Trench, "was the cross-examination of hostile witnesses." With great good humour, O'Connell would coax and confide, "from time to time rolling his large, blue-grey eyes at judge and jury," until he trapped the witness in a lie or contradiction, and nailed him to the wall.

A Roman Catholic, born and raised, Daniel O'Connell became politically active. Ireland's Catholics had been subject to discrimination since England had gained control of the country in the seventeenth century. They were barred from holding public office or serving in the army. Members of the government had to be Anglican. Even Presbyterians, almost all Scottish, did not qualify to govern. By the early 1700s, the Anglican ruling class, known as the Protestant Ascendancy, had enacted the Penal Laws to ensure their own dominance over Catholics and Dissenters of all stripes.

By the early 1800s, some of the worst excesses had been rescinded. Catholics could serve in the armed forces or enter the legal profession, for example. Yet still they could not inherit Protestant land, own a horse valued at more than five pounds, become court judges, or be elected to serve in the British House of Commons, which had governed the country since the 1801 Act of Union between England and Ireland.

O'Connell set out to change all this, and to induce "Catholic emancipation" by democratic means. He would later express this succinctly, insisting "that all ameliorations and improvements in political institutions can be obtained by persevering in a perfectly peaceable and legal course, and cannot be obtained by forcible means, or if they could be got by forcible means, such means create more evils than they cure, and leave the country worse than they found it."

Rejecting the revolutionary approach of the French, the Americans, and the United Irishmen of Wolfe Tone, Daniel O'Connell insisted that the only way forward ran through evolutionary democracy—a position that would resonate with Michael Collins, Thomas D'Arcy McGee, and the vast majority of Canadians. In 1811, O'Connell leveraged his reputation as a barrister to establish the Catholic Board to campaign specifically for emancipation, or the right of Irish Catholics to become Members of Parliament.

A dozen years later, O'Connell turned this board into the Catholic Association, a broadly focused organization that sought to improve the Catholic situation generally. Gradually, he gained a massive following and built a war chest to support pro-emancipation candidates standing in Ireland for election to the British House of Commons. Yet because a discriminatory oath of office demanded the renunciation of Catholicism, all of these elected men were propertied Protestants.

In 1828, O'Connell decided to promote the election of an Irish Catholic who would go to Westminster but refuse to take the offensive oath. When the 1828 by-election was called in County Clare, he anticipated that a prominent Catholic, an ally from that county, would contest the election. When that candidate withdrew, he agreed to stand himself—not out of personal ambition, he insisted, but "to advocate a principle, which may in my person be vindicated."

The old courthouse, where Daniel O'Connell won his first election, is long gone from the heart of Ennis. Today, this painting of the scene hangs in the window of a nearby shop.

The election was to be held in Ennis, County Clare, in the Irish mid-west. On Monday, June 30, 1828, after travelling day and night by coach from Dublin, 240 kilometres away, Daniel O'Connell arrived at two o'clock in the morning. At the courthouse a few hours later, his opponent, William Vesey Fitzgerald, gave a tour-de-force speech that reduced most of the audience to tears. As he rose to answer it, O'Connell, already considered the greatest Irish orator of the age, knew he had his work cut out for him. He did not dislike Fitzgerald, a Protestant who supported Catholic emancipation. But if he were going to win this election, he had to demolish him verbally.

In *King Dan,* Geoghegan shows how he did this with a speech that was "nasty, brutish, and brilliant, without doubt one of the greatest of his life." O'Connell charged that Fitzgerald belonged to a government which treated Catholics with contempt. He lamented that he himself could not rise in his chosen profession because he was a Catholic. Building a good head of steam, he claimed that Protestants could murder Catholics with impunity, and that Catholics were not permitted even to mobilize. Fitzgerald's conduct was "barefaced and miserable hypocrisy." The speech ended, Geoghegan writes, "with a volley of execration for the combined enemies of the Catholic cause" that left the crowd cheering, roaring, and laughing.

The formal vote began the next day and, with people pouring into the town from the countryside, lasted almost a week. When the polling ended, O'Connell had won in a landslide, 2,057 votes to 982. The people had elected a Roman Catholic to confront the British House of Commons.

Today, Ennis is a colourful, musical town of twenty-five thousand. The old courthouse, where O'Connell won his first election, is long gone. In its place we find O'Connell Square, which features a sky-high, seventy-four-foot tower topped by a statue of the great man himself. A local historian, Jane O'Brien, conducts guided walks around Ennis, sprinkling them with anecdotes about O'Connell. The main street of Ennis, she tells visitors, which has taken the name O'Connell, was once called Jail Street. And, this being Ireland, O'Brien leads us past a lively pub called Dan O'Connells.

In February 1829, O'Connell went to London to take his seat as a Catholic Member of Parliament. By now, the elected British government was ready to accept this development. But King George IV was still bent on preventing it. Finally, in April, the emancipation bill gained royal assent. Because of a technicality—the bill did not become law until after the Ennis election—O'Connell had to get himself re-elected. This he did, unopposed, the following July. And when Parliament resumed in February 1830, he took his seat in the British House of Commons.

The town of Ennis, County Clare, is a thriving regional centre that celebrates Irish traditional music and remembers Daniel O'Connell in the names of its streets and pubs.

Having planted a flag on behalf of Irish Catholics, Daniel O'Connell became known as "the Liberator." He would go on to fight many battles, and would even spend three months in jail for non-violent political agitation. But as biographer Charles Chenevix Trench observes in *The Great Dan*, "the reputation of this greatest of Irishmen deserves to rest not on what he might have done, nor on what he failed to do, but on his wonderful achievement in 1828, which raised his people's heads and straightened their backs after generations of subjection and failure."

From the start, O'Connell had two main objectives. The first, Catholic emancipation, involved overthrowing Penal Laws which ensured that Catholics would remain second-class citizens. The second, summed up in the word "repeal," meant repealing the 1801 Act of Union, which had abolished the separate Irish Parliament established by Henry Grattan in 1782. O'Connell regarded the union of England and Ireland as a direct result of the failed rebellion of 1798, a view that underlay his passionate adherence to the principle of non-violence. He wanted to transform the country, and to achieve the liberation of the Catholics, by democratic means.

O'Connell proved unable to repeal the Act of Union, though he fought for Home Rule through the 1830s and '40s. But during this period, as Trench observes, there was "not the slightest chance of repeal being conceded, either to his moral force or to the physical force of Young Ireland," a nationalist movement that arose in the 1840s. O'Connell also proved unable, despite furious and sustained efforts, to secure British relief from the Great Potato Famine that engulfed Ireland in 1845.

Yet even in his late fifties and sixties, O'Connell made significant contributions and innovations. In keeping with the logic of Catholic emancipation, he became active in the anti-slavery movement. He offended many Americans by highlighting the contradiction between celebrating liberty and keeping slaves. "In the midst of their laughter and their pride," he declared at one meeting, "I point to the negro children screaming for the mother from whose bosom they have been torn. America! It is a foul stain on your character!" He called George Washington a hypocrite and ignored a challenge to a duel he received after calling another American a slave breeder.

In 1843, O'Connell began holding "monster meetings" across Ireland, with a view to showing the British government that the Irish people wanted to repeal the Act of Union: they wanted to be free. He dreamed of using these monster meetings, a new political weapon, to achieve Home Rule. He hoped at least to improve the lot of the poor by changing certain laws—those mandating the export of food, for example. He insisted that these monster meetings be peaceful, and so they remained, though many of the forty he held that summer attracted more than a hundred thousand people. They became so sensationally popular—more than one million turned out at the Hill of Tara—that the British authorities, alarmed, banned an October monster meeting set for Clontarf, near Dublin, which was expected to be the largest yet.

Fearing violence and bloodshed, and despite the furious protests of some of his supporters, O'Connell cancelled that gathering. Even so, he was arrested, was charged with conspiracy, and spent several months in jail. This was more like house arrest, but it did not improve his now fragile health. On his release in September 1844, he enjoyed what would be his last great public moment—a triumphal procession. Accompanied by hundreds of men wearing top hats, and cheered on by adoring crowds, O'Connell rode through the streets of the city in the largest procession Dublin had ever seen.

Three years later, while on a pilgrimage to Rome at age seventy-one, Daniel O'Connell died of cerebral softening (usually the result of a stroke) exacerbated by the cold weather he encountered during his southward journey. His democratic ideals would soon take root and flourish—not just in Ireland, but most notably in Canada. Many disciples would transport the O'Connell legacy to this country. The greatest among them was the silver-tongued Thomas D'Arcy McGee. He turned away from O'Connell as a young man, but then, in his maturity, turned again and, at the cost of his life, championed the creation of a Canadian democracy in the tradition of the Great Dan. He did so in anticipation of yet another influential Irish constitutionalist: Charles Stewart Parnell.

Charles Stewart Parnell

In his classic first novel, *A Portrait of the Artist as a Young Man*, James Joyce writes nothing of Daniel O'Connell, even though he could claim a family connection with the Liberator through his maternal grandmother, Ellen O'Connell. Instead, and intriguingly, the author devotes pages to a Christmas-dinner argument about Charles Stewart Parnell, who built upon the work of O'Connell.

Joyce's point-of-view character, Stephen Dedalus, is present as a boy at an emotional exchange between his father's friend Mr. Charles, an avid supporter of the Protestant Parnell, and his aunt Dante, who defends the antagonistic position taken by the Roman Catholic Church. The scene ends with Dante throwing aside her chair and storming out of the room, stopping only to shout, flushed and quivering with rage: "Devil out of hell! We won! We crushed him to death! Fiend!"

Joyce had already written about Parnell in his story collection, *Dubliners*, and would invoke his name repeatedly in both *Ulysses* and *Finnegans Wake*. Irish writers as different from Joyce as Augusta,

Lady Gregory, and William Butler Yeats would also wrestle with the significance of Parnell, exploring what he represented and who was to blame for his political collapse, and, above all, regretting what he might have achieved if events had unfolded differently.

One British prime minister, William Gladstone, called Parnell the most remarkable person he ever met, and another, H. H. Asquith, declared him one of the greatest men of the nineteenth century. That Parnell should have registered so profoundly while also becoming extraordinarily controversial would have seemed a miracle to those who knew him as a youth.

Born into an Anglo-Irish family in 1846, during the onset of the Great Potato Famine in western Ireland, he grew up on a country estate in the east at Avondale in County Wicklow, seventy kilometres south of Dublin. The Georgian mansion in which he was born and raised is today open to visitors. While it cannot compare to the estate O'Connell inherited in the west, called Derrynane, it is certainly impressive. The displays and an audiovisual presentation trace the route Parnell took while becoming an Anglo-Irish champion of democracy.

The Parnells had arrived from England in the early 1600s, and had since produced several free-thinking individuals. Parnell's great-grandfather had served as a senior figure in Henry Grattan's Irish Parliament until 1799, when he opposed the Act of Union with Great Britain. His grandfather had written a pamphlet tracing Irish unrest to the Elizabethan conquest, and to the confiscation of lands that culminated in the Flight of the Earls. As a Protestant Member of Parliament for four years, he had supported Daniel O'Connell and Catholic emancipation.

Parnell's mother was an American of Ulster Presbyterian (Scottish) heritage, and the daughter of naval hero Admiral Charles Stewart, better known as Old Ironsides, who had captured two British ships during the War of 1812. His parents separated in

1852, when he was six, and at boarding school, the shy and retiring Parnell showed an aptitude only for science and mathematics. He spent three and a half years at the University of Cambridge, where he enjoyed carousing. He also discovered that he was Irish, and developed a distaste for what he viewed as English hypocrisy, arrogance, and superciliousness.

Charles Stewart Parnell insisted that democratic means could answer Irish nationalist demands. We see his resolve in this portrait by Czech painter Jan Vilímek.

In his early twenties, Parnell seemed well on his way to becoming an Irish country squire with a penchant for playing cricket and shooting grouse. But a visit to the United States, where he was jilted by a woman as lacking in enterprise, awakened the latent rebel in him. Later, his wife, Katherine O'Shea, would write that he was absolutely self-controlled, "and few knew of the volcanic force and fire that burned beneath his icy exterior."

Having absorbed the writings of his ancestors, Parnell concluded that the Anglo-Irish landlords, those men of his own class, could play a crucial role in resolving the "Irish question." In *Enigma: A New Life of Charles Stewart Parnell*, biographer Paul Bew observes that, unlike many others, Parnell could "rebel against his class in his political life without rebelling against his family." Like Daniel O'Connell before him, Parnell rejected violence. He believed that constitutional and democratic means could answer Irish nationalist demands for independence, and that the way forward lay through progressive land reform.

Having served briefly as High Sheriff of Wicklow, Parnell joined the Home Rule League, a moderate organization founded in 1873 by Isaac Butt. Initially unimpressive as a speaker, Parnell ran for election in 1874 and lost. But in April 1875, backed by a prominent Fenian, Patrick Egan, he won an election to represent County Meath in the British House of Commons.

Parnell allied himself with the more radical MPs from the Home Rule League, and led them in developing a campaign of obstructionism. This involved using technical procedures and giving irrelevant speeches to disrupt the House of Commons, so forcing it to pay more attention to Irish issues. It was Parnell's effectiveness as a parliamentarian that, in recent times, prompted a member of Britain's Conservative government to denounce Alex Salmond as "the new Parnell." MP Bill Cash warned that if the former leader of the Scottish National Party were re-elected to the

House of Commons, he would "ruthlessly and recklessly" disrupt the functioning of government. Salmond himself, that proud Scot, has revelled in comparisons with the earlier Irish politician.

By 1877, Parnell deposed the less effective Isaac Butt and became leader of the Home Rule Confederation of Great Britain. Never an inspirational orator in the tradition of O'Connell, Parnell excelled as an analyst, an organizer, and a tactician. He had a genius for finding a middle way, for acting constitutionally and democratically while maintaining the support of those who advocated violence and revolutionary action. In 1879, following yet another economic depression, he became leader of the New Departure and toured the country addressing poor tenant farmers who could not afford to pay their rent: "You must show the landlord that you intend to keep a firm grip on your homesteads and lands. You must not allow yourselves to be dispossessed as you were dispossessed in 1847."

At this time, as Paul Bew explains, there were two classes of tenant farmers—those with tiny holdings, who paid rents of between 1 and 20 pounds, and those with superior holdings who paid more. The first class included 538,000 farmers who paid an average of 6 pounds each, and the second 121,000 who averaged 56 pounds. At the same time, 300 individuals owned more than 540 million acres, and 12 of them possessed 1.3 million acres. Another 5 million people owned no land at all.

Parnell perceived that to achieve Home Rule, he had to demolish the class barriers created by land ownership. He argued that destroying such barriers had always increased self-respect and a sense of nationality: "I am convinced that nothing could more effectively promote the cause of self-government for Ireland than the breaking down of these barriers between different classes." In October, Parnell was elected president of a newly formed Irish National Land League, which linked a mass movement for land reform not to revolution but to parliamentary agitation.

That December, he embarked on a fundraising drive in North America. Over the next three months, he spoke in more than sixty cities around the continent, including in Montreal and Toronto, and raised seventy thousand pounds (worth today about six million pounds, using the retail price index, or roughly nine million Canadian dollars). In Toronto, he elicited such enthusiasm that people dusted off a title once applied to O'Connell and began calling Parnell "the uncrowned king of Ireland."

Like John A. Macdonald, who was three decades older, Parnell was a master of pragmatic ambiguity. In North America, carried away by the moment, he famously declared that all Irishmen yearned for Ireland "to take her place amongst the nations of the earth . . . None of us whether we be in America or in Ireland . . . will be satisfied until we have destroyed the last link which keeps Ireland bound to England." Yet later, and indeed almost always, he articulated an essentially federalist position, with the Irish retaining a link to the empire while participating in two parliaments, one in Dublin, the other in London.

Early in 1880, with an election announced, Parnell hurried home. That April, sixty-three Home Rulers were elected to the British Parliament, among them Parnell and twenty-seven of his supporters. Now, as tensions mounted between Irish landlords and tenants, he became leader of a new Home Rule League Party. He sought to replace violent agitation with mass meetings and "boycotts," or the shunning of any tenants who took over the farms of those evicted. British prime minister William Gladstone brought in a land act that halted evictions except where rents remained unpaid.

A newspaper Parnell owned, the *United Ireland*, denounced the land act and, as proprietor, together with several supporters, he was arrested and imprisoned for sabotaging it. Today, visitors to Dublin can visit Kilmainham Gaol and see the double cell in which he was held in relatively genteel conditions. From Kilmainham, Parnell released a document known as the "No Rent Manifesto," calling for a national rent strike by tenant farmers. In April 1882, using a then-friendly Member of Parliament, Captain William O'Shea, as intermediary, Parnell negotiated to withdraw the manifesto if the government would allow a hundred thousand tenants to appeal before the land courts for fair rents. On May 2, Parnell signed this deal, known as the Kilmainham Treaty. It highlighted his approach as constitutional and democratic, and so cost him some support among revolutionary Irish Americans. But he was freed.

Days later, amidst the euphoria engendered by his release, nationalist assassins murdered two senior British officials. This terrorist act became infamous as the Phoenix Park Murders. Shocked, Parnell offered to resign as an MP. He denounced the outrage, broke with the radical Land Leaguers, and, ironically, began the long process of forging an alliance with the man who had jailed him in Kilmainham: British prime minister William Gladstone. In October, Parnell resurrected the Land League as the Irish National League, which advocated parliamentary constitutionalism, moderate land reform, and Home Rule.

A man of scientific bent, Parnell had never shown much interest in religion. But recognizing that the Roman Catholic Church wielded influence, he made overtures and gained its help in expanding the Irish National League. By the end of 1885, the INL had 1,200 branches around the country. Over the next three decades, the League would transform land ownership in Ireland, replacing most of the large Anglo-Irish estates with tenant ownership.

In 1882, having turned the Home Rule League Party into an efficient, grassroots organization—and a harbinger of future political parties—Parnell renamed it the Irish Parliamentary Party (IPP). During the election of 1885, he gave a notable speech in Cork, when he clearly implied that Home Rule would be a gradual process: "We cannot ask the British constitution for more than the restitution of Grattan's parliament, but no man has the right to fix the boundary of a nation. No man has the right to say to his country, 'Thus far shalt thou go and no further,' and we have never attempted to fix the 'ne plus ultra' to the progress of Ireland's nationhood, and we never shall."

By the end of 1885, with eighty-six seats, Parnell's IPP held the balance of power in the British Parliament, where Liberal seats exceeded Conservative ones by exactly that number: eighty-six. Bent on re-establishing a Dublin-based legislature, Parnell supported first the Conservatives and then William Gladstone's Liberals. By April 1886, he had inspired Gladstone to introduce the First Irish Home Rule Bill to establish a separate Irish legislature. Opposition came from the newly formed Irish Loyal and Patriotic Union, which would give rise to the Irish Unionist Alliance or Party, and also from the Conservatives, with Lord Randolph Churchill declaring: "The Orange card is the one to play."

The defeat of the bill, by a count of 341 to 311, led to an election fought largely over Irish Home Rule. This time, with the backing of anti-Gladstone Liberal Unionists, the Conservatives won a majority. Parnell was still regrouping when, in the spring of 1887, he became the target of a scurrilous media campaign. The *Times* published a letter, allegedly written by Parnell, commending the 1882 Phoenix Park Murders.

He denounced this missive as "a villainous and bare-faced forgery" and "an audacious and unblushing fabrication," and requested a commission of inquiry. This commission exonerated him in February 1889, when the forger—an anti-Parnellite journalist named Richard Piggott—confessed under cross-examination (he later committed suicide). The commission did not publish its thirty-five-volume report until early 1890. But that March, when Parnell entered Parliament, he received a standing ovation from the entire house, led by William Gladstone.

With Gladstone, who was widely expected to regain power, Parnell had begun preparing a second Home Rule Bill. In mid-December 1889, he had visited Gladstone at Hawarden Castle, his spectacular residence in Wales, directly across the Irish Sea from Dublin. To a contemporary viewer, it recalls Downton Abbey. The two men had got along splendidly and nailed down all but the final details. By this time, Parnell had sat for more than a dozen years in the British Parliament, and had emerged as unchallenged leader of the Irish Parliamentary Party. He had developed an alliance with that Liberal statesman Gladstone, who had already served three times as British prime minister. With the help of Gladstone, Parnell believed he would soon succeed in establishing a separate Irish parliament in Dublin, and so achieve Home Rule for Ireland.

But on December 27, 1889, the *Times* of London reported that Parnell was being accused of adultery. An Irish captain, a former ally named William O'Shea, had filed for divorce and named Parnell as co-respondent. The politician reacted with controlled fury. He was celebrating Christmas in Eltham, ten miles southeast of London, with Katherine O'Shea and their two surviving children. He was outraged, yet also felt certain that he could find a way through this crisis. Never had he wielded more power.

Nor did he feel himself to be in the wrong. Nine years before, when Parnell had begun his relationship with Katherine, she and her husband had long since separated and were living independently. And William O'Shea was serving as a Member of Parliament for County Clare. Since then, Katherine had borne Parnell three children, one of whom had died. O'Shea had known about their relationship almost since the beginning. He had also known that, for the past three years, Parnell had resided in Eltham with Katherine in the family home she had inherited.

While technically involved in an adultery, the two were married in all but name. In recent years, thanks to her family connections with the British Liberal Party, Katherine had acted as Parnell's intermediary with Gladstone, clearing the way for the introduction in 1886 of the First Irish Home Rule Bill—an act narrowly defeated in Parliament. But now Parnell was ready to launch a second initiative.

Five months before, Gladstone—himself of Scottish ancestry—had hailed Parnell's welcome in Edinburgh, where thirty thousand people had cheered him in the streets. The Irishman had been falsely accused of writing letters condoning a terrorist act, the Phoenix Park Murders, but had been vindicated when the forger confessed. Edinburgh had offered him the freedom of the city, and Parnell had responded with moderate speeches that Gladstone applauded.

In Edinburgh, omitting calls to sever links with the British Empire, Parnell had advanced a version of Irish Home Rule more in keeping with the Dominion status accorded Canada in 1867: "Justice to Ireland so far from weakening the greatness of the Empire must consolidate and increase its strength," he said. His country would henceforth "be united in the bonds, the strong and enduring bonds of friendship, mutual interest and amity," and would "prove a source of strength to the Empire instead of a source of weakness."

Parnell would not allow the conniving O'Shea to destroy this latest Home Rule initiative. The man wanted money. Rather than subject Katherine to the scandal that, in Roman Catholic Ireland, would inevitably arise from contesting allegations of adultery, Parnell would pay the man off. All he needed was twenty thousand pounds. O'Shea had waited almost a decade to file for divorce because he had known that Katherine's rich aunt would leave her an estate. As long as he remained officially her husband, and as long as her deeply religious aunt learned nothing untoward, O'Shea expected that he would lay hands on a tidy sum.

But Katherine's aunt, who had died a few months before at age ninety-six, had left less than expected, and had arranged her will so that O'Shea would receive nothing. He had just discovered this, and that was why he had acted now. But for twenty thousand pounds, Parnell felt certain, O'Shea would confess to one of his own seventeen identified infidelities and end the marriage quietly.

In that calculation, Parnell was probably correct. He was wrong, however, to imagine that he would quickly be able to procure the requisite sum, which today, in Canadian terms, would be roughly three million dollars. For years, Parnell had lived beyond his means. As a landlord, he had proven overly generous, forgiving many tenants their rents. His estate, Avondale, was heavily mortgaged. Six years before, supporters had become aware of his financial situation and had raised "a tribute" of thirty-seven thousand pounds by subscription. But that money was long gone.

Discreet inquiries revealed that, in the present circumstances, he could not hope to be rescued again. Nor could Katherine, who had inherited mainly real estate, readily lay hands on such a sum. Biographer Paul Bew summarizes succinctly: "Parnell was eventually destined to lose his unique position of power and authority for the want of a ready 20,000 pounds in 1890."

The rest is tragically anticlimactic. An inspirational constitutionalist, a democratic champion, Parnell had stood on the verge of achieving All-Ireland Home Rule. He had the requisite ally in William Gladstone. He had the enthusiastic support of Catholic Ireland. If Katherine O'Shea's aunt had survived one more year, he would almost certainly have succeeded, and so changed Irish history. There would have ensued no Easter Rising, no War of Independence, no Irish civil war, no partition of the country—a radically different Irish history.

As it happened, despite the pleas of his supporters, Charles Stewart Parnell refused to contest the claims of adultery. Initially, the

Irish National League voted to uphold his leadership. But then—and this is what so enraged and alienated James Joyce—the Christian moralists decided to pronounce judgment. In England, the "non-conformist conscience" rebelled against Parnell. Gladstone sought to warn him that their project was in danger, but Parnell, bent on protecting Katherine O'Shea, refused to change his strategy.

He found some support among Catholic clergymen, but when, after the uncontested divorce, he married Katherine, Irish Catholic bishops condemned him almost unanimously. They declared that Parnell, "by his public misconduct, has utterly disqualified himself to be . . . leader" of the Irish Parliamentary Party. Given no chance of succeeding with their joint initiative, Gladstone withdrew his support. The Irish Parliamentary Party split into two factions, Parnellites and anti-Parnellites. And the Second Home Rule Bill never reached the British House of Commons.

The city of Dublin has a street and a square named after Charles Stewart Parnell, and also this Parnell Monument, installed at the north end of O'Connell Street in 1911.

Could Charles Stewart Parnell have made a political come-back? Probably not, though he believed he could. In any event, he died within months, at age forty-five. For years, he had suffered from ill health, probably kidney disease. In the west of Ireland in September 1891, campaigning despite heavy rain, he had insisted on addressing a crowd of supporters. He got soaked. He returned to Dublin and caught the mail boat to his new home in Brighton, promising: "I shall be all right. I shall be back next Saturday week." But on October 6, 1891, he died in the arms of his wife.

Five days later, in Dublin, after a funeral procession attended by more than two hundred thousand people, Parnell was laid to rest in Glasnevin Cemetery. In the 1930s, William Butler Yeats wrote a four-stanza paean that begins: "Come gather round me, Parnellites, / And praise our chosen man." Today, his statue presides over the north end of O'Connell Street, and his grave in Glasnevin Cemetery is marked by a large stone of unhewn granite taken from his home county. It reads, simply, "Parnell."

One of the most memorable grave markers at Glasnevin Cemetery in Dublin is the unhewn granite stone brought from County Wicklow and inscribed simply "Parnell."

Canadian visitors, knowing that Charles Stewart Parnell died just four months after Sir John A. Macdonald, are wont to see in that stone not just a commemoration of a towering Irish statesman, but also a symbol of the foundational value for which both Parnell and Macdonald stood—that of constitutional democracy, and of effecting political change not through violent revolution, but by political means. No wonder James Joyce could never forgive and forget.

PART THREE

PLURALISM

The town where I grew up is described today as "an off-island suburb of Montreal" located in the county of Deux-Montagnes. Situated on the Lake of Two Mountains, Sainte-Marthe-sur-le-Lac shares a border with Saint-Eustache, the site of a significant battle between French Patriotes and English redcoats during the Lower Canada Rebellion of 1837. In recent years, the population has swollen to more than fifteen thousand full-time residents. But in the 1950s and early 1960s, when I was growing up there, Sainte-Marthe was a resort town of maybe fifteen hundred persons. Then, as now, fewer than 10 per cent spoke English as a first language. Everybody else spoke French.

In winter, when I wasn't at school in Two Mountains / Deux-Montagnes, I hung out mostly with French-speakers. But every summer, when the local population exploded with Montrealers escaping the heat and humidity of the city, I became one of *les Anglais* or, more often than not, in the world of teenagers, one of the *maudits Anglais*, or "damned English." Not for my French friends, with whom I remained close, but for those we called "the summer people." It irritated me. I was one-quarter French Canadian, for starters, descended from *pure laine* immigrants who arrived in the early 1600s. Also, I had no English ancestors. I was Scottish and Irish and French. How could I be a *maudit Anglais*?

As a teenager, I gave up trying to figure it out. This was the world. I never wondered if growing up in a minority situation might make me different from the majority of Canadians, even those with whom I shared a first language. I never dreamed that it would sharpen my sense of kinship with the Scots and the Irish, who, in the context of the British Isles, represent cultural minorities. And I never imagined that it would predispose me to develop a pluralistic world view. I did not begin to think about any of this until the mid-1990s, when, after the death of my friend Samuel Selvon, an expatriate Caribbean writer, I wrote an appreciation of him for a literary magazine called *ARIEL: A Review of International English Literature*.

I had never analyzed my friendship with Selvon, or wondered about its psychological underpinnings. But while preparing to write about him, I read a book called *Interviews with Writers of the Post-Colonial World,* in which a scholar observed that "cultures designated as minorities have certain shared experiences by virtue of their similar antagonistic relationship to the dominant culture, which seeks to marginalize them all." I thought of how, in Quebec, people of Scottish, Irish, Jewish, or Italian heritage, as well as English, are frequently lumped together as "Anglos," admittedly an improvement over *maudits Anglais*. Yet surely it is reductive and marginalizing when, every election, we hear the same question: How will the "Anglos" vote?

One reason Selvon and I became friends, I came to think, is that we both grew up into marginality. And we responded to this complex, shaping predicament in similar ways. A man of Indian background, Selvon told me once that a lot of his boyhood friends "were mixed blacks and Indians." And I found myself reflecting that race, like language, can be a huge divider. And wondering whether the cultural divide between Caribbean blacks and Indians, most of whom are English-speakers, is greater than that between people of the same race but with different languages, as in Quebec.

Growing up first-language-English in a French world created in me a certain sense of self—one more like Sam Selvon's, in many ways, than like that of other Caucasian Canadians who grew up in an anglophone milieu. I would suggest that in Quebec, an English-speaking Caucasian marginalized by a dominant French culture would naturally develop an outlook similar to that of someone who, like Selvon, felt racially marginalized, and clearly identified with the "post-colonial world." Over the centuries, a similar marginalization played a role in shaping both the Scots and the Irish.

Numerous literary scholars have approached the literature of Ireland and Scotland through post-colonial theory. This is not the place to wrestle with their work. But I would make two points. First, as we have seen in Part One, the Scots and the Irish both have long traditions of resisting assimilation and homogenization. Such resistance teaches an appreciation of the importance of cultural difference: that is what they are fighting for—their right to be themselves. The Québécois mirror that struggle. Second point: here in Canada, at least outside Quebec, Celtic resistance to assimilation has blossomed into an acceptance of multiculturalism and pluralism generally. Our long, slow, evolutionary development enabled this to happen. Canada emerged into independent nationhood not in the eighteenth or nineteenth century but in the twentieth. As a result, instead of one nation, one identity (a modern concept), we celebrate one nation, many identities (a postmodern one).

If we have yet to succeed in accommodating everybody, and face special challenges with aboriginal peoples, Canada remains committed to pluralism—to developing a society in which citizens of different backgrounds can hold different beliefs and competing ethical views without coming under attack or threat of assimilation.

I was reminded of this on Canada Day 2014, when the mayor of Calgary turned up on the front page of the *Toronto Star*.

Challenged to account for Calgary's success and prosperity, Naheed Nenshi, the son of South Asian immigrants from Tanzania, acknowledged that having "oil in the ground certainly helps . . . But there are lots of places with lots of oil that have not managed to create a successful, resilient society." Speaking more broadly, Nenshi cited this country's openness, tolerance, and sense of diversity: "We've figured something out in Canada that other people in other places haven't figured out."

That diversity is reflected in Canadian literature. One of the key figures in pioneering this reality was publisher Jack McClelland. His father was a Glasgow-born Irishman who immigrated to Toronto in 1882 at age five. In the early 1960s, when most mainstream Canadian publishers were unabashedly "white-bread," McClelland published not just Scottish and Irish Canadians, from Farley Mowat to Brian Moore and Margaret Atwood, but also a large contingent of Jewish writers, among them Irving Layton, Leonard Cohen, Henry Kreisel, William Weintraub, Peter C. Newman, Matt Cohen, and Mordecai Richler. McClelland published such openly gay writers as Scott Symons, and also the early works of Austin Clarke, who immigrated from Barbados and has been called "Canada's first multicultural writer."

The power of Canadian society, as Dr. James Orbinski, humanitarian activist, once suggested, has "everything to do with diversity in all of its forms: geographic, cultural, linguistic, spiritual. Here we have a framework, both legal and normative, that allows this diversity to thrive." That framework, as I hope to show here in Part Three, has arisen out of Canada's Celtic heritage, as imported by such figures as McClelland. The Scots and the Irish have battled assimilation and intolerance for centuries, including within their own societies, and even their failures have proven instructive.

Both the Scots and the Irish have long embodied a mix of peoples—Celts, certainly, but also Picts, Vikings, Normans, and Anglo-Saxons. Pluralism begins with accepting and embracing a single "other." After the Protestant Reformation, in both Ireland and Scotland, Gaelic-speakers tended to remain Roman Catholic. They were "other." In both countries, anglophone Protestants reached out to them, and so began the long, slow evolution to postmodern pluralism. The man who pointed the way was a patriotic Scot who adored history: Sir Walter Scott.

13.

Sir Walter Scott

✖✖✖

Author Bill Bryson once described the Scott Monument in Edinburgh as looking like a "Gothic rocket ship," and who could improve on that? It soars skyward from Princes Street Gardens in the New Town area, a short walk from Waverley railway station, which is named after Scott's breakthrough novel. The monument is just over two hundred feet high, and features a narrow, spiral staircase that leads to a series of viewing platforms. Smart visitors are content to examine the statue of Sir Walter Scott from the base of the monument.

Others, like myself, feel duty-bound to climb to the top. To reach the highest platform, you mount a total of 287 steps. What you might not know when you start stepping is that the stairway gets narrower as you climb—so narrow, eventually, that a man who stands just over six feet tall, say, will find it difficult to squeeze onto that last platform. Somewhere, I have a piece of paper attesting to my accomplishment. The panorama of Edinburgh is splendid, but to do it all again, I would choose a calm day rather than a windy one.

Climbing the monument provided me with one Walter Scott moment, but a finer one awaited at Edinburgh Castle, when we entered the Crown Room. This was where, in 1818, Scott led the disinterring of the ancient honours of Scotland: a crown, a sword of state, and a sceptre that had been locked away since 1707, when the Acts of Union joined Scotland and England into a single, united "Great Britain." Today, visitors encounter a tableau of Scott rediscovering the relics. For him, the occasion was a sacred moment. When one of the commissioners suggested placing the newly recovered crown on the head of a young woman present, an appalled Scott roared, "By God, no!" As John Buchan observes in his biography of the man, "That day Edinburgh learned that its genteel antiquarianism was a very different thing from Scott's burning reverence for the past."

Walter Scott's passion for history led him to create Abbotsford, a spectacular mansion near Melrose. It contains countless relics, including some from medieval Edinburgh.

Thanks partly to that reverence, Scott contributed to Canada without ever visiting. Some declare flatly that, beginning with *Waverley* (1814), Walter Scott invented the historical novel, which plays a notable role in our literary tradition. If that had been his sole contribution to Canadian culture, Scott would have warranted attention here. But in 1822, he organized a hotly debated pageant that gave Scotland symbols of identity unique in the world—symbols that now play a major part in Canadian life. Yes, we are talking about kilts and bagpipes.

Earlier that year, when King George IV announced a state visit to Scotland, Edinburgh went into a tizzy. George would be the first reigning monarch to set foot in the country since 1650. How was the city to celebrate such an occasion? The movers and shakers realized that the only man who could hope to organize an appropriate national pageant was Sir Walter Scott, recently named a baronet.

Originally a lawyer, Scott had become world-famous through his poetry and historical novels. But he met this new challenge head-on, and worked himself to the brink of illness while turning the occasion into an unprecedented celebration of all things Scottish. During the fourteen days King George spent in Scotland, more than three hundred thousand people turned out to see him. Great numbers of them wore symbolic tartan, formerly forbidden, and marching bands paraded around to the ubiquitous skirling of bagpipes.

The pageantry sparked controversy. Scott's son-in-law and first biographer, John Gibson Lockhart, praised the extravaganza as "Sir Walter's Celtification of Scotland," while the *Scotsman* complained that the celebration went too far in giving "a Highland complexion to the whole . . . as if nothing were Scottish but what is Highland." In the twentieth century, author John Prebble, who grew up in the Canadian west, took this criticism to its apogee in *The King's Jaunt*.

Prebble decried "the Highland dress and spurious tartans" as having little connection with ancient costume, and complained that no laments were heard "for the evictions, the burnings and the white-sailed ships that were emptying the glens while the men who profited from this diaspora formed their highland societies and solemnly debated the correct hang of a kilt and the exact drape of a plaid."

The author had a point. The Highland Clearances were a tragedy and an outrage. But nobody knew that better than Walter Scott, who had written about them. From the perspective of the twenty-first century, those critics who take Prebble's line are missing something essential. The most significant aspect of Scott's pageantry was its pluralism.

Sir Walter Scott was an English-speaking Protestant—a Lowlander who, as a child, had been weaned on the stories of heroic Covenanters. When he called for bagpipes and kilts, he was reaching out to Gaelic-speaking, Roman Catholic Highlanders—to those who, in his world, represented "the other." He was making a gesture for which he had been preparing all his life, and expressing a generosity of spirit which, brought forward by those who learned from him, would become a cornerstone of Canadian nationhood.

※※※

Walter Scott was born in Edinburgh in 1771, the son of a solicitor. At age two, after surviving a bout of polio that left him lame in one leg, he went to live in the Borders region at his grandparents' farm, near the ruin of Smailholm Tower, which had once been the family home. Here, besides learning to read, the boy heard tales and legends that influenced his later work. He returned to the city at age seven and, the following year, began attending the Royal High School of Edinburgh.

Scott read voraciously: poetry, chivalric romances, works of history and travel. He explored the city on foot to exercise his bad leg. And a private tutor, James Mitchell, taught him arithmetic, writing, and the history of the Protestant Church, highlighting the Covenanters as heroes who would not compromise their faith. In 1783, at age twelve, Scott began studying classics at the University of Edinburgh.

Three years later, while visiting a school friend at the home of a professor, Adam Ferguson, he met the poet Robert Burns at the height of his fame. A well-known painting illustrates an incident from this meeting. Burns admired a print called *The Justice of the Peace* and asked who had written the poem that inspired it. In the august company of Edinburgh intellectuals, only the bookish young Scott could tell him the name of the author (John Langhorne). Burns gave the youth a nod that Scott would remember with pride.

At university, the young Walter Scott became friends with Thomas Douglas (1771–1820), who inherited estates and became well-known in Canada as Lord Selkirk. Douglas toured the Scottish Highlands during the clearances, and was so appalled by what he witnessed that he devoted his wealth and energies to creating colonies of immigrant Scots in Canada. The most successful of these, which he established at Red River, got him embroiled in a protracted battle with fur-trading Scots, but evolved into the city of Winnipeg.

Walter Scott, born not into nobility but into the middle class, turned to the study of law. As a law clerk, while visiting the Scottish Highlands, he witnessed an eviction—an event that shocked him. Not long afterwards, in 1792, he gained admittance to the Faculty of Advocates. By this time, he had learned to read French, Spanish, Italian, and German, and at twenty-five, while practising law, he translated and published a collection of rhymed ballads by German romantic G. A. Bürger. Influenced by Robert Burns, who had devoted years to collecting folk songs, Scott compiled a three-volume collection of old ballads, *The Minstrelsy of the Scottish Border*. One of those who assisted him in collecting tunes was James Hogg, a poet who later became famous as "the Ettrick Shepherd." Hogg's mother was related to William Laidlaw, whose descendants would include Alice Munro, Canada's first winner of the Nobel Prize for Literature.

❊❊❊

At age twenty-six, after surviving a failed love affair, Walter Scott married Margaret Charpentier, a woman of French descent who would bear him five children. Two years later, he became sheriff deputy of the County of Selkirk. This position, together with his wife's income and money from his father's estate, would have given him financial security, had he been able to control his antiquarian yearnings to celebrate Scottish history in art and architecture.

At this time, the turn of the nineteenth century, poetry was considered the highest of the literary arts. In 1805, Scott published *The Lay of the Last Minstrel*, a first book of poems, and so began his climb to celebrity. During the next few years, he published a series of long narrative poems, among them *Marmion* (1808), *The Lady of the Lake* (1810), *Rokeby* (1813), and *The Lord of the Isles* (1815). The first of these inspired Schubert's "Ave Maria," and another poem included the oft-quoted lines "Oh! what a tangled web we weave / When first we practice to deceive!"

Although regarded as a major poet, Scott perceived that his work was slipping out of fashion. In an astute critical biography, *Sir Walter Scott*, writer John Buchan—later Governor General of Canada—captured Scott's quandary as that romantic rambler Lord Byron emerged as a poet: "How could a middle-aged Scottish lawyer compete . . . against a young and handsome lordling, who had about him the glamour of a wild life and a broken heart? How could the homely glens of his own land vie with the glittering cities of the South and the magic of the ancient East?"

A few years before, Scott had begun working on a prose narrative set against the Jacobite rebellion of the 1740s, when a Highland uprising against the British king culminated in what, for most Highland Scots, was the disastrous Battle of Culloden. Having discovered and admired *Castle Rackrent* by Maria Edgeworth, Scott had written the first few chapters of *Waverley*. But a friend voiced doubts about the work, and convinced him that publishing a historical novel might damage his reputation as a poet. He set the book aside. But in 1813, while rooting around in an attic, he chanced upon the manuscript. He decided to finish it—"and thereby," Buchan tells us, "entered into his true kingdom."

The next year, still worried about harming his reputation as a man of letters, not to mention as a sheriff and lawyer, Scott released *Waverley* anonymously. At this time, as Buchan notes, great novels were expected to be studies of contemporary life: "The historical tale was a lifeless thing, smothered in tinsel conventions, something beneath the dignity of literature."

Waverley, however, was clearly serious: entertaining, yes, but also educational, challenging, even provocative. The novel proved hugely successful. Walter Scott had created a new literary genre with an international future: the realistic historical novel. The protagonist of his first such work, an English Tory named Edward Waverley, is sympathetic to the rebellious Scottish-Gaelic Jacobites—and here we see the author's empathy, and the seeds of his incipient pluralism. Edward Waverley does decide finally to remain loyal to the British king, but clearly he is torn. Scott makes his point.

Following hard on the success of *Waverley*, Scott produced a series of historical novels: *Guy Mannering* (1815), *The Antiquary* (1816), *Rob Roy* (1817). He published these works anonymously, so giving rise to endless speculation. People called him "the Wizard of the North." But gradually his identity became known, and as early as 1815, he was invited to dine with George, Prince Regent of Britain, who had expressed a desire to meet the author of *Waverley*.

Scott kept writing, producing *Ivanhoe* (1819), *Kenilworth* (1821), and *The Pirate* (1822). The first of these, set in twelfth-century England, was especially notable for its sympathetic depiction of a major Jewish character, Rebecca. This emerged at a time when people in England were still struggling to achieve Jewish emancipation, which meant the lifting of legal restrictions and the passing of laws that put male Jews on an equal footing with other men. This represented yet another instance in which Scott demonstrated his avant-garde acceptance of otherness.

Scott's reputation has varied as fashions changed, and few today would argue that he is a literary novelist of the first rank. Yet Scott is widely recognized as the father of serious historical fiction, a genre that has an unusually strong presence in Canadian literature. *The Oxford Companion to Canadian Literature* tells us that of foreign authors who influenced early English Canadian writers, "the most important was Sir Walter Scott." Through the late nineteenth and early twentieth centuries, many Canadian home libraries included *Rob Roy*, *Ivanhoe*, and *The Pirate*, parts of which are said to have been influenced by a visit Scott made to Orkney, where he was entertained by the father of Arctic explorer John Rae.

In recent times, some literary critics have suggested that Canadian writers produce far too many historical novels. Certainly, an abridged list of the happily guilty would begin in the 1830s with John Richardson and *Wacousta*, and swell to include such contemporary figures as Timothy Findley, Margaret Atwood, Katherine Govier, Lawrence Hill, Jane Urquhart, Joseph Boyden, Anne Michaels, Dennis Bock, Steven Galloway, Karen X. Tulchinsky, Fred Stenson, Ronald Wright, Helen Humphreys, and Sean Michaels, to name just a few.

Sir Walter Scott invented the realistic historical novel, but did not foresee that it would
thrive into twenty-first-century Canada. This engraving derives from Evert A. Duyckinck's
Portrait Gallery of Eminent Men and Women in Europe and America *(1873).*

The disgruntled critics would appear to be using American literature as a yardstick. Unlike the U.S., Canada never deliberately
severed ties with Scotland or Ireland. So why wouldn't the literary
traditions of those countries exert a lasting influence? Whatever
the explanation, here in Canada, the historical novel has remained
continuously alive all the way back to its origins in the works of
Maria Edgeworth and Sir Walter Scott.

As for Scott's fourteen-day pageant, certainly it was extravagant. But that is one reason why it has resonated down through

the decades and across oceans. And if the diversity among Scottish plaids dates back no farther than Walter Scott, yet those tartans today create a sense of continuity and proclaim a respect for history and tradition. Working with a state visit, Walter Scott turned the kilt and the bagpipes into symbols of Scottish identity that continue to colour every major parade in Canada, and today are recognized around the world.

Biographer John Buchan summarized this way: "John Knox gave his land the Reformation, which led to high spiritual exaltations, but also to much blood and tears . . . [Robert] Burns, with a Greek freedom in his soul, gave Scotland her own French Revolution." And Scott, he writes, "completed what eighteenth-century philosophers had begun and gave [Scotland] her own Renaissance. He is, with Burns, her great liberator and reconciler." Buchan adds that Scott gave his fellow countrymen a new confidence by reconnecting them with their history, and also found a way to communicate the distinctiveness of Scotland to the world.

Some latter-day critics have sought to position Scott as standing in opposition to Burns, portraying the former as a High Tory Unionist contending against a Scottish nationalist. Yet this is too simple. From the perspective of the twenty-first century, their commonalities far outweigh their differences, most notably with regard to their broadly based empathy.

For contemporary Canadians, Scott still resonates beyond pageantry because, with his novels, he showed that the future lies hidden in the past. As a Lowland Scot, an English-speaking Protestant who celebrated the culture of Gaelic-speaking, Roman Catholic Highlanders, Sir Walter Scott also planted an early flag for pluralism. He anticipated the emergence in Ireland of William Butler Yeats, who would follow Scott in launching a parallel Celtic Revival, and win the Nobel Prize for Literature while he was at it.

14.

William Butler Yeats

※※※

few decades after one literary giant restored all things
Celtic to Scotland, another led the national embrace of
a Celtic identity in Ireland. The Anglo-Irish poet William
Butler Yeats engendered the "Celtic Renaissance" that gave rise to
the Abbey Theatre and revived the Irish (Gaelic) language. Both
Scott and Yeats modelled an acceptance of "otherness" that, transported to the wide-open spaces of Canada, would find room to
grow, and to evolve into a broadly based pluralism.

Some trace the birth of Ireland's Celtic Revival to April 1902,
when the Dublin staging of one of Yeats's plays led to riots in the
streets. Others point to December 1904, when that same play,
Cathleen ni Houlihan, was mounted to launch the Abbey Theatre.
But both these moments have their origins in 1897, when at age
thirty-two, Yeats began collecting folk tales preserved in the Irish-
Gaelic language.

That year, Yeats wrote to an Edinburgh-based Scot about creating literary societies to mount plays: "They would be far more
effective than lectures and might do more than anything else we

can do to make the Irish, Scots, and other Celts recognize their solidarity." In 1897, finally, Yeats drafted a manifesto for a Celtic Theatre that would perform Celtic and Irish plays, moving beyond "dramatic journalism" to draw on "an ancient idealism" and present work "outside all the political questions that divide us."

As a unilingual English-speaker rooted in the Protestant Ascendancy, Yeats was doing precisely what, in Scotland, Walter Scott had done. He was looking to ancient history—to pre-Christian legends and folk tales preserved by Irish-Gaelic-speakers—as a way to transcend division. In advancing the notion that Irish identity was broader and deeper than any separation between Protestant and Catholic, Yeats was urging the acceptance of otherness. He was laying the foundations of pluralism. As T. S. Eliot wrote, Yeats was "one of those few whose history is the history of their own time, who are part of the consciousness of an age which cannot be understood without them."

❈❈

Born in Dublin in June 1865, William Butler Yeats could trace his ancestry on both sides to Protestants who arrived from England in the seventeenth century. He spent his early years in a comfortable family home in County Sligo, on the west coast of Ireland. Later, he would describe this area as his spiritual home and his "country of the heart." His father studied law but then became a semi-successful artist. A bookish man, he read stories aloud to the young W. B.—notably, those of Walter Scott—and taught him that dramatic poetry was the highest form of literature.

As an artist, Yeats's father moved his family back and forth between Dublin and London, and so Yeats attended a number of different schools. Instead of going to Trinity College, that bastion of Protestant education, he studied art at the Metropolitan School of Art and the Royal Hibernian Academy School. Already he was fascinated by Irish legends and mysticism generally and, while still in his teens, moved from painting into poetry.

William Butler Yeats grew up during the political heyday of Charles Stewart Parnell. He lived through Parnell's rise as leader of the Land League in the 1870s; his imprisonment at Kilmainham Gaol in 1881; his drive for Irish Home Rule in the 1880s; his mistreatment and betrayal by large segments of the populace in 1890; and his death in 1891. Like Parnell, Yeats came of Anglo-Irish stock. Like Parnell, he favoured evolution over revolution. And perhaps most significantly of all, like Parnell, Yeats reached out to Gaelic-speaking Irish Catholics.

Later, Yeats would write poems remembering Parnell, the best known of which begins:

> Come gather round me, Parnellites,
> And praise our chosen man;
> Stand upright on your legs awhile,
> Stand upright while you can,
> For soon we lie where he is laid,
> And he is underground;
> Come fill up all those glasses
> And pass the bottle round . . .

Yeats published his first poems in 1885, while still studying art. These showed the influence of such English poets as Percy Bysshe Shelley and William Blake, but soon enough the young man was drawing on Irish mythology and folklore. At twenty-four, he published *The Wanderings of Oisin*, a long narrative poem that, according to biographer R. F. Foster, features "obscure Gaelic names, striking repetitions, and unremitting rhythm." It draws heavily on Irish mythology and is considered his first notable work.

In 1889, Yeats fell obsessively in love with Maud Gonne, a charismatic Irish nationalist slightly younger than he was. Over the next dozen years, he would propose to her four times, and four times be rejected. Gonne was a fiercely committed activist who would at one point advocate violence against landlords. Yeats remained a classic Parnellite who sought non-violent solutions to Ireland's problems. Eventually, after she married a revolutionary and then separated from him, Yeats got over her.

His platonic relationship with another woman—Augusta, Lady Gregory, thirteen years his senior—ultimately proved more constructive. He recognized this only later, after she fell seriously ill, causing him to realize that to him she meant "more than kin," for she was mother, friend, sister, and brother. She introduced him to influential people and at times provided funds and even furniture. Yeats met her in London in 1894 at the house of a friend. They found common ground in their keen interest in Celtic legend and mythology, and Lady Gregory, a wealthy widow, invited Yeats to visit her estate, Coole Park, near Galway on the west coast of Ireland. Today, the mansion is long gone, but visitors can wander the grounds and visit a tree on which Yeats and other writers etched their initials.

The library at Westport House, County Mayo, features wax figures of the writers and artists of western Ireland, including William Butler Yeats and Augusta, Lady Gregory.

Lady Gregory, too, was Anglo-Irish, but having acquired some fluency in the Irish-Gaelic language, she began collecting Celtic folk tales for Yeats. During the summer of 1897, he joined her in gathering legends from country people in Kiltartan village near her estate. To record these, she developed a colloquial, idiomatic style she called Kiltartanese, and later used it to help Yeats climb down out of what he called "that high window of dramatic verse." As first reader and editor, she helped translate his vision into "the English of the West of Ireland, the English of people who think in Irish."

Yeats could not have launched the Irish Literary Revival, part of the broader Celtic Revival, without Lady Gregory (1852–1932), hailed by George Bernard Shaw as "the greatest living Irishwoman." Yeats and Gregory were joined by numerous other writers in seeking to assert a distinct Irish identity. This did not mean abandoning the English language, but writing poetry and plays drawing on Irish myths, legends, and politics. Without Lady Gregory, the Abbey Theatre, Ireland's national theatre, would not be thriving today in Dublin. She was the one who brought that theatre into existence.

Lady Gregory, who wrote books and plays, had been born in Galway into a prominent Anglo-Irish family. She became an Irish cultural nationalist after she visited the Aran Islands, where she awoke to the beauties of the Irish (Gaelic) language. Unlike many of her revivalist allies, including Yeats, she studied and learned to speak it. One of her plays, *The Deliverer*, focused on Charles Stewart Parnell, and Colm Tóibín recently published a biographical essay, *Lady Gregory's Toothbrush*, celebrating her as Ireland's First Lady of the Theatre.

By the late 1890s, according to biographer A. Norman Jeffares, Yeats had already set up Irish literary societies in Dublin and London, and had written articles and speeches calling for a new kind of Irish literature. But he did not feel that he was reaching a broad enough audience. "I wanted a Theatre," he wrote later. "I had wanted it for years." But "knowing no way of getting money for a start in Ireland," he had spoken with theatrical friends of renting "some little London hall, where I could produce plays. I first spoke to Lady Gregory of my abandoned plan for an Irish Theatre," he explained, while they were walking in the garden of a friend's house.

Yeats was thinking still of London, but Lady Gregory, "with her feeling for immediate action, for the present moment, disapproved of my London project." She offered to collect or give the money for the first Irish performances. In that moment, Yeats would recall, "the Irish National Theatre was born."

Before long, with a number of like-minded writers—Edward Martyn, George Moore, John Millington Synge, George Russell, Sean O'Casey, Padraic Colum, and Douglas Hyde—Yeats and Lady Gregory had begun forging an Irish Literary Revival, which is sometimes referred to as the Celtic Twilight. Originally, Yeats had proposed to establish a Celtic Theatre focusing on dramatic literature, but biographer R. F. Foster tells us that he changed the name to Irish Literary Revival partly for political reasons, and partly because he "had recently discovered that 'Celticism' was a highly problematic concept in historical or cultural terms."

Indeed, Yeats had learned that the Irish-Gaelic Celtic culture had much in common with the Scottish-Gaelic culture of the Highlands and islands. More than that, this Celtic culture had long since incorporated Norse and Anglo-Norman elements. The idea of "Celtic" was far more complex and, yes, problematic, than he had initially imagined. Yeats had discovered Celtic pluralism. In developing a voice to articulate this new-found complexity, he would push beyond Victorian versifying into modernism.

This evolution influenced the Montreal or McGill Group of Canadian poets who emerged in the 1920s. In the *Encyclopedia of Literature in Canada*, William H. New put it this way: "The McGill Group sought to modernize Canadian poetry writing, and its members drew eclectically on the influences of imagism and symbolism as manifested in the works of poets such as William Butler Yeats . . . They wished to freshen the craft conventions of Canadian poetry and therefore committed themselves to a new realism of expression, to tonal wit and irony, as opposed to merely effusive lyricism, and to a view of the poet as a responsible and intelligent commentator on culture and society."

From 1921 to 1929, W. B. Yeats lived with his family in this fifteenth- or sixteenth-century Norman tower, Thoor Ballylee, in County Galway, not far from Coole Park.

Where Yeats eulogized Parnell, the Montreal Group lambasted the Canadian Authors' Association for using "publicity, advertising and the methods of big business" to foster Canada's young literature. Group members went on to win a Pulitzer Prize and five Governor General's Awards, among other accolades. According to the *Encyclopedia*, the Montreal Group of poets "continued to influence the writing of poetry in Canada until the end of the 20th century." Indeed, because that group and Yeats himself had a major impact on the work of poet and singer-songwriter Leonard Cohen, the Yeatsian influence would appear to be alive and thriving in twenty-first-century Canada.

▨▨▨

In 1899, with Edward Martyn, George Moore, and Lady Gregory, William Butler Yeats established the Irish Literary Theatre, a collective committed to presenting Irish and Celtic plays. Yeats had already published *The Countess Cathleen*, a verse drama that unfolds during an unspecified famine and finds the countess of the title selling her soul to the devil to save her starving people. In May 1899, the theatre collective rented the Antient Concert Rooms in Dublin to present it. The play, previously published, offended some Roman Catholic authorities. It had to be mounted under police protection, and drew both cheers and jeers.

This reaction was mild compared with the response Yeats elicited three years later, in April 1902, with his one-act play *Cathleen ni Houlihan*. That work revolves around the 1798 Rebellion, whose leaders included Theobald Wolfe Tone, and finds young men sacrificing their lives for the title character, who clearly symbolizes an independent Irish state. Maud Gonne played the heroine in this production, which was mounted in Dublin at another rented hall. The besotted Yeats wrote that "her great height made Cathleen seem a divine being fallen into our mortal infirmity."

He was not alone. Stephen Gwynn, a journalist/biographer who later became a Member of Parliament, wrote that he had never seen an audience so moved. According to Norman Jeffares, Gwynn wondered whether such plays should be produced "unless one was prepared for people to go out to shoot and be shot." Yeats himself would one day ask the same question in a poem called "The Man and the Echo," with an allusion to the 1916 uprising: "Did that play of mine send out / Certain men the English shot."

Also in 1902, Yeats met the twenty-year-old James Joyce, recognized his youthful genius, and in London introduced him to as many influential literary men as he could. That year, as well, he helped set up a press—run by his two sisters—to publish works by writers of the Irish Revival. Two years later, it became the Cuala Press. Over the next four decades, it produced more than seventy titles, forty-eight by Yeats himself.

But now, the year after he met Joyce, Yeats undertook a lecture tour in North America. He ranged from Berkeley, California, to Toronto, Kingston, and Montreal. Addressing audiences as large as two thousand, he highlighted the intellectual revival in Ireland, and marvelled at the lack of religious prejudice in North America. The old hatreds and divisions lived on, of course, but flared less often and with less ferocity.

Back home, Yeats had begun seeking a permanent home for the Irish theatre. With Lady Gregory and his allies, he located a suitable building in Dublin. He also turned up a wealthy patron, an Englishwoman named Annie Horniman who in London had produced work by another eminent Irish writer, George Bernard Shaw. Having come to Dublin to assist Yeats, she designed costumes for one of his plays, and then donated the money to hire professional managers and turn the vacant building into the upscale Abbey Theatre.

Opening night, December 27, 1904, featured two short plays by Yeats—one was *Cathleen ni Houlihan*—and a third by Lady Gregory. The next night, a play by John Millington Synge replaced *Cathleen*, and these two bills alternated for five nights. Over the next couple of years, the theatrical collective frequently sparked controversy. Conservative outrage reached a crescendo in January 1907, when riots erupted after the opening of another play by Synge, *The Playboy of the Western World*.

Years before, Yeats had urged Synge, six years younger, to visit the Aran Islands. Synge had done so, and on one of them heard a story about a young man being sheltered after he killed his father. In *Playboy*, Synge had exaggerated this story into a fabulous comedy focusing on a yarn-spinner who had not killed his father after all. But in 1907, Irish nationalists viewed the play as offensive, immoral, and insulting. Riots broke out inside the theatre and then spread into the street. Nationalist leader Arthur Griffith, who advocated a more political theatre, denounced the play as "a vile and inhuman story told in the foulest language we have ever listened to from a public platform."

Newspapers and public opinion turned against the "Playboy Riots," and they abated. But two decades later, when a pacifist drama by Sean O'Casey, *The Plough and the Stars*, evoked a similar reaction, Yeats harked back to this moment, telling the unruly critics: "You have disgraced yourself again. Is this to be the recurring celebration of the arrival of Irish genius?"

Yeats stood apart from the 1916 Easter Rising, which drew most of its support from Catholics. But later, in a poem called "Easter 1916," he recognized that the failed revolution had transformed Ireland: "All changed, changed utterly: / A terrible beauty is born." One century after the Rising, Alex Salmond, the Scottish nationalist politician, has grown fond of quoting Yeats to describe contemporary Scotland. As a result of the 2014 referendum, he says frequently, Scotland is "changed, changed utterly." Right or wrong, Salmond's declaration illustrates the transmission of ideas through time and across national borders.

In 1916, after proposing to Maud Gonne one last time—half-heartedly, feeling more moral obligation than love—Yeats married a younger woman, Georgie Hyde-Lees, who shared his burgeoning interest in spiritualism and stayed with him through several brief affairs.

An evocative bronze statue of William Butler Yeats, created by Rohan Gillespie, stands outside the Ulster Bank on Stephen Street in Sligo. It was unveiled by his son in 1989 to mark the fiftieth anniversary of the poet's death.

In 1922, after the emergence of the Irish Free State, Yeats was appointed to Ireland's first Senate. Three years later, he was reappointed for a second term. And between those occasions, in December 1923, William Butler Yeats received the Nobel Prize for Literature. In his acceptance address, he positioned himself as a champion of Irish cultural independence, and reiterated this in responding to letters of congratulation: "I consider that this honour has come to me less as an individual than as a representative of Irish literature; it is part of Europe's welcome to the Free State."

Meanwhile, as a senator, when a debate on divorce arose, he took a stand against the all-encompassing refusal promulgated by the Roman Catholic Church, arguing that "it seems to us a most sacrilegious thing to persuade two people who hate each other to

live together, and it is to us no remedy to permit them to part if neither can remarry." In the face of aggressive intolerance, Yeats flew
the flag for pluralism: "If you show [that] this country, southern
Ireland, is going to be governed by Roman Catholic ideas and by
Catholic ideas alone, you will never get the North . . . You will put
a wedge in the midst of this nation."

This he fiercely resisted. William Butler Yeats, like Sir Walter
Scott, championed acceptance and accommodation while battling
attempts to stifle dissent and eradicate difference. In so doing,
Yeats followed an unlikely Irish prophet—a clergyman satirist who
launched no societal transformation, but who, nevertheless, made
an overwhelming case for pluralism. In Canada, that satirist is still
famous as the author of *Gulliver's Travels*.

15.

Jonathan Swift

⬚⬚

At an event during my cross-country promotional tour for *50 Canadians Who Changed the World*, somebody asked me, "Have you had any second thoughts? Spotted any omissions? What about Mordecai Richler?" This was in Calgary at Pages on Kensington, and I thought a moment. Richler was one of my all-time favourite novelists, I said. But he worked in the great North American Jewish tradition that includes Saul Bellow, Norman Mailer, and Philip Roth. Given such peers, how could I argue that Richler changed the world? So no: I had no second thoughts.

Later, however, when I stopped into the Oak Room at the Palliser Hotel to unwind, I felt sick as the truth hit me: I had wrongly omitted one of Canada's finest writers. At the Palliser, where several times I had taken strong drink with Mordecai, I realized that I should have realized that he added a Canadian dimension to the North American Jewish tradition—a satirical streak that harks back, ironically, to that Irish clergyman Jonathan Swift.

In *Oh Canada! Oh Quebec!*, Richler launched a cannonade against ethnic nationalism in Quebec, a *cri de coeur* on behalf of pluralism. But as with Swift in the eighteenth century, his sardonic ferocity was widely misunderstood. In reviewing a later Richler work, Joel Yanofsky noted that "satirical writers are frequently misunderstood—Swift was just kidding about eating babies after all—and that's been especially true in this country. It's a fact of life Richler has had to put up with from the beginning of his career."

Elsewhere, Yanofsky added that "Richler knows what Jonathan Swift knew: the first rule of satire is to offend everyone. That way no one is spared and no one is singled out. As satirists go, Swift was a true democrat ('I have ever hated all nations, professions, and communities,' he wrote to Alexander Pope); so is Richler." No question, the Montreal writer (1931–2001) evoked many a comparison with Jonathan Swift.

A Jewish friend of mine argues that Richler's humour is rooted in the eastern European shtetls, or small Jewish villages, that existed before the Holocaust. Like the humour of Canadian Morley Torgov, it owes much to the works of Sholem Aleichem and Isaac Bashevis Singer. And with that I have no argument. But all of us have two parents, four grandparents, and more than one ancestral lineage. One of the last things Richler wrote was an introduction to a new edition of *Sunshine Sketches of a Little Town* by Stephen Leacock. In that piece, Richler describes that book as "the first work to establish a Canadian voice."

In an introduction to *Leacock on Life*, editor Gerald Lynch suggests that this observation "weightily bears comparison with Hemingway's landmark claim that all modern fiction flows from *Huckleberry Finn*." Lynch writes also of a video clip in which Richler "invoked Leacock's boundless Lord Ronald to characterize Canada's directionally challenged Parliament." Here we see Richler's familiarity with the work of his Canadian precursor. Stephen Leacock's Lord Ronald, who turns up in a 1911 story called "Gertrude the

Governess," was a fictional character who "flung himself upon his horse and rode madly off in all directions."

Stephen Leacock himself, Lynch tells us, "learned from such predecessors as Jonathan Swift, Henry Fielding, and Mark Twain the comic rewards of the mock-epic and mock-heroic, mainstays of his style. He also learned from them (especially Swift) the comic impact of making the metaphoric literal." And that, of course, is precisely the strategy Richler deploys in *Oh Canada! Oh Quebec!* Without disputing Richler's Jewish heritage, I would suggest that the Montreal writer also embodies a distinctly Canadian lineage rooted in the work of Jonathan Swift.

In writing *Oh Canada*, Richler drew on a thirty-one-page article about Quebec nationalism that he published in the *New Yorker* magazine in 1991. At the time, I was working as books editor at the *Calgary Herald*, and I hailed Richler's article as a journalistic tour de force: "There's passion here, controlled anger, yet also fairness and a sense of responsibility." Some Québécois wanted the book banned as "hate propaganda," but Richler was directing his righteous anger not at a people, but at "a virulent strain of nationalism that has taken root in *la belle province*."

His sardonic wit drives the book that ensued in 1992. Richler describes how, for example, following the introduction of Bill 178 and its infamous dictates about the relative size of English and French on signs, the denizens of Woody's Pub, himself included, created the Twice as Much Society—a prime example of the Swiftian strategy of "making the metaphorical literal." The society planned to lobby for an amendment, Richler writes, that "would call for French to be spoken twice as loud as English inside and outside.

"Inspectors from the language commission would be armed with sound meters to detect Anglophones who spoke above a whisper, sending offenders to the slammer. A Francophone hockey player scoring a goal for *le Club de hockey canadien* would have to be cheered twice as loud as a minority group teammate. A member of the collectivity, ordering a meal in a restaurant, would have to be served a double portion, and so forth and so on."

With this scathing parody of Quebec language laws, Mordecai Richler was advancing a tradition that Swift established in the early 1700s. Three centuries after he became dean of Saint Patrick's Cathedral in Dublin, Swift is still celebrated not as an Anglican churchman, but as the foremost satirist in the English language. In what today we recognize as a repressive era, Swift found a way to express a humanistic pluralism that was far ahead of his times. By giving voice to his private beliefs—usually anonymously by virtue of necessity—Swift showed himself to be a giant among men, a Gulliver in the land of Lilliput.

Jonathan Swift was dean of St. Patrick's Cathedral in Dublin from 1713 to 1745. Swift battled discrimination and satirized wars fought over differences of religious opinion.

As dean of Saint Patrick's, Swift adhered to the High Church doctrine that the national religion of England (and Ireland) was one and indivisible. Biographer Leo Damrosch tells us that he saw the Church's authority "as essentially legal rather than spiritual." In the early 1700s, in both Britain and Ireland, Catholics and dissenting Protestants "were free to worship as they pleased, but not to enjoy the same civil rights as Anglicans." That religious discrimination raised his hackles.

When majority opinion, and even Daniel Defoe, supported the slave trade, Jonathan Swift denounced it. And in 1720, despite his own Anglo-Irish background, he published a pamphlet arguing that, since England would never treat Ireland fairly, the Irish should boycott English goods. Three years later, after travelling around the south and west of Ireland, he wrote of the wretched conditions in which most Irish Catholics lived, and declared that "all these evils are the effects of English tyranny."

His subversive analysis would find its way into *Gulliver's Travels*, in which, anonymously, he savaged intolerance by ridiculing wars fought over differences of religious opinion. In that satirical work, published in 1726, Swift presents the allegory of a destructive war between Little-Endians and Big-Endians. The two groups fight a long, murderous war over whether a soft-boiled egg should be cracked open at the little end or the big end. Scholars have teased out local specifics. But as with Richler's Twice as Much Society, the universal meaning of that allegory is unmistakably a cry for pluralism.

▨▨

Jonathan Swift was born in Dublin in 1667. The official story has always been that his father, a man of the same name, died soon after his birth. But in his authoritative new biography, Damrosch makes the compelling case that Swift was really the son of Sir John Temple, an Irish lawyer and sometime Member of Parliament. Swift attended the prestigious Kilkenny College, and then Trinity College, Dublin.

He was taking a master's degree at Trinity when upheavals arising from the Glorious Revolution of 1688, which brought the Protestant William of Orange to the British throne, caused him (and many other Anglo-Irish figures) to retreat to England.

There, with the intercession of his mother, Swift became secretary and personal assistant to the wealthy Sir William Temple, a diplomat and essayist who would appear to have been his much older half-brother. Swift, already gaining a reputation as a stylist, completed his master's degree at Oxford while assisting Sir William. Then, unhappy at his lack of advancement, he became an ordained priest in the Anglican Church of Ireland.

After spending 1695 as a vicar in the obscure parish of Kilroot, near Carrickfergus in northern Ireland (County Antrim), Swift returned to Sir William and his Moor Park estate northwest of London, and assisted the older man in writing his memoirs. He also made influential friends, and in 1700, the year after Sir William died, he became a prebendary, or senior clergyman, at Saint Patrick's Cathedral in Dublin.

Articulate and persuasive, Swift shunted back and forth between Dublin and London, negotiating church business. Always he was writing, and in 1704, at age thirty-seven, he published *A Tale of a Tub*, his first major work. It is a satirical parody that highlights a tale of three brothers, each of whom represents one of the main branches of western Christianity. Swift published the work anonymously, but people deduced who had written it. Some saw it as an attack on religion, and others watched it sail high over their heads—the fate of many a satire. Enormously popular, *Tale of a Tub* offended enough powerful people that it ruined Swift's chance of advancement within the Church of England.

A peerless polemicist, Swift published regularly in the influential *Examiner*. He wrote plainly and clearly, and when he needed more space, he churned out pamphlets. He divided his time between

Ireland and England, where he moved in literary circles. After 1713, when he became dean of Saint Patrick's, he stayed mostly in Ireland. Meanwhile, he developed what we might call "special friendships" with two younger women, and would famously nickname them Stella and Vanessa. According to Damrosch, probably he married Stella in 1716. But he buried that secret after he discovered, to his horror, that she was almost certainly the daughter of his older half-brother, Sir William Temple, which meant they were related by blood.

Over the years, two of his best friends were the poet Alexander Pope, who was Roman Catholic, and playwright Richard Sheridan, whose Catholic forebears had converted to the Protestant Church of Ireland a hundred years before. Swift himself was suspected of having Jacobite sympathies, and might have preferred to see the Stuart dynasty restored.

In 1720, Swift published his anonymous *Proposal for the Universal Use of Irish Manufacture*, urging the Irish to resolve "never to appear with one single shred that comes from England." This was a voice, Damrosch observes, that "the Irish public had not heard before, straightforward and persuasive, but with an undercurrent of controlled anger—and sometimes more than undercurrent."

Decades before Maria Edgeworth wrote *Castle Rackrent*, in which she looked askance at her fellow Anglo-Irish landlords, Swift took aim at "our country landlords, who by unmeasurable *screwing* and *racking* their tenants all over the kingdom, have already reduced the miserable people to worse condition than the peasants in France, or the vassals in Germany and Poland." Jonathan Swift was an early supporter of a separate Irish parliament that would have equal authority with the one in England.

Starting in 1724, Swift wrote a series of seven pamphlets under the pseudonym M. B. Drapier, in which he assailed the imposition and corrupt licensing of a minted copper coinage of inferior quality. Known collectively as *Drapier's Letters*, they inspired a nationwide boycott which forced the British government to withdraw the patent. As a result, Swift was hailed as a hero, and some observers have described him as the first to establish "a more universal Irish community." Pluralism, again.

Meanwhile, Swift had begun working on a narrative of four imaginary voyages, a work that would become that literary classic *Gulliver's Travels*. Published first in 1726, immediately acclaimed, and never since out of print, this early novel satirizes human nature and parodies travellers' tales. It also presents a systematic rebuttal of Daniel Defoe's *Robinson Crusoe*, published seven years before, and finds "Lemuel Gulliver" encountering not barren islands but established societies.

An 1850 image of Jonathan Swift, who used exaggeration to powerful effect while denouncing greed, selfishness, and an inability to accept anyone different or other.

Countless critics have written books analyzing *Travels*, and the theme that interests us here is that of the stupidity of fighting wars over petty differences of religion. In Lilliput, Gulliver learns that differences between Big-Endians (those who broke their eggs at the larger end) and Little-Endians had given rise to "six rebellions . . . wherein one Emperor lost his life, and another his crown." Swift alludes to conflicts between Protestants and Catholics, as well as between different branches of Protestantism, and communicates a clear message: Instead of waging war over petty differences, why not give tolerance a try?

For his last great moment as a writer, which came in 1729, Swift presented a scathing variation on this same theme. With his friend Sheridan, he had been writing for a weekly periodical called the *Intelligencer*. Having contributed a series of lucid but ineffective commentaries on the plight of the rural Irish following recent bad harvests, Swift resorted to his rhetorical bag of tricks. He produced a sixteen-page pamphlet entitled *A Modest Proposal for Preventing the Children of the Poor People in Ireland from Being a Burden to Their Parents or Their Country, and for Making Them Beneficial to the Public.*

He begins by mimicking the earnest, objective tone of conventional commentaries, but soon moves to wild exaggeration. He suggests that some Irish women have been "murdering their bastard children . . . more to avoid the expense than the shame." But since colonial plantation owners know "all about buying and selling human beings"—a sideswipe at slavery—why not make infanticide commercially profitable?

Swift takes his readers over the top, "confessing" anonymously that a knowing American of his acquaintance assures him "that a young healthy child, well nursed, is at a year old a most delicious, nourishing, and wholesome food, whether stewed, roasted, baked, or boiled." It is difficult to imagine a more scathing denunciation of the English exploitation of Ireland—a circumstance that, for Swift, had a great deal to do with greed, selfishness, and an inability to empathize with anyone different or "other." In short, with an absence of pluralism. Mordecai Richler would have understood. So would anyone who straddled cultures, fitting in easily neither here nor there. I think of Cuthbert Grant, part Scottish, part aboriginal, who would father the Metis nation.

16.

The Metis Scots

※※

From Winnipeg's Fort Garry Hotel, where we stayed during our book-tour extravaganza, we could look out over the ruins of a stone gate to Upper Fort Garry, built by the Hudson's Bay Company. This location has a written history dating back to the 1730s. The HBC built here first in 1822, naming its "fort" after Nicholas Garry, the company's deputy governor. Four years later, a severe flood destroyed this original Fort Garry. The HBC rebuilt in 1835, and this time used the name Upper Fort Garry to distinguish the settlement from Lower Fort Garry, which it had erected roughly thirty kilometres south down the Red River four years before.

But what kept my imagination whirring, as I looked down from our ninth-floor hotel room, was the image of Cuthbert Grant arriving here as a young man. Grant turned up at this HBC fort in 1823, when it was newly built and thriving. Born forty-eight years after the death of Jonathan Swift, and fifty-one years before Louis Riel, he embodied the reality of Scottish pluralism, the forging of close relationships between Scots and native peoples, as it took root in Canada. Nobody said it would be easy. But other English-speaking

Metis followed Grant to prominence. They came to be called Anglo-Metis, but most in fact were Scottish or Scottish-Orcadian Metis. They rejected the prevailing racism and assumptions of Caucasian superiority. And they included many leading individuals, among them:

- James Isbister (1833–1915), an HBC interpreter who spoke five languages—English, Gaelic, Cree, Dene, and Mischif—and founded Prince Albert, Saskatchewan.
- John Norquay (1841–1889), who played a minor role in Riel's Red River Rebellion and later served as the first premier of Manitoba to be born in the region.
- Thomas McKay (1849–1924), who sided with the federal government during the Northwest Rebellion of 1885 and later represented Prince Albert for a decade in the legislature of the Northwest Territories.

Cuthbert Grant cleared the way for all these figures. Born in 1793 in a fur-trade post called Fort de la Rivière Tremblante, halfway between Winnipeg and Saskatoon, he was the fluently bilingual son of a Scottish wintering partner, also named Cuthbert Grant, and a mother of Cree and French heritage. His uncle Robert Grant had been one of the original Montreal traders who formed the North West Company in 1779. His father, who died when he was six, provided for his education in Montreal, where he was baptized into the Scottish Presbyterian Church.

After a few years of schooling under the supervision of William McGillivary, a leading Montreal fur trader, Grant went to work for the North West Company. In 1812, when he was nineteen, he travelled west to Fort William (now part of Thunder Bay) with the annual brigade, and then took charge of a small outpost on the Qu'Appelle River. Here the beaver had been virtually eradicated, and the post served mainly to organize the buffalo hunt and provide pemmican for Athabasca country traders. The arrival of the Scottish "Selkirk Settlers" at Red River not only put additional strain on area resources, but also raised questions about how the lands would be used from now on. The fur traders believed that agricultural settlement—which was underwritten by Lord Selkirk, that well-meaning Scottish colonizer—would disrupt and destroy traditional supply lines that carried food (mostly pemmican) one way and beaver pelts the other.

Selkirk appointed Miles Macdonell to establish the Red River Colony, and warned him not to antagonize the Nor'Westers. But in January 1814, facing a food shortage, Macdonell issued a proclamation outlawing the export of pemmican from the area—food the fur traders farther west desperately needed.

Two more Scots arrived in the colony to lead the Nor'Westers in opposing Macdonell's initiative. One of them, the wily veteran Duncan Cameron, rode into the colony in August "dressed in regimentals," according to an HBC witness. Calling himself a captain, Cameron declared that Macdonell had no authority there, and that he himself was "Chief of this Country." He announced that he wished to hire all the freemen in the neighbourhood, "to prevent them," according to Peter Fidler of the Hudson's Bay Company, "from killing Buffalo for the support of the Settlement." Who was going to go hungry? The traders or the would-be farmers?

To oust the settlers, Cameron and the Nor'Westers would need the broad support of people who lived in the area—mainly people who straddled cultures, the so-called half-breeds of mixed native and Scottish or French heritage. Historian George Woodcock writes that this community had taken no position in the dispute between the two groups of Scots represented by the Nor'Westers and Macdonell's Selkirk Settlers. They had not done so because they as yet lacked a sense of identity and recognized leaders. Led by the astute Cameron, who himself maintained an Ojibwa wife and family, the Nor'Westers proceeded to cultivate, and in fact were the first to voice, the idea of a Metis nation with aboriginal rights to the land and special interests as hunters.

By doing so, Woodcock notes, they were exploiting ill-defined sentiments of Metis identity and giving them shape and direction. The transformation that had happened in Scotland and Ireland a thousand years before, when a mixed Norse-Gaelic culture emerged as a result of an influx of Scandinavian settlers, must have involved similar shaping, and also similar tensions, mistakes, occasional battles, and slow realizations. In Canada, we can trace the emergence of the Metis almost step by step.

From among the mixed-blood clerks of the North West Company, Cameron chose four who might become leaders able to channel the energy and provoke the anger of the Metis on behalf of the NWC. By March 1816, one of these four captains of the Metis—twenty-three-year-old Cuthbert Grant—had emerged as notably daring and resourceful. Cameron named him "Captain-General of all the Half-Breeds."

During the next couple of years, as a cavalry captain who could inspire a following in both English and French, Grant recruited a large number of Metis to the North West Company cause. In March 1815, after the HBC arrested and charged an ally with assault, Grant led two dozen Metis in taking four colonists hostage—an action that led to a prisoner exchange. That spring, while encamped four miles from Red River, Grant and his men harried the settlers, stealing horses and plows. By the end of June, he had convinced the settlers to leave the area.

Later that summer, almost incredibly, fifty of the stubborn Scottish colonists returned to try again. Grant had gone back to the Qu'Appelle River valley, and he dismissed overtures from the Hudson's Bay Company. In May 1816, Grant rode out with about sixty horsemen to put an end to the Red River Colony. He ambushed some boats and ransacked a fort belonging to the HBC, and then proceeded west through Portage la Prairie with pemmican he had stolen to supply North West Company brigades.

On June 19, while returning eastward, and seeking to go around the well-defended Fort Douglas, Grant and his men were confronted at Seven Oaks, now a suburb in north-central Winnipeg. Robert Semple, the newly arrived governor of the Red River Colony (and the HBC), had emerged from Fort Douglas on horseback, hotheaded and unthinking, with a small group of armed men. Most historians agree that one of Semple's men fired the first shot. Cuthbert Grant fired the second and wounded Semple in the thigh, rendering him helpless. Then ensued the battle of Seven Oaks, during which the Metis killed about twenty men while losing one or two.

With the Red River Colony destroyed, Grant withdrew to Fort Alexander on Lake Winnipeg. When, a couple of months later, he learned that Selkirk had captured the North West Company headquarters at Fort William and revived the agricultural settlement yet again, he could only shake his head at the obstinacy of these colonizers.

In August 1817, after a new commissioner arrived from Lower Canada to investigate the violence, Grant gave himself up, made his depositions, and was taken back to Montreal to face a trumped-up murder charge. Released on bail, he got wind early in 1818 that he would soon face better-grounded charges relating to the massacre at Seven Oaks. In a light canoe, Grant paddled west out of Montreal.

North West Company officers, influential in both Upper and Lower Canada, eventually got the charges against him shelved. In June 1820, Grant was among those who fought at the last battle between the two Scots-dominated trading companies, when

Nor'Westers ambushed a fur-laden HBC brigade returning from Athabasca country. The following year, on the far side of the Atlantic, pragmatic Scottish businessmen finally contrived an end to the profit-killing war between the rival fur-trading concerns. When they folded the NWC into the HBC, Cuthbert Grant figured as one of the leaders who could not easily be integrated into the new arrangement.

In February 1822, however, when the newly appointed governor, George Simpson, ventured west on his first tour of Rupert's Land, he met the twenty-nine-year-old Grant at Fort Hibernia on the Swan River, just west of Lake Winnipegosis. Simpson was impressed with Grant's historical and geographical knowledge, and realized that the bicultural young man—both Scottish and Cree—could prove a useful ally. "I am therefore of the opinion," he wrote the London committee, "that it might be policy to overlook the past and if you did not object to it [he] might be smuggled quietly into the Service again."

Cuthbert Grant accompanied Simpson to Red River, where the Metis had become surly and unpredictable. The following July, at the newly built Fort Garry—the site we could see from our window at the Fort Garry Hotel—Grant was made HBC clerk and special constable. This appointment outraged colonists who remembered how effectively he had fought on behalf of fur traders. In 1824, after surviving an assault, Grant "retired" from the HBC. With the company's blessing, he created a settlement thirty kilometres west, where from White Horse Plain on the Assiniboine River he continued to wield influence. With one hundred Metis families, he founded the village of Grantown (now St. François Xavier). Designating himself Seigneur of White Horse Plain, he put thirty-four acres under cultivation and ran an ostensibly independent fur-trading concern.

In 1828, the HBC made Cuthbert Grant "Warden of the Plains

of Red River" and authorized him to prevent "the illicit trade in furs within that district." The Metis community continued to elect him captain of the annual buffalo hunts. Grant became a justice of the peace, and then a territorial councillor and sheriff. In 1844, as "Chief of the Half-Breeds and Warden of the Plains," the multi-lingual Grant negotiated a peace treaty between the Metis and the Sioux, who had been fighting over buffalo-hunting territories— though a few years later, when the two groups renewed hostilities, Grant could not engineer a workable peace.

Among the Metis, a new generation of leaders had emerged. A split would develop between Grant's mostly English-speaking followers in White Horse Plain and the predominantly French-speaking people from around Red River Colony. But there begins a tale that leads in a different direction. Our present theme, how the Scottish-run fur trade fostered biculturalism and so pluralism in Canada, carries us like a mountain river around a bend towards a slightly younger contemporary of Cuthbert Grant, a culture-straddling fur trader who would prove still more influential: James Douglas, the so-called "Scotch West Indian" who became the father of British Columbia.

17.

Sir James Douglas

▨▨▨

When Cuthbert Grant, having officially withdrawn from the Hudson's Bay Company, was flourishing as a Metis leader west of Fort Garry, young James Douglas was establishing an HBC trading post far to the north-west in present-day British Columbia. In 1827, Douglas was thinking about retiring from the fur trade when his three-year contract expired. He was tired of the isolation, of the lack of good books and companionship, of the hostility of some of the nearby tribes, and of the hunger that ensued when the salmon run failed. He was "bent on leaving the country."

The chief factor at Fort St. James, William Connolly, responded with alacrity. Soon after meeting Douglas, he had judged him a "fine steady active fellow good clerk & trader, well adapted for a new country." Now, rather than lose him, Connolly not only increased his salary by two-thirds, but allowed him to marry, according to the custom of the country, his beautiful half-aboriginal daughter. Amelia Connolly was a "shy, sweet and lovable girl," not yet sixteen, known as the "little snowbird." She would give Douglas thirteen children, five of whom would not survive infancy. And she would help turn Douglas into one of the most progressive figures of the age.

With his complex heritage, marriage to a Scottish Metis, and championing of aboriginal peoples, James Douglas sought to make British Columbia a model of multiculturalism.

Born in 1803 in British Guiana, now Guyana, Douglas was the son of a wealthy Glasgow merchant, John Douglas, and a Creole woman named Martha Ann Telfer. Like Cuthbert Grant and the other Metis cited above, the half-Scottish Douglas not only would demonstrate that a person of mixed race could flourish in the fur trade, but would also illustrate in his very person how the Scots brought pluralism to Canada.

As a boy, Douglas attended preparatory school in Lanark, Scotland, where he excelled as a scholar. He was also a big, strapping fellow who got into fights "with all sorts of boys," as he wrote later, and learned "to get on by dint of whip and spur." Douglas received additional education from a French tutor at Chester, England, and people in later years would remark on his fluency in French, both oral and written. At sixteen, he joined the North West Company as an apprentice.

He sailed from Liverpool to Quebec, proceeded to Fort William, and spent the winter learning the fur trade. The following summer, he was transferred to Île-à-la-Crosse in present-day Saskatchewan. No shrinking violet, he sparked a warning from the Hudson's Bay Company to cease parading around provocatively with "Guns, Swords, Flags, Drums, Fifes, etc., etc." In 1822, when George Simpson merged the competing fur-trading companies, young Douglas made a smooth transition, joining the HBC as a second-class clerk. He impressed Simpson and everyone else who met him, and in 1825, he travelled north and west to take charge of Fort Vermilion.

With him he carried his library of books from Scotland, among them forty-five volumes of what he called "British classics," as well as a history of England, a French dictionary, and textbooks in geometry, arithmetic, and grammar. In this rugged world, his bookishness set him apart, and Douglas could be both superior and pedantic. Later in life, he would complain that slang was "essentially vulgar and to me unbearable," and edit letters from his young-adult daughter: "Observe how it is improved by the process."

After one winter at Fort Vermilion, Douglas crossed the Rockies to Fort St. James, fording flooding rivers and traversing cliffside mountain passes on a journey he would describe as perilous, exhausting, and exciting. From that outpost, headquarters of the New Caledonia district, Douglas travelled 3,200 kilometres while leading a pack-horse brigade in a return journey to Fort Vancouver on the Pacific coast—present-day Vancouver, Washington.

In 1828, after he married, and while in charge of Fort St. James, Douglas—"furiously violent when aroused"—seized and executed a Carrier native who had been involved in murdering an HBC man five years before. This prompted several attempts on his life, and his father-in-law wrote to George Simpson that "Douglas's life is much exposed among these Carriers." Douglas "would readily face a hundred of them," he added, "but he does not like the idea of being assassinated." William Connolly recommended that the young man be transferred to Fort Vancouver to help expand the coastal trade.

After a second meeting, the astute Simpson had described Douglas as "a stout, powerful, active man of good conduct and respectable abilities—tolerably well-educated, expresses himself clearly on paper, understands our Counting House business and is an excellent trader. Well qualified for any service requiring bodily exertion, firmness of mind, and the exercise of sound judgment . . . Has every reason to look forward to early promotion and is a likely man to fill a place at our Council board in the course of time."

Simpson sent Douglas to take up a post as the HBC's chief accountant at Fort Vancouver. In January 1830, accompanied by his wife and carrying his cherished library, the Scotch West Indian travelled south to his new home, where a wooden palisade enclosed eight substantial buildings and overlooked the north side of the

Columbia River. Here, about a hundred HBC employees lived and worked. A number of smaller buildings lay beyond the walls, where three hundred native people had settled. In addition to trading in furs, this district centre included a farm that grew food for export to Alaska and also a small shipyard, a lumber mill, and an active salmon fishery.

Douglas reported to yet another formidable Scot—Dr. John McLoughlin, "the white-headed eagle" in charge of the HBC's Columbia department. Within a year, a fellow fur trader relayed word that Douglas was "at Vancouver and is rising fast in favour." Two years in a row, Douglas was entrusted with carrying considerable coastal revenues east to York Factory. And in 1835, while still serving as McLoughlin's right-hand man, he travelled to Red River and was commissioned a chief trader.

Three years later, with McLoughlin on leave, Douglas ran Fort Vancouver for a year. In 1839 he became a chief factor, which doubled his income and brought financial security. During McLoughlin's absence, Douglas sought to eradicate slavery at the HBC settlement. "With the Natives," he wrote, "I have hitherto endeavoured to discourage the practice by the exertion of moral influence alone. Against our own [HBC] people I took a more active part, and denounced slavery as a state contrary to law; tendering to all unfortunate persons held as slaves, by British subjects, the fullest protection in the enjoyment of their natural rights."

Douglas was in tune with the most progressive people of the age. In London, the British Parliament had passed the Slavery Abolition Act in 1833, abolishing slavery in most of the British Empire. The process had begun in Upper Canada in 1793, with Lieutenant Governor John Graves Simcoe insisting that the British constitution did not admit of any law "that discriminates by dishonest policy between natives of Africa, America or Europe."

In 1840, with Simpson seeking to expand trade throughout

the Pacific, Douglas sailed north to Sitka, Alaska, where he dealt with Russian authorities and established Fort Taku. Then he travelled south to California and negotiated a trading arrangement with Mexican officials. The following year, this time with Simpson, Douglas again journeyed to Sitka to deal with the Russians.

During this trip, Simpson decided to abandon the HBC's far northern outposts. Instead, he opted to expand the steamboat-based trade along the coast and, in response to American expansion around Fort Vancouver, to establish a new port farther north on Vancouver Island. In 1842, James Douglas explored that island and chose a site. The following March, with the help of friendly Songhees people, he began building Fort Victoria.

By now, Douglas wrote, countless people "of a class hostile to British interests" were pouring into Oregon. Also, the U.S. government was seeking seaports on the Pacific coast. Douglas worried that every port would "be converted into a naval arsenal and the Pacific covered with swarms of Privateers, to the destruction of British commerce in those seas." In 1845, with six thousand settlers in Oregon, the provisional United States government unilaterally extended its jurisdiction north of the Columbia River over territory that included Fort Vancouver.

Later the next year, when British negotiators accepted the 49th parallel as the U.S. border, James Douglas orchestrated the HBC's northward retreat. He reorganized canoe routes and, in 1849, moved the company's west-coast headquarters to Fort Victoria. By agreement with Britain, the HBC was to establish a colony there within five years. In 1851, while remaining a chief factor, Douglas became governor and vice admiral of Vancouver Island and its dependencies.

Not surprisingly, given that his wife was half-native, Douglas devoted considerable attention to aboriginal policy. From the outset, he aimed "to conciliate the goodwill of the native Indian tribes by treating them with justice and forbearance, and by rigorously protecting their civil and agrarian rights." He allowed First Nations peoples to choose their own reserves of land. He ordered surveyors to include fishing stations, burial grounds, cultivated land, and "all the favourite resorts of the Tribes, and in short to include every piece of ground to which they had acquired an equitable title through continuous occupation, tillage or other investment of labour." He also allowed aboriginal individuals to buy property on the same terms as everyone else.

To develop the colony, Douglas had recommended free land grants of two to three hundred acres. Both the HBC and the Colonial Office rejected this. But where some HBC men bridled at the high land prices, the relatively wealthy Douglas bought lands at the going rate, the most valuable of which were situated near the government reserve at James Bay. In 1856, the Colonial Office ordered Douglas to establish an assembly. He complied, though he lacked experience or expertise as a legislator. He also actively developed Vancouver Island, building roads and schools and encouraging farming, sawmills, coal mines, and salmon fishing.

Late in 1857, following the discovery of gold along the Fraser and Thompson Rivers, large numbers of Americans began pouring into the country. Acting without instructions from London, Douglas proclaimed British control of mineral rights and announced that all miners required licences. The following April, with Californians streaming into Victoria and heading for the mainland, Douglas put a gunboat at the mouth of the Fraser River to collect licensing fees. More than eight thousand miners made their way up the Okanagan Valley. On the mainland as a whole, the influx approached twenty-five thousand. This tidal wave worried the native people and threatened the region with lawlessness.

Early that summer, Douglas went upriver to assess the situation. To the Colonial Office, he reported that he "spoke with great

plainness of speech to the white miners who were nearly all for-
eigners representing almost every nation in Europe. I refused to
grant them any rights of occupation to the soil and told them distinctly that Her Majesty's Government ignored their very existence
in that part of the country, which was not open for the purpose
of settlement, and they were permitted to remain there merely on
sufferance, that no abuses would be tolerated, and that the Laws
would protect the rights of the Indians no less than those of the
white men."

In August, Douglas made a second visit. Accompanied by
twenty sailors and sixteen royal engineers, he relied on the force of
his personality for safety. Later, he reported that he had never seen
"a crowd of more ruffianly looking men." When he ordered them to
give three cheers for the queen, they complied "with a bad grace."

Douglas drew up mining regulations, hired constables, and put
aboriginal men in charge of policing their own peoples. He raised
volunteers to build a road to Lillooet and a mule track from Yale to
Lytton. And he not only outlawed squatting, but also surveyed the
land near Langley and Hope and put lots up for sale—though only
to British subjects. "If the majority of the immigrants be American,"
he wrote, "there will always be a hankering in their minds after
annexation to the United States . . . They will never cordially submit
to English rule, nor possess the loyal feelings of British subjects."

Douglas could not hope to check immigration, but he wanted
settlers loyal to the crown, and he offered naturalization to anyone who sought it. Meanwhile, with affairs growing increasingly
complex, the Colonial Office and the Hudson's Bay Company
found themselves occasionally at odds. Late in 1858, when mainland British Columbia became a colony, Douglas resigned from the
HBC to become governor.

The next year, when Vancouver Island became a crown colony,
he added a second governorship. In July 1859, an American military

force occupied San Juan Island, the second largest of those islands situated between southern Vancouver Island and the continental mainland. Douglas wanted to expel the occupiers by force, and he had the British naval power available to do it. He was, however, overruled by the Legislative Assembly and a British rear admiral who chanced to be on hand.

After a while, the British ceded San Juan Island and its neighbours to the United States. A son-in-law wrote later that if James Douglas "had had his way, the affair would have been quickly settled, the Island occupied by the British, and then diplomacy would have settled the matter—he thought possession of great importance." In other words, the San Juan Islands would today belong to Canada.

By the early 1860s, Douglas was envisaging the development, within a decade, of "an overland Telegraph, *surely*, and a Railroad on British Territory, *probably*, the whole way from the Gulf of Georgia to the Atlantic." But now he found himself at odds with a citizenry that wanted responsible government. This he regarded as American, "associated with revolution," and ultimately menacing. He would have preferred "wise and good despotism," yet he acted to introduce representative government in 1862. The following year, faced with mounting unrest, the Colonial Office urged Douglas to accept a knighthood and retire from both governorships.

Douglas did so the following spring. He then set out alone on a voyage to the Auld Sod, enjoying a once-in-a-lifetime holiday. Here and there he saw relatives, and also, most poignantly, he visited Lanark—the schoolboy home he had not seen in fifty years. He reported that the town had grown in size, and that the old houses were "not improved by age. The old people are all gone . . . and their very memory has perished . . . As it is with them, so it will be with us."

In the New World, James Douglas had laid out towns, built

a consolidating highway, and established order in rough country. In 1871, as Sir James Douglas, he saw British Columbia enter Confederation, and so complete the process he had launched. This Scotch West Indian had retained the Pacific seaboard for the British crown. And when, in 1877, he passed away, more than three thousand people attended his funeral.

During the next century, British Columbia would flare at times with racial intolerance, enforcing anti-Asian immigration legislation and banishing Japanese Canadians to internment camps. James Douglas would have been appalled. With his multicultural background, his marriage to a Scottish Metis, and his ferocious defence of the rights of aboriginal peoples, he had established B.C. as a model of multiculturalism.

As he finished his work on the Pacific coast, another equally singular figure, then completing his education on the east side of the Atlantic, was preparing to make a courageous stand for yet another kind of tolerance and diversity—one that is often overlooked in discussions about pluralism. By insisting on the right to be different, Oscar Wilde pointed the way to a broad-mindedness that would lead, eventually, to a more pluralistic Canada.

18.

Oscar Wilde

❏❏❏

The year after James Douglas died, Oscar Wilde graduated from Oxford University with a rare double first. Having also won the Newdigate Prize for a poem called *Ravenna*, Wilde told one friend that the dons were astonished at "the Bad Boy doing so well in the end." Now twenty-four, he returned to his hometown, Dublin, and embarked on a career as unlike that of James Douglas as can be imagined—except that Wilde, too, would plant a flag for diversity. He would take a pioneering stand in a seemingly endless battle to gain acceptance of sexual difference, a struggle that still surfaces occasionally in twenty-first-century Canada.

Born on October 16, 1854, Oscar Wilde was the son of two Anglo-Irish intellectuals. His surgeon-philanthropist father, Sir William Wilde, had published books on medicine, archaeology, and Irish folklore. His Irish nationalist mother, Jane Wilde, had written revolutionary poetry as "Speranza" for the Young Irelanders of 1848, with whom Thomas D'Arcy McGee had been involved. Wilde himself is not usually associated with the Celtic Revival, but early on, while dazzling the English-speaking world with his brilliance, he reworked many of the myths and legends of western Ireland.

In 1882, at the Grand Opera House in Toronto, Oscar Wilde told a full house, "It is better to live without art than to live with bad art." He pointed the way to broadening our definitions of tolerance, diversity, and pluralism.

Wilde grew up in a home where regular visitors to his mother's celebrity salons included Joseph Sheridan Le Fanu, a leading writer of Gothic tales; the Ulster-Scottish poet Samuel Ferguson, whose interest in Irish mythology made him a forerunner of the Irish Literary Renaissance; and lawyer Isaac Butt, founder of a number of Irish nationalist parties. Educated privately until age nine, Wilde learned French and German from native speakers. He attended a prestigious boarding school, Portora Royal School in Enniskillen, northern Ireland, and summered at a family villa in western Ireland, where he played with George Moore, later an influential novelist who worked with William Butler Yeats and Lady Gregory.

After graduating at the top of his class, Wilde spent three years immersed in Greek and Latin at Trinity College, Dublin. There, he became a leading member of the University Philosophical Society and won several academic awards, including a scholarship to Oxford University. A striking figure who stood more than six feet tall, he became a long-haired dandy and a flamboyant Freemason.

From Walter Pater's *Studies in the History of the Renaissance*, passages of which he learned by heart, Wilde gleaned a lifelong devotion to art. He flirted with converting to Roman Catholicism. Instead, he became a prominent aesthete bent on turning himself into a work of art. A lavish entertainer, like his mother, but also a wit, he famously sighed: "I find it harder and harder every day to live up to my blue china."

Back in Dublin after Oxford, Wilde wooed a childhood sweetheart. She let him down gently in favour of Bram Stoker, who would later write *Dracula*. And Wilde moved to London, where he lived on an inheritance from his father, who had recently died. In 1881, Wilde published a collection of poems that won faint praise as lacking in originality. The following year, as an apostle of aestheticism—beauty for beauty's sake—Wilde undertook a lecture tour of North America, stating on arrival: "I have nothing to declare but my genius."

Originally scheduled to last four months, the tour proved so popular (and controversial) that it ran for a year. Wilde covered fifteen thousand miles and gave a hundred and forty lectures, including two in Toronto. There, at the Grand Opera House on May 25, 1882, dressed entirely in black—velvet coat, knee breeches, silk stockings—the flamboyant young genius opined, characteristically, "It is better to live without art than to live with bad art."

Early in 1883, while sojourning in Paris, Wilde finished a five-act, blank verse play called *The Duchess of Padua*. But the actress for whom he wrote it turned it down, and it would not be produced until 1991, when it ran in New York for three weeks. In May 1884, Wilde married Constance Lloyd, whose income, as the daughter of a wealthy Queen's Counsel, provided a decent living. He had produced two sons by 1886, when he began regularly contributing reviews and articles to various high-end publications.

Wilde was the only literary figure to sign a petition, organized by fellow Irishman George Bernard Shaw, seeking a pardon (unsuccessfully) for anarchists charged with the 1886 Haymarket massacre in Chicago. And the following year, he wrote a series of articles defending Charles Stewart Parnell when that politician came under attack. Wilde became editor of *The Lady's World* magazine. Renaming it *The Woman's World*, he revamped it to treat "not just what women wear, but what they feel and think." He ran that publication for just over two years, while also publishing the first of several collections of fairy tales.

In 1889, Wilde published a short story playing with the idea that William Shakespeare wrote his love sonnets for a boy actor named Willie Hughes. Years later, author Arthur Ransome would write that Wilde "read something of himself into Shakespeare's sonnets." By this time, while still a doting father, Wilde had succumbed to a precocious young man named Robert Ross who, according to biographer Richard Ellmann, had been "determined to seduce Wilde." The wit himself would explain, "I can resist anything but temptation."

Tiring of journalism, Wilde began writing longer pieces on aesthetics, arguing that art should be both subversive and redemptive or developmental. In *The Soul of Man under Socialism*, he envisaged a society where humans were freed from necessity, and could devote themselves to artistic creation: "The only thing that can console me for having no money is extravagance." In 1891, Wilde published three collections of essays and dialogues and also his controversial novel, *The Picture of Dorian Gray.*

That work opens with the title character, a gorgeous young man, realizing that his beauty will fade while a portrait of himself remains unchanged. He strikes a Faustian bargain to reverse roles with the picture, then embraces a hedonistic lifestyle whose ravages show up only on the portrait. Reviewers of the work in serial publication criticized its decadence and suggestions of homosexuality, and Wilde revised the novel extensively before publishing it in book form.

Returning to Paris as an established writer, Wilde moved easily in literary circles because he spoke such fluent French. After one soiree, he wrote a play in French, *Salomé,* about the real-life woman who, in exchange for doing a seductive dance, requested the head of John the Baptist on a silver platter. In short order, Wilde then wrote several witty and subversive yet popular comedies: *Lady Windermere's Fan, A Woman of No Importance,* and *An Ideal Husband.*

Late in 1894, Wilde produced *The Importance of Being Earnest,* a send-up of late Victorian society which is generally regarded as his finest achievement. First performed in February 1895, this comedy about shifting identities proved a magnificent triumph. But as the professional Wilde moved from one success to another, personally the man was sliding towards disaster. In 1891, his marriage having dissolved into friendly cohabitation, Wilde began a flagrant affair with Lord Alfred Douglas, son of the Marquess of Queensberry. The rebellious young lord introduced Wilde to the world of gay prostitution, and the playwright took to indulging himself. Later, he wrote to Douglas that "it was like feasting with panthers; the danger was half the excitement."

The Marquess of Queensberry, an arrogant, aggressive man who devised the rules of boxing, disapproved of his son's relationship with Wilde and accosted the two of them more than once. In June 1894, he called on Wilde at home and, cursing and swearing, threatened, "If I catch you and my son again in any public restaurant I will thrash you." The following February, the bullying Queensberry left his card at Wilde's private club, the bohemian Albemarle: "For Oscar Wilde, posing as sodomite."

This constituted a public accusation that Wilde had committed the crime of sodomy. Urged on by Lord Alfred, the playwright made the mistake of launching a private prosecution for criminal libel. Facing a possible sentence of two years in prison, Queensberry hired private detectives to prove the truth of his accusation. At a meeting at the Café Royal witnessed by George Bernard Shaw, the writer Frank Harris urged the playwright to flee the country while he still could.

In a preface to one of his plays, *The Dark Lady of the Sonnets*, Shaw wrote: "Wilde, though under no illusion as to the folly of the quite unselfish suit-at-law he had been persuaded to begin, nevertheless so miscalculated the force of the social vengeance he was unloosing on himself that he fancied it could be stayed by putting up the editor of *The Saturday Review* (as Mr. Harris was then) to declare that he considered *Dorian Grey* a highly moral book, which it certainly is." When Harris foretold what would happen, Shaw added, Wilde declared him a faint-hearted friend and stormed out of the café with young Douglas in tow.

With *Earnest* drawing raves on the London stage, private detectives led by Queen's Counsel Edward Carson—who eventually became the pro-Britain leader of northern Ireland—turned up salacious details about Wilde's encounters with would-be blackmailers and male prostitutes. On the advice of his lawyers, Wilde dropped the prosecution. That rendered him bankrupt, as now he was liable for Queensberry's legal expenses.

Soon after he left, the court issued a warrant for his arrest on a charge of gross indecency. At the upscale, newly opened Cadogan Hotel, where he had taken a room, friends again urged him to flee to France. Wilde refused. And on April 6, 1895, two plainclothes policemen arrived and arrested him.

At his trial, which began three weeks later, Wilde pleaded not guilty. He had convinced Lord Alfred to leave London for Paris, and several of his other friends, fearing prosecution, had also departed. Now, on the witness stand, and under prosecution for illegal homosexual activity, Oscar Wilde defined "the love that dare not speak its name" as "such a great affection of an elder for a younger man as there was between David and Jonathan, such as Plato made the very basis of his philosophy, and such as you find in the sonnets of Michelangelo and Shakespeare. It is that deep spiritual affection that is as pure as it is perfect. It dictates and pervades great works of art, like those of Shakespeare and Michelangelo, and those two letters of mine [in evidence], such as they are."

The date was April 26, 1895, and the playwright went on: "It is in this century misunderstood, so much misunderstood that it may be described as 'the love that dare not speak its name,' and on that account of it I am placed where I am now. It is beautiful, it is fine, it is the noblest form of affection. There is nothing unnatural about it. It is intellectual, and it repeatedly exists between an older and a younger man, when the older man has intellect, and the younger man has all the joy, hope and glamour of life before him. That it should be so, the world does not understand. The world mocks at it, and sometimes puts one in the pillory for it."

With those words, bravely spoken in a London courtroom, one of the finest writers of the late nineteenth century sealed his own fate. Having written such works as *The Importance of Being Earnest* and *The Picture of Dorian Gray*, and established himself as the prince of the epigram, Wilde would become a martyr in the cause of pluralism, and specifically to the right to belong to that minority of human beings attracted to persons of the same sex.

The colourful statue of Oscar Wilde in Merrion Square, Dublin, faces the poet's family home. Sculptor Danny Osborne divides his time between Cork and Iqaluit, Nunavut.

Oscar Wilde advanced the cause of pluralism when, at the cost of his literary reputation and even his freedom, he stood tall for the right to be different. Nine decades later, Canada would legally recognize that right when Prime Minister Pierre Elliott Trudeau declared, "The state has no place in the bedrooms of the nation." In 2005, Canada would become the fourth country in the world to legalize same-sex marriage. But in England in 1895, as Wilde well understood, his principled stand would probably lead to a harsh imprisonment.

The jury proved unable to reach a verdict. Freed on bail, Wilde went briefly into hiding. Prosecutor Edward Carson, to his credit, asked the Solicitor General, "Can we not let up on the fellow now?" But that official said the matter had become too politicized. At a second trial, on May 25, Wilde was convicted of gross indecency and sentenced to the maximum allowed: two years' hard labour. The judge described this as "totally inadequate for a case such as this." Cries of "Shame!" drowned out Wilde when he said, "And I? May I say nothing, my Lord?"

Jailed in one harsh prison and then a second, the brilliant Oscar Wilde, that refined and stylish aesthete, was relegated to "hard labour, hard fare and a hard bed." In November, he collapsed during chapel and ruptured his right eardrum—an injury that contributed to his death. A Liberal reformer, Richard B. Haldane, managed to get him transferred to the marginally more humane Reading prison, but during the transfer, a crowd jeered and spat at him. Early in 1897, Wilde wrote a fifty-thousand-word letter to Douglas, in which he cast himself as a martyr, yet took responsibility for this own fall: "I am here for having tried to put your father in prison."

Later published as *De Profundis*, the letter traces Wilde's spiritual journey through his prison readings, which included some ancient Greek texts, the Bible in French, Dante's *Divine Comedy*, and essays by Saint Augustine and Cardinal Newman. Released on May 19, 1897, after two years in jail, Wilde sought a six-month Catholic retreat, and wept when he was denied. He left England for the continent, where he wrote *The Ballad of Reading Gaol*, focusing on the brutalizing punishment meted out to all convicts, regardless of crime. It went through seven editions in less than two years, but brought him little money.

Denied contact with his young sons, Wilde ended his days in a dingy hotel in Paris. He corrected proofs of two of his plays and wrote to his publisher, "This poverty really breaks one's heart: it is so *sale* [dirty], so utterly depressing, so hopeless. Pray do what you can." Not long afterwards, at a Paris café, he sipped absinthe and told a friend: "My wallpaper and I are fighting a duel to the death. One or the other of us has to go."

Wilde's French physicians diagnosed cerebral meningitis. They attributed it to an old infection in his right ear, the result of the injury he sustained when, in prison, he was driven to collapse. Oscar Wilde died on November 30, 1900. The epitaph on his tomb comes from his own *Reading Gaol*:

> And alien tears will fill for him
> Pity's long-broken urn,
> For his mourners will be outcast men,
> And outcasts always mourn.

If Oscar Wilde were alive and writing as a Canadian today, he would be no outcast—certainly not in Toronto, which is proud of its annual Gay Pride Parade. Here Wilde would stand, first and foremost, as a literary giant, period. But also he would surely be the flag-bearer for this country's flourishing LGBT literature, which encompasses works that treat LGBT (lesbian, gay, bisexual, or transgender) themes, characters, or issues.

LGBT literature springs from a more closeted tradition that runs from Wilde through such Canadians as John Glassco and Timothy Findley. Today, contributors include Wayson Choy, Marie-Claire Blais, Emma Donoghue, Brad Fraser, Bert Archer,

Marnie Woodrow, Shyam Selvadurai, Jane Eaton Hamilton, Michel Tremblay, Farzana Doctor, Morris Panych, Sky Gilbert, and Elizabeth Ruth. That LGBT writers have been able to thrive in this country—as much as any writer can be said to thrive—is owing first and foremost to Oscar Wilde, who cleared a space for difference and pointed the way to broadening our definitions of tolerance, diversity, and pluralism.

PART FOUR
AUDACITY

That cross-country promotion I mentioned above? We called it "The VIA Rail, Cross-Canada, Ocean-to-Ocean, Book Tour Extravaganza." We rode a westbound train known as "the Canadian," Sheena and I, from Toronto to Winnipeg, Saskatoon, Edmonton, and Vancouver. Then we flew home and travelled east, from Toronto to Ottawa, Montreal, and Halifax. Along the way, we got off at each city and checked into a historic railway hotel. I beat the drum for my book *50 Canadians Who Changed the World*, madly holding forth to anyone who would listen, and then we boarded VIA Rail's next "Canadian."

Following in the tracks of the trailblazers, among them such men as John Palliser, Sandford Fleming, and William Cornelius Van Horne, we rumbled and roared through a landscape alive with history. We traced the path of what was probably the single most audacious act in Canadian history: the building of the Canadian Pacific Railway. This was the cross-Canada rail adventure of a lifetime.

Wait: Canadian audacity? Isn't that what they call an oxymoron, or at least a contradiction in terms? Aren't Canadians modest and self-effacing? Timid, cautious, and apologetic rather than audacious? Yes, you've heard this before. But the Trans-Siberian Railway had yet to be conceived. So imagine a struggling, newborn nation of fewer than four million citizens setting out in the 1870s to build the world's longest railway across a wilderness that includes the Rocky Mountains. A contemporary politician called the undertaking "an act of insane recklessness." Yet by 1885, thanks to the leadership of Sir John A. Macdonald—and to a multifarious army of contractors, politicians, financiers, surveyors, and workers—Canada had driven steel rails from Ontario to British Columbia.

The Canadian Pacific Railway is an act of staggering temerity. And Canadian history turns up a great many more. Consider Vimy Ridge. During the First World War, in April 1917, Canadian troops wrested that high escarpment from the Germans after other Allied forces had tried and failed. Military historians tell us that, fighting together for the first time, the four divisions of the Canadian Expeditionary Force succeeded thanks to their preparedness, organization, and, above all, tactical boldness.

Think of the Canadian Caper of 1979, when this country's ambassador to Iran helped six Americans escape during a hostage crisis. Ken Taylor and his people procured Canadian passports for the six and spirited them out of the country, passing them off as members of a Canadian film crew scouting locations. That escapade was so outlandish that it inspired *Argo*, a Hollywood movie starring Ben Affleck.

You want more? Perhaps, above all, Canada is the land of audacious women. This came home to me during my cross-country book-tour extravaganza, because at stop after stop, I talked about *50 Canadians Who Changed the World*. And that, as we see from the table of contents, meant talking about women:

- A literary superstar doubles as an activist: Margaret Atwood
- A spirited Muslim calls for an Islamic Reformation: Irshad Manji

- A Nobel Prize winner creates her own country: Alice Munro
- A law reformer brings war criminals to justice: Louise Arbour
- A global activist leads the charge against "disaster capitalism": Naomi Klein
- A Picasso of song refines self-expression: Joni Mitchell
- A Japanese Canadian clears the way for minorities: Joy Kogawa
- A transnational filmmaker gives voice to marginalized women: Deepa Mehta
- A globe-trotting doctor does her work in war zones: Samantha Nutt
- A feminist champion warns of a global water crisis: Maude Barlow
- An Inuit activist links climate change to human rights: Sheila Watt-Cloutier
- A Haitian immigrant proves that pluralism works: Michaëlle Jean

This list is incomplete, but you get the idea: Canada is a breeding ground for what would once have been called "overstepping" women. Only some of those cited above come from a Scottish or Irish background. But all have been influenced and empowered by living in Canada. And all can be understood as emerging from a broadly defined Celtic tradition of audacity that has evolved here after originating in Scotland and Ireland—a tradition that includes a conspicuous female component.

19.

Grace O'Malley

ff the south coast of Ireland, in choppy seas, we sailed around Skellig Michael, a rocky island that rises, volcano-like, seven hundred feet into the air. We marvelled to think that, for centuries, Christian monks lived in beehive meditation huts near the top, and would reach them in the wind by clambering out of their coracles and climbing six hundred stone steps, narrow, steep, and often wet.

We were circumnavigating Ireland, Sheena and I, going ashore once or twice a day in Zodiacs. Off the west coast, on Inishmore in the Aran Islands, where children learn Gaelic as their first language, we debarked and followed a rugged footpath uphill to Dun Aengus, a ritual site from the Bronze Age. Here one of us determined that, yes, we could terrify ourselves by lying on our stomachs, crawling to the edge, and looking straight down to where, a hundred metres below, white waves smashed into the black rock face.

At nearby Inisheer, where hand-built stone walls and winding one-lane roads made us feel we were wending through a maze, we heard a nighttime concert by the Begleys, a father-son duo from

West Kerry, who brought foot-stomping life to the traditional music of Ireland, music that has long since made its way into pubs and community halls across Canada.

Voyaging around Ireland with Adventure Canada meant visiting the Aran Islands and Inishbofin, where in the 1500s the Irish Pirate Queen, Grace O'Malley, had a fortress.

But the most evocative moment of the circumnavigation of Ireland came on Inishbofin, which is located north up the west coast, off Connemara. In the prologue to this book, I have already described riding in a Zodiac past Dun Grainne, the remains of a fortress used in the 1500s by legendary Pirate Queen "Grainne" or Grace O'Malley. Her enemies denounced her for having "overstepped the part of womanhood." The Celtic tradition which produced O'Malley—the tradition of the dauntless woman, known today as feminism—has never been short of exemplars.

Besides the Irish Pirate Queen and the Scottish Flora MacDonald, saviour of Bonnie Prince Charlie, we will soon meet Maria Edgeworth, who has been called the Irish Jane Austen and the female Sir Walter Scott. She kicked down doors through the early 1800s. And later that century, after seeing Irish tenants evicted from their lands, the activist-actress Maud Gonne inspired William Butler Yeats and thousands of Irish nationalists.

In Scotland, the first champion of Scottish independence to be elected to the British House of Commons was a woman, Winifred Ewing, leader of the Scottish National Party. Five years later, in 1972, and in that same hallowed house, a twenty-year-old Irish MP, Bernadette Devlin, delivered "a slap heard round the world" when the home secretary claimed that on Bloody Sunday, British troops had shot more than two dozen unarmed protesters in self-defence. Having witnessed the massacre—thirteen died that day, and one later—Devlin crossed the floor and slapped his face.

In this unbroken Celtic tradition of "overstepping women," which extends backwards to Saint Brigid of Kildare (451–525) and forward to its flowering in contemporary Canada, Grace O'Malley came early. In June of 1593, as she sailed up the River Thames to meet Queen Elizabeth I, she would have known little about what her privateering English counterparts were doing. Walter Raleigh was organizing an expedition to discover the Lost City of Gold in South America. Martin Frobisher, having conducted three expeditions to North America, was plundering ships off the coasts of France and Spain. Francis Drake, circumnavigator of the world, was ranging around North Africa, the Caribbean, and South America, seizing booty wherever he found it.

Grace O'Malley, commander of a fleet of galleys and several hundred sailors, had sailed from the west coast of Ireland to seek the removal of the ruthless Richard Bingham, the English-appointed governor of Connaught. Bingham was the one who had denounced her as "a woman who overstepped the part of womanhood," and labelled her "the most notorious sea captain in Ireland." She sought the release from Bingham's jail of a half-brother and of her son,

Tibbot. Also, she hoped to secure the right to maintain herself "by land and sea," by which she meant forcibly collecting "tax" from any ships that plied the waters she patrolled. The merchants of Galway were allowed to do this: why was she prevented?

Earlier in the year, Grace had written to Elizabeth requesting a meeting. She spoke little English, and knew that the queen spoke no Irish, so had communicated in Latin. As a descendant of Irish nobility, the privileged daughter of a prominent chieftain, she had learned the language as a child, probably from a priest. Intrigued, Elizabeth had responded, through her ministers, with the Eighteen Articles of Interrogation. Several of these focused on antecedents and familial relations, but others sought information about who owned what lands and how the Irish Brehon law treated wives and widows, a subject Grace had raised: how were widows to survive after their husbands died?

Ancient Brehon laws were more egalitarian and democratic than the English common law. Under the Irish system, administered by Brehons or itinerant judges, a ruler not only would be elected, but could be male or female. He or she could also be voted out of office and replaced. In the mid-1600s, Oliver Cromwell would put an end to all that.

But now, in her early sixties, Grace O'Malley wrote that Bingham had been persecuting her since 1586. He had hanged one of her sons, who had been faithful to Her Majesty, and had jailed Grace herself. He had built a gallows from which to hang her, but had released her after receiving a pledge from a powerful ally. When Bingham briefly left the country, she had secured a pardon from the English governor in Dublin, and then retreated to her stronghold, Rockfleet Castle. But Bingham had taken almost all her cattle and horses, and had also seized most of her ships. He had driven her into poverty. Surely Queen Elizabeth, a powerful woman of almost precisely her own age, would lend a sympathetic ear?

Grace O'Malley locked herself into Rockfleet Castle and, when her husband arrived home, called down from the battlements: "Richard Bourke, I dismiss you." Later, she relented.

⊠⊠⊠

Grace O'Malley was born at Belclare Castle near Westport around 1530. During her lifetime, King Henry VIII of England had begun the Tudor conquest of Ireland. This had led, under his daughter Queen Elizabeth, to the Nine Years War, the Flight of the Earls, and the Plantation of Ulster. During Grace's youth, her elders escaped the worst depredations of the England-based Tudors. A seafaring clan, the O'Malleys controlled the waters off the west coast of Ireland. They taxed and plundered those who came within reach, and also conducted raids in foreign lands.

As a girl, when her father refused her permission to join him in a Spanish expedition, ostensibly because her long hair would get caught in the ropes, she chopped off her hair and changed into male clothing. This incident inspired her nickname, Grainne, which means "crop-haired." It also convinced her father to teach her to sail. Still, she was a female. And when she was sixteen he gave her a substantial dowry in cattle, horses, sheep, and ships, and married her off to Donal O'Flaherty, the warrior son of a clan chieftain.

With "Donal of the Battles," as he was called, she would have two sons and a daughter. While Donal engaged in feuding on land, notably against the neighbouring Joyces, Grace combined her own vessels with those of the O'Flahertys to create a growing fleet of well-armed ships. With this fleet, she controlled shipping lanes to the west-coast port of Galway. She practised a type of piracy she euphemistically called "maintenance by land and sea." Either captains of merchant vessels would pay her a toll for safe passage or she would seize their ships and add them to her fleet.

When Grace was in her early thirties, she lost her marauding husband to an ambush. The rugged O'Flahertys laughed at her demands under Brehon law and installed a new chieftain. Grace returned to her father's lands, bent on reasserting her primacy at sea. With her she brought some two hundred sailors who chose to remain with her—not just O'Flahertys but also scores of elite "gallowglass" mercenaries, Norse-Gaelic warriors from Scotland and northern Ireland.

As Judith Cook writes in her biography, *Pirate Queen*, "There was no precedent for what she achieved as a woman in a man's world." That so many men followed Grace O'Malley at this juncture "is almost beyond belief. That she retained their continuing loyalty . . . suggests that she had a truly charismatic personality. But even that would have been insufficient had she not earned their respect by proving herself a master mariner, a brilliant strategist, and, above all, successful."

Now, while based at Clare Island in Clew Bay, due west of Westport, Grace O'Malley became known as the Pirate Queen. She commanded several hundred fighting men and reigned supreme over the coastal waters. Because she frequently visited Scotland, especially Kintyre and the southern Hebrides, and sailed also into ports along the northern coast of Ireland, O'Malley was well aware that Elizabeth I, queen of England since 1558, had begun a campaign to force English law on Ireland. Grace needed a powerful alliance and so took a second husband, "Iron Richard" Bourke, who was likely to become a clan chieftain: the MacWilliam.

Legend has it that, when she was in her mid-thirties, she turned up at his stronghold, Rockfleet Castle, and proposed a trial marriage. After one year, if it did not work out, either partner could withdraw. A corollary legend, one that highlights her bravado, finds Grace locking herself in the castle after a year and a day. When Iron Richard arrives home, she calls down from the battlements: "Richard Bourke, I dismiss you."

In fact, the two remained allies until his death two decades later. In 1567, Grace gave birth to his son, Tibbot. Again according to legend, she did so while leading a trading mission to the Middle East. A day after she gave birth, off the Mediterranean coast of North Africa, Grace was resting below decks when her ship was attacked by pirates. Fighting raged until one of her men appeared and told her they were being boarded.

Grace leapt out of her bunk, pulled a blanket around herself, and grabbed a pair of blunderbusses. She emerged on deck playing the madwoman, dancing and capering. As the invading officers stood gaping, she pulled out her muskets and blasted away. She killed all the leaders, told her men to seize their followers, and sailed home to hang the lot at Rockfleet.

In 1571, her husband, Iron Richard, became *tánaiste* or second-in-command to the MacWilliam. Not long afterwards, the English began exerting control over the western counties. They were taking direct aim at the Irish system of communal land tenure. Sir Henry Sidney, the English lord deputy, was inducing the Irish chieftains to surrender their lands, to take them back under the queen's authority, and then to rule according to English law. Grace O'Malley opposed this because it would disinherit her husband. But she was sly. When Henry Sidney visited Galway, she sailed into the harbour with three galleys and two hundred fighting men. She pledged allegiance to Queen Elizabeth, gave Sidney a boat tour of the harbour (for a price), and, when he was gone, resumed her old ways.

Weeks after Sidney departed, the Pirate Queen made a miscalculation. She sailed south and began raiding the estates of the Earl of Desmond. She was captured by Desmond's men and spent the next two years in jail—first in Limerick, then in Dublin Castle. Early in 1579, Grace O'Malley regained her freedom, possibly in exchange for information regarding Spain's plans to use Ireland as a stepping stone to invade England. Four years later, after her husband died of natural causes, she claimed one-third of his estates and retreated to Rockfleet Castle with hundreds of retainers and a thousand head of cattle and horses.

At age fifty-three, with a ferocious army, a hard-to-reach castle, and a fleet of ships, Grace O'Malley looked set to sail blithely into the future. She did not anticipate the appointment, in 1584, of Sir Richard Bingham as English governor of Connaught. Probably, as Anne Chambers suggests in *Ireland's Pirate Queen*, Bingham was "no more cruel than his contemporaries." The brutal methods he used to subdue western Ireland were "the accepted rules of sixteenth-century warfare," she writes, though they were "reinforced by his own racist attitudes towards the Irish in general."

Unlike his conciliatory predecessor, Henry Sidney, Bingham believed in colonization by the sword. Born in Dorset, trained in military service from his youth, he took a hard line with Irish clan leaders who resisted English incursions. He detested Grace

O'Malley, who in his view had no right, as a widow, to the estates she controlled, and still less right, as a woman, to rule.

Soon after being appointed, he introduced the Composition of Connaught, a complex document that asserted English control, pre-empting Gaelic law and custom, abolishing tributes paid to Irish chieftains, and fixing land rents payable to the English crown. It abolished this Irish business of the MacWilliamship, ending Grace's dream of bequeathing that legacy to her son Tibbot, now eighteen. As a precaution against Grace, Bingham captured Tibbot and sent him to England as a hostage to his brother, George Bingham.

In the face of such aggression, former enemies created alliances, and these Bingham quashed ruthlessly. He executed hostages and murdered Grace's oldest son, Owen. He promised Grace O'Malley safe conduct to Rockfleet Castle, but when she set out with a few men and cows, he ambushed her and took her prisoner.

Bingham built a special gallows from which to hang the Pirate Queen. He denounced her as a "drawer in of Scots" and insisted that she had been "nurse to all rebellions in the province for forty years." At the last moment—almost incredibly, given that he had killed so many without a second thought—Bingham let her go. Legend has it that, just as Grace O'Malley was about to climb onto the gallows, or in some versions when she was standing with a rope around her neck, a messenger arrived on horseback bearing a royal warrant for her release.

Grace O'Malley sailed north to Ulster to raise Scottish forces. Her galleys were damaged in a gale and needed repairs. As a result, she spent three months visiting with the Great O'Neill and the O'Donnell, leaving them in no doubt as to what they might expect when the English turned their attention to Ulster. In May 1587, Queen Elizabeth ordered Bingham to lead a force in Flanders. While he was in France, Grace made her way to Dublin

Castle, and there secured an official pardon for both herself and her remaining sons.

The Pirate Queen lives again at Westport House, County Mayo. The estate includes a Pirate Adventure Park, dungeons that date from the 1500s, and related displays.

When Bingham returned to Ireland, he seized much of her property, enforced an embargo, and resumed making life difficult for all of the Irish. Early in 1593, Grace O'Malley sent a letter to Queen Elizabeth, complaining of Bingham. She outlined her personal history, highlighting her two marriages. She noted that the Composition of Connaught neglected to make provision for the widows of chieftains, and asked the queen "to grant her some reasonable maintenance for the little time she has to live."

Grace O'Malley offered to submit to "surrender and regrant." The Tudors used this legal mechanism to establish control over

Irish clans, who owned their lands collectively as extended families under an ancient system of Brehon law. Those clans surrendered their holdings and were regranted control under the English common law. In a clever attempt to circumvent Bingham's embargo, Grace O'Malley also sought permission "to invade with sword and fire all your highness's enemies wheresoever they are or shall be . . . without any interruption of any person or persons whatsoever." Soon after she sent this petition, she learned that Bingham had arrested Tibbot and charged him with treason on the grounds, probably justified, that he had conspired with the Great O'Neill to repel English expansion.

With Tibbot's life in the balance, and without waiting for an answer to her petition, Grace O'Malley gathered a few of her more prestigious allies and sailed for London. That she met and had an audience with Queen Elizabeth is well documented. But the details of the meeting of these two women, both in their early sixties, are lost. Probably they met at Greenwich Palace, and certainly they conversed in Latin, the only language both spoke well.

With this visit, Grace O'Malley achieved a spectacular success. She waited, anchored in the Thames among ships from around the world, while Queen Elizabeth followed court protocol and received a reply from Richard Bingham. He responded furiously but to no effect. Towards the end of September, Queen Elizabeth ordered him to release Tibbot. She wrote that, because Grace had become a widow without livelihood, Bingham should provide for her out of her sons' estates.

Elizabeth urged him, further, "to have pity for the poor aged woman" who had visited, noting that she "departs with great thankfulness and with many more earnest promises that she will, as long as she lives, continue a dutiful subject, yea and will employ all her power to offend and prosecute any offender against us."

Back at Rockfleet Castle, Grace O'Malley built three massive new galleys and, as she neared seventy, set about plying her old trade of "maintenance by land and sea." She lives on today not just in novels, biographies, plays, concert pieces, dances, and movies, and not just in the statues erected at Westport House, but in the "overstepping" audacity of countless Canadian women—a boldness encountered, as well, in any number of Scottish heroines, among whom we discover the dauntless Flora MacDonald.

20.

Flora MacDonald

⬚⬚⬚

I n the winter of 1778, one of my ancestors slept with Flora
MacDonald. That "overstepping" Celtic woman had long since
become legendary as the saviour of Bonnie Prince Charlie—a
distinction she achieved in 1746, after the Battle of Culloden and
Charles's devastating defeat at the hands (primarily) of the English.
Two hundred and sixty-eight years after that cataclysm, in August
2014, Sheena and I drove sixty-five kilometres north out of Halifax,
Nova Scotia, to the national historic site where Flora encountered
my maternal ancestor Thomas Laffin.

During the American Revolution, as a young officer with the
Royal Highland Emigrants, Laffin had been posted to Fort Edward
in Windsor, Nova Scotia. For a time, both he and Flora were
ensconced in the long wooden rectangle that served as the officers'
quarters. Flora had arrived after these premises were established.
But perhaps I have not been clear. Flora's husband was the senior
officer in charge of the fort, and he took her into his private com-
partment at one end of the low-lying wooden building. Young Laffin
slept with Flora in that he bunked down under the same roof at the

same time, though he did so with the other officers at the far end of the barracks.

Flora MacDonald spent one winter at Fort Edward as a refugee from the American Revolution. In 1922, most of the fort burned down, leaving only the blockhouse.

By this time, Flora MacDonald was a Loyalist refugee from the American Revolution. Earlier that year, she had sailed up the coast of the U.S. from North Carolina to New York "in the dead of winter," as she wrote later, "being in danger of our lives for most of the voyage by a constant storm." In addition to Laffin, an Irish volunteer from the Limerick area, two of her sons were already serving in Nova Scotia with the newly created Royal Highland Emigrants (the 84th Regiment of Foot).

Earlier in 1778, Flora's husband, Allan MacDonald, having exhausted all other options, went north in their wake. At Windsor, he took command of the garrison at Fort Edward. Here on a hill overlooking Minas Basin, a four-cornered wooden palisade enclosed several buildings: a barracks, officers' quarters, a bakery, kitchens, stores, and a two-storey wooden blockhouse, the last of which is all that remains today.

Granted permission to join her husband, Flora sailed after him from New York. By the time she reached Halifax, she "was very nigh death's door, by a violent disorder the rough sea and long passage had brought on." After eight days in Halifax, she journeyed overland through "woods and snow" for five days. At Fort Edward, even the officers' quarters were cramped, spartan, and miserable. "There we continued all winter and spring," she wrote later of her Nova Scotia sojourn, "covered with frost and snow, and almost starved with cold to death, it being one of the worst winters ever seen there."

Probably Flora did not stay at the fort for more than a few weeks. A letter in the archives at the West Hants Historical Society Museum, just down the hill from the historical site, indicates that the officers' barracks "were in very poor repair, and that because of crowded conditions at the fort, some of the officers and their families had obtained lodging in the village of Windsor." Flora MacDonald and her husband, Allan MacDonald, were almost certainly among that number.

※※※

Roughly three decades before, when she was twenty-three, Flora MacDonald had become a Scottish heroine by enabling Bonnie Prince Charlie, the most wanted man in Europe, to escape from British government forces. The twenty-five-year-old prince had fled after the Battle of Culloden, when on April 26, 1746, the British had decimated the Jacobites, those Highlanders and islanders bent on helping Charlie regain the crown. The English had put an extraordinary price on his head: thirty thousand pounds, the equivalent today of seven million Canadian dollars.

With hundreds of ruthless, money-hungry soldiers on his heels, the prince had fled to the westernmost Hebrides, the "Long Island" comprising North Uist, Benbecula, and South Uist. He had

found shelter there courtesy of Ronald MacDonald, the chief of
Clanranald, who had hidden the prince in a gamekeeper's hut in
the woods. Flora had grown up not far away. She was visiting the
wife of Clanranald when Felix O'Neil, one of the prince's men,
approached her asking what she would give for a sight of the prince.

*The Culloden Battlefield Memorial features a 360-degree film that places the viewer at
the heart of the 1746 action. Modest stones mark the areas where clans fought and fell.*

Flora MacDonald wrote later, referring to herself in the third
person, that "a sight of him would make her happy, though he was
on a hill and she was on another." Later that day, without revealing his reasons, her older brother, now master of the family home,
insisted that she spend the night at a hillside "shieling" or shepherd's hut a couple of kilometres from the house.

Realizing that some scheme was afoot, Flora did as he asked.
That night, she was wakened by Neil MacEachain, a fellow islander
who, along with O'Neil, was one of the two men assisting the Young

Pretender. Neil had hurried ahead to waken her, and later reported that "she got scarcely on the half of her clothes, when the prince, with his baggage upon his back, was at the door, and saluted her very kindly; after which she brought to him a part of the best cheer she had." This was "a large bowl full of cream, of which he took two or three hearty-go-downs, and his fellow travellers swallowed the rest."

O'Neil explained that the plan was to spirit Prince Charlie to the Isle of Skye, nearer the Scottish mainland, dressed as a maid-servant. He asked if she would accompany them as the lady to the servant. At first Flora refused, "with the greatest respect and loyalty." She feared that such an action would ruin the Chief of Sleat, Sir Alexander MacDonald, who owned Skye and North Uist.

O'Neil assured her that Sir Alexander would not be implicated because he was still on the mainland, working ostensibly with the British. He added that, by undertaking this "glorious action" to save the prince, she would gain honour and immortality. Flora protested that to help might ruin her reputation. "You need not fear for your character," O'Neil answered, "for by this you will gain an immortal character." He added that he would, by an oath, "marry you directly, if you please."

Flora responded that she could live without immortality, and certainly without Felix O'Neil as a husband. At this point, the Bonnie Prince spoke up, and told Flora of the gratitude "he would always retain for so conspicuous a service." The young woman relented. After learning the details of the plan, she set out across the fields in the darkness.

Here we see courage in action. Flora MacDonald knew that this errand could lead to arrest and imprisonment, and yet away she went. She could not know that this undertaking would lead also to a marriage, to emigrating, and to entanglement in the American Revolution. It would lead to sojourning in Nova Scotia, where she would cross paths with Thomas Laffin. And it would make her famous throughout the English-speaking world, so famous that James Boswell and Dr. Samuel Johnson would visit the Isle of Skye to meet her. She could not know that this undertaking would secure her a prominent place in the Scottish parade of heroes and heroines.

※※

To separate truth from mythology, a biography by Hugh Douglas, *Flora MacDonald: The Most Loyal Rebel*, has proven especially useful. Flora was born in 1722 on South Uist at Milton, where today a lonely cairn marks the rough location of the house. Her father, Ranald, was a tacksman, or leaseholder, who sublet small holdings for their owner, the clan chieftain. Her mother was the daughter of a Presbyterian minister whose ancestors included the founder of the MacDonalds of Sleat, and so also Somerled of Argyll, as well as Robert the Bruce. She came by her courage naturally. Her father died the year after she was born, and his "tacks" had gone eventually to his eldest son, Angus. In 1728, her mother took another husband, Hugh MacDonald, of a different branch of the family.

Flora usually spent a lot of time at Lady Clanranald's house in Nunton, some distance north across a narrow channel on Benbecula. Here she learned enough social graces that those who later met her insisted that one "could not discern by her conversation that she spent all her former days in the Highlands." In 1744, she lived with relatives for ten or eleven months at Largie in Argyll.

By this time, according to early accounts, she was "easy and cheerful, yet she had a certain mixture of gravity in all her behaviour which became her situation exceedingly well, and set her off to great advantage." Clearly well-bred, she spoke both Gaelic and English. When she returned home early in 1745, she found the Long Island roiling and divided over news that a Jacobite uprising was imminent.

The political problem dated from the Glorious Revolution of 1688–1689, which ended with the exile of the Roman Catholic Stuart king, and the adoption of Presbyterianism as the Protestant state religion of Scotland. The English throne went to the Protestant House of Hanover, and the 1707 Acts of Union, despite opposition, brought England and Scotland together in the single unified kingdom of Great Britain. In 1715, the son of the exiled Stuart king, the Old Pretender, incited a first Jacobite uprising in a disastrous attempt to regain the throne. Now, in 1745, his son—the Young Pretender, or Bonnie Prince Charlie—was trying again.

The prince raised a considerable force in the Highlands and marched into Edinburgh to the cheers of twenty thousand people. His Jacobites won a victory at Prestonpans, just outside Edinburgh, and began marching south. They crossed the border into England, hoping to gain support as they went. They did not. In early December, when they reached Derby, they realized that they faced insurmountable odds.

Despite protests from the prince, the Jacobites turned back. By now the British had gathered a formidable, well-equipped army. Over the next three months, they tracked the Jacobites northward, all the way back to the Highlands. On April 16, 1746, near Inverness, the Jacobites suffered a crushing final defeat at the Battle of Culloden. They lost between fifteen hundred and two thousand men, while the British lost one-tenth of that number. Bonnie Prince Charlie narrowly escaped.

In June 1746, the prince sought refuge on South Uist. With the British hunting furiously, Clanranald hid him in a wooded glen called Corodale. After one narrow escape, the prince sent away his few remaining men and kept just two with him—Felix O'Neil and Neil MacEachain, who had come to Flora MacDonald. As she strode off into the night, these two and the prince returned to Corodale to wait.

After one brief stop, Flora set out to hike thirty-two kilometres to Nunton on Benbecula to finalize arrangements with Lady Clanranald. She crossed the narrow channel from South Uist, but then soldiers detained her overnight as she had no travel permit. By sheer good luck, her stepfather, Hugh MacDonald, arrived next morning. As a captain in the British army, he was nominally on the other side of the conflict. He ordered Flora's immediate release, and did the same for Neil MacEachain, who had also been captured. Before resuming her northward journey, Flora said she was going to get food and costumes, and told Neil to bring the prince to Rossinish on the west-coast of Benbecula.

At Nunton, Flora and Lady Clanranald created the prince's disguise: a quilted petticoat and calico gown patterned with sprigs of lilac flowers, to be worn with a white apron and a hooded cloak. They added stockings, garters of blue velvet, and shoes. Finally, on June 27, they summoned Prince Charles from the woods, where he was suffering from hunger, cold, and the first signs of scurvy. While the conspirators were dining, word came that the ruthless General Campbell had landed nearby with fifteen hundred men.

Flora's stepfather, Captain Hugh MacDonald, now actively engaged in the conspiracy, had written Flora a letter of safe passage. He addressed it to his wife on Skye, and said he was sending Flora to her because of the dangers on Uist: "She has got one Bettie Burke, an Irish girl who, she tells me, is a good spinster. If her spinning please you, you may keep her till she spin all your lint; or if you have any wool to spin, you may employ her." He added that he was sending Neil MacEachain along to take care of these two.

This trio—Flora, Neil, and the disguised prince—collected a couple of crew members and set out rowing across the water to Skye. After a long night, they landed on the coast. Leaving the prince in the boat, Flora and Neil went over a rise to seek help from Lady Margaret MacDonald, who expected them. They found a British officer, Lieutenant Alexander Macleod, in the house.

Flora went inside and distracted Macleod while Neil and Lady MacDonald arranged to take the prince south to safety. After Macleod left, she followed the prince to Kingsburgh, the house of another ally, Alexander MacDonald. In the morning, she and Neil walked sixteen kilometres south to Portree to make further arrangements. That afternoon, in a driving rain, the prince followed.

Flora and Neil waited in Portree at Charles MacNab's Inn. They had arranged for a small boat to ferry Charles to the island of Raasay, from where he would make his escape from Scotland.

To Flora, the prince said a fond farewell: "For all that has happened, I hope, Madam, we shall meet in St. James's yet." Then, still in a heavy downpour, the prince got into the boat and was rowed away into the fog, eventually to return to France. As Hugh Douglas observes, without Flora's assistance, "he could never have escaped from the trap that was on the point of snapping shut on him on the Long Island."

Flora never saw the prince again. Two weeks after waving him goodbye, she was arrested and taken aboard a notorious prison ship, HMS *Furnace*. This was a converted bomb ketch, a single-deck wooden vessel designed to lob explosive shells at fixed positions. Flora was kept on deck, though most captives were driven below into the hold, where they slept on coils of rope and survived on half rations amidst filth and slop buckets.

Flora remained a prisoner for fifty-one weeks. She made an honest, unashamed "confession" early on, impressing her questioners, and was treated with respect. Still, she was continually under threat—numerous Jacobites were tortured and executed, their severed heads displayed publicly in London and Manchester—and moved several times from one ship to another. For a few months, while held aboard a vessel off Edinburgh, she was allowed to receive visitors. Eventually, in London, she was kept onshore at one of several private houses where prisoners were held.

By the spring of 1747, Flora MacDonald had become a folk hero, thanks to the publication of an allegorical thirty-page pamphlet called *Alexis, or The Young Adventurer*. Written almost certainly by Neil MacEachain, it told the story of a beautiful young girl named Heroica, who showed courage and resourcefulness in leading a princelike figure to escape his dastardly pursuers. Then came a second pamphlet, this one by a government supporter. In *The Female Rebels* (1747), James Drummond wrote that Flora was "of graceful person, good complexion and peculiar sweetness mixed with majesty in her countenance."

Anti-Jacobite feeling subsided and, on July 4, 1747, the government declared an amnesty. Released, Flora travelled north by post-chaise to Edinburgh, where among friends she stayed nine months. When she did return to Skye, she received a less-than-warm welcome, probably because she had been treated leniently while others had died. She divided most of the next year between Edinburgh and London. Then, while visiting Skye in 1750, she accepted a marriage proposal from Allan MacDonald, who lived at Kingsburgh and was in line to become the chief factor of Lord MacDonald of Sleat.

Flora settled into life as a tacksman's wife. Through the 1750s, she gave birth to six children, and in 1766, she added a seventh. By this time, with the infamous clearances beginning, Highlanders and islanders had begun emigrating of their own accord to the American colonies. They were lured by promises of better climate and cheap land, and encouraged by landlords who hoped to make a killing by trading crofters for sheep. Flora and her husband talked of leaving but stayed to care for her husband's aging father.

They were still at Kingsburgh in September 1773, when James Boswell guided Dr. Samuel Johnson, England's foremost man of letters, around the Highlands and the Hebrides. Both gentlemen were appalled by the scale of the Scottish exodus, and tired of hearing, as Boswell wrote, of "racked rents and emigration, and finding a chief not surrounded by his clan."

Flora MacDonald became a legend in her own time. A contemporary Welsh painter Richard Wilson, known mainly for landscapes, created this likeness.

They endured an argumentative sojourn with the latest Chief of Sleat, who was keen to see the back of his crofters. The visitors offended this man greatly when they revealed, as he wrote later in a missive to Boswell, that their "only errand into Skye was to visit the Pretender's conductress, and that you deemed every moment as lost which was not spent in her company."

At Kingsburgh, the fifty-one-year-old Flora and her husband, who donned his kilt and cockaded bonnet, entertained the two travellers royally. Flora installed Johnson in the bed where Bonnie Prince Charlie had slept, and he hugely enjoyed the whole visit. He insisted that Flora tell him the story of her singular adventure, and encouraged Boswell to take notes. Johnson was saddened to learn that, her father-in-law having recently died, she and her husband were preparing to join their extended family in North Carolina. Later, he described her as "a woman of soft features, gentle manners, kind soul and elegant presence." And he added, using words that would one day be engraved on her memorial at nearby Kilmuir, that hers was "a name that will be mentioned in history, and if courage and fidelity be virtues, mentioned with honour."

In August 1774, Flora and her husband sailed from Campbeltown, Kintyre. After a miserable two-month voyage, they landed at Cape Fear, North Carolina. Established immigrants welcomed Flora as a celebrity symbol of Scottish bravery, and the moment Allan strode off the ship in his Highland finery, he stepped into the role of clan leader.

The American Revolutionary War would not be declared until April 1775, but skirmishing had already begun. As the family settled into a new home west of Cape Fear, Captain Allan MacDonald emerged as a key Loyalist figure in the struggle to retain British control of North Carolina. But in February 1776, after he and his men suffered a devastating defeat at Moore's Creek Bridge near Wilmington, he was taken prisoner. Back in her new home, her dreams broken, Flora waited for news . . . and then entered a dark night of the soul.

By April 1777, Loyalist families, manifestly unwelcome in North Carolina, had begun streaming northward out of that colony. Flora waited, moving house more than once. That October, she received word that Allan had negotiated his release and, while raising a company of "gentlemen volunteers," was trying to arrange for her to join him in New York. She eventually did so, and then followed him to Nova Scotia, where she spent that dreadful winter—though she did get to meet Thomas Laffin, one of my mother's forebears.

After the war, when Allan MacDonald received a land grant of seven hundred acres near Kennetcook, Nova Scotia, Laffin received five hundred acres in the same vicinity. But in October 1779, before the fighting ended, and rather than endure a second winter at Fort Edward, Flora sailed back to Scotland. That voyage would spawn mythical tales of how her ship came under attack and Flora was wounded in the arm while rallying the troops. In fact, as the ship turned and fled from attackers, Flora fell and dislocated her shoulder. Having landed in England, she took ill, suffering "a violent fit of sickness which confined me to my bed in London for half a year." Jacobite friends cared for her, and in the spring of 1780, she travelled north to Edinburgh and then to Skye.

For the next few years, she moved among her relatives on the Long Island. Meanwhile, after the war ended in 1783, Allan MacDonald received his land grant. He cleared woodlands and built a house, hoping to send for Flora and create a new home. But he received far less money for his military services than he had hoped, and in 1785, he returned to Skye. The couple stayed with one of their daughters at Dunvegan. Then one of their sons, John, who had amassed a small fortune in Sumatra, relieved them of any financial worries. They settled into a home on Skye near four of their five surviving children.

In January 1788, according to biographer Hugh Douglas, the erstwhile Bonnie Prince Charlie died "a fat, drunken, pathetic old man." He had never sent another word to Flora MacDonald. On

March 4, 1790, attended by the surgeon who had drawn up her marriage contract, Flora went to the grave herself. She was buried at Kilmuir Cemetery on the north Skye coast, less than two miles from where, in 1746, she had landed with the prince.

She is commemorated, more than two centuries after she died, in song, dance, poetry, and stone. In Canada, visitors to Fort Edward can walk where once she walked. And in so doing, we can honour the intrepidity of the woman who, at age twenty-three, strode alone into the night, risking her life to save the most wanted man in Europe. But here is a sign of the times: in that same month, June 1746, an audacious Scottish intellectual had begun having second thoughts about remaining at Oxford University. By August, disgusted with the rise of anti-Scottish sentiment, and with Flora MacDonald imprisoned on a ship, Adam Smith left Oxford for home.

21.

Adam Smith

※※※

The Jacobite rising that began in 1745, and which later called forth Flora MacDonald, was no singular event. From 1689 onward, Scotland had gone through a series of rebellions, revolutions, and wars. Then came the Highland Clearances, spawned by an agricultural revolution. Yet against this background of continual upheaval, the country produced a staggering array of pioneering figures in science and technology. The Scottish Enlightenment of the eighteenth century is rightly famous for its many audacious theorists, inventors, and engineers.

At the University of Glasgow, electrical engineer James Watt (1736–1819) created the steam engine, which fostered the Industrial Revolution. William Murdoch (1754–1839) of Ayrshire invented gas lighting, the steam tricycle, and waterproof paint. Charles Macintosh (1766–1843), a Glasgow chemist, produced a raincoat for an Arctic expedition, and even today people speak of wearing a macintosh.

Continuing into the 1800s, the Enlightenment produced James Clerk Maxwell (1831–1879), a mathematician and physicist from

Edinburgh, who formulated an electromagnetic theory that dazzled Albert Einstein and laid the foundations of quantum physics. And after emigrating to Canada, Alexander Graham Bell (1847–1922) invented the telephone, a communications advance that would spawn the digital revolution.

Against this background, Adam Smith stands as one of many. Born in 1723, one year after Flora MacDonald, he shone as philosopher, literary critic, historian, and anthropologist. But he made his enduring mark as a pioneering economist, writing a book that would earn him a nickname: Father of Capitalism. Smith was the first to analyze free-market forces, and to argue that alone, supply and demand can regulate an economy. Thanks to his intellectual temerity, Adam Smith established economics as a field of scientific study, giving rise to the kind of analysis that identifies Canada as one of the world's wealthiest nations. That analysis highlights the country's diversified economy, which includes a dominant service industry and an unusually strong primary sector (logging and oil).

Two and a half centuries ago, when in 1763 Flora MacDonald was raising a family on the Isle of Skye, Adam Smith was tutoring the son of a nobleman in Toulouse, France. To his best friend, the philosopher David Hume, who was serving as secretary to the British Embassy in Paris, the forty-two-year-old intellectual wrote: "The life which I led at Glasgow was a pleasant, dissipated life in comparison to that which I lead at present. I have begun to write a book to while away the time."

Published in 1776 as *An Inquiry into the Nature and Causes of the Wealth of Nations*, that work—which today is recognized as an economic manifesto and a foundational text in classical economics—investigates the links between productivity, division of labour, and free markets. No page-turner, *Wealth of Nations* appeared just as the Industrial Revolution was taking off. It sold out within six months and began influencing government policy almost immediately. In 1777, British prime minister Frederick North introduced two new taxes based on the book. Within two years, politicians were consulting Smith on the subject of giving Ireland free trade. And, as we have already noted, that was just the beginning.

Born in 1723, Adam Smith grew up into the burgeoning Age of Reason. The leading Scottish figures of the later 1700s made creative advances not just in philosophy and economics, but in engineering, architecture, medicine, geology, archaeology, law, chemistry, and sociology. Among them, in addition to those mentioned above, were Francis Hutcheson, Thomas Reid, Adam Ferguson, James Hutton, and Robert Burns.

Smith grew up in Kirkcaldy, north of Edinburgh, as the son of the city comptroller, and so he was raised among the children of merchants, professionals, and landed gentry. Legend has it that, when he was three or four, Smith was carried off by "tinkers," or travelling gypsies, but was soon rescued. The boy received an excellent education, thanks to the way Presbyterianism had fostered high rates of literacy. He was not a vigorous boy, and in an earlier age, his passion for books would almost certainly have marked him out for the ministry.

Instead, he found a vocation as a moral philosopher and man of letters. Frugal, disciplined, and hard-working, he rebelled against religion and, in an age when most people were farmers, focused on improving agriculture. At fourteen, Smith went to Glasgow University, and there studied with several outstanding scholars: Greek with Alexander Dunlop, logic with John Loudoun, and mathematics with Robert Simson, renowned as the restorer of ancient geometry. Also, he learned philosophy, jurisprudence, and political reasoning from that charismatic Irishman Francis Hutcheson.

In 1740, at age seventeen, Smith received a scholarship from the Church of England to attend Oxford University. He had no intention of entering any church, but happily set out on horseback for Oxford, a few days' journey south from Edinburgh. Already interested in economics and agriculture, he noticed as he travelled that the English looked healthier than the Scots, and attributed this to the difference in diet: "wheaten bread" instead of porridge.

At Oxford, Smith entered Balliol College, which had been founded in 1263 by John de Balliol, whose son caused the Bruce family so much trouble. Having been taught by some of Scotland's leading scholars, Smith disdained Oxford for failing to teach the philosophy and science of John Locke and Isaac Newton, and characterized it as a sanctuary in which "exploded systems and obsolete prejudices found shelter and protection, after they had been hunted out of every corner of the world."

During his second year at Oxford, Smith got his first taste of English opulence when he spent fourteen days at Adderbury House, which was run by his guardian William Smith. Though he took a dislike to Oxford, the young man continued studying there until August 1746, when he departed for home. One of his later students claimed that he "left in disgust." The previous April, an English army had decimated a ragtag force of Highland Scots at the Battle of Culloden. As a Scot, Adam Smith had come up against prejudice, suspicion, and discrimination.

Back in Kirkcaldy, he spent two years living with his mother while working occasionally as a private tutor. During this period, he developed a four-stage theory of forms of society, identifying them mainly by their chief means of subsistence: hunting and fishing, pastoralism, agriculture, and commerce. He judged the Scottish Highlands to be at the pastoral stage, with a warrior society and patriarchal leaders, and saw the Scottish Lowlands as more like England, organized for agriculture and commerce and requiring a professional army for defence.

As an emerging intellectual, Smith attracted the attention of Henry Home, Lord Kames, an Edinburgh-based lawyer, philosopher, writer, and agricultural improver. Born in 1696, Home was an early leader of the Scottish Enlightenment, and his proteges included philosopher David Hume and James Boswell, the lawyer who would transform the art of biography. As a founder and influential figure in the Philosophical Society of Edinburgh, Kames invited Smith to lecture regularly on rhetoric in Edinburgh.

Smith's systematic, rigorously logical teachings, based on years of study, demonstrated that rhetoric, which had been discredited, needed to be part of any liberal curriculum. And in 1750, when the chair of logic came open at Glasgow University, the twenty-seven-year-old Smith was elected unanimously to fill that post. David Hume was another candidate, but already he had a reputation as a skeptic and was, in fact, disqualified by his well-warranted reputation as an atheist. Two years later, Hume became keeper of the legal library in Edinburgh.

Smith was an engaging lecturer, and in Glasgow, his early lectures on jurisprudence treated price and money in the context of contracts. He grew increasingly sophisticated in economic analysis, and in 1761, a renowned thinker and physician from Geneva, Theodore Tronchin, visited Glasgow expressly to study with him. Smith taught numerous other intellectuals, merchants, and incipient luminaries. He helped establish the Literary Society of Glasgow and attended the Political Economy Club, where discussions probably influenced his *Wealth of Nations*.

He also attended meetings of the Poker Club, founded to champion the creation of a Scottish militia, which had been denied to Scotland after the 1745 uprising. Hume and others favoured a militia over an army of paid soldiers, though he and Smith maintained that professionals would usually defeat volunteers. Smith linked standing armies with the commercial stage of society, and saw them as an extension of the principle of division of labour.

Scottish philosopher Thomas Carlyle, who dubbed economics "the dismal science," wrote that he "heard Adam but once" at the Poker Club. Carlyle described him as "the most absent man in company that I ever saw, moving his lips and talking to himself, and smiling . . . If you awake'd him from his reverie, and made him attend to the subject of conversation, he immediately began a harangue and never stop'd till he told you all he knew about it, with the utmost philosophical ingenuity." According to Smith's biographer Ian Simpson Ross, Carlyle added that Smith's travels abroad with the third duke of Buccleuch "cured him in part of these foibles."

Those travels began in 1763 when, having accepted to tutor the eighteen-year-old duke, Smith spent two years travelling with him and his entourage in France and Switzerland. Five years before, he had published his *Theory of Moral Sentiments*, which offered a unique analysis of the nature of virtue. In this acclaimed work, which laid the foundations of *Wealth of Nations*, he divided moral philosophy into four parts: ethics and virtue; private rights and natural liberty; familial rights (economics); and state and individual rights (politics). Then, from Toulouse, Smith wrote to David Hume of beginning a new book "to while away the time."

Through the 1760s, Smith worked continuously on *Wealth of Nations,* adding material until it ran more than a thousand pages— not unusual for the Scottish Enlightenment. He finished writing by 1773, and then stayed in London to shepherd the book into print three years later. The massive work begins with the idea that division of labour creates wealth or prosperity, and proceeds to show how that happens. It dazzled contemporary thinkers.

Historian Edward Gibbon hailed *Wealth of Nations* as offering "an extensive science in a single book, and the most profound ideas expressed in the most perspicuous language." In the British

Parliament, Whig leader Charles James Fox cited Smith's simple but indisputable maxim "that the only way to become rich was to manage matters so as to make one's income exceed one's expenses." He added that this "applied equally to an individual and a nation."

Economists credit *Wealth of Nations* with originating the idea that given competition, owners of resources will deploy them logically and profitably. Here we discover the roots of free-market capitalism, the system that underpins the economies of the entire Western world. In Canada, that system is indisputably foundational, though Canadians have ameliorated some of its worst effects.

Today, Naomi Klein argues that the capitalist system is due for a radical correction, one that involves controlling the free market, reducing the power of global corporations, and rebuilding local economies. With such ideas, the socially conscious Adam Smith would be enthralled. As an intellectual adventurer, Smith would be thunderstruck to find Klein arguing, in *This Changes Everything*, that our economic system is responsible for global warming, and that galloping greed and a rampaging free-market economy are giving rise to floods, fires, storms, and droughts, and even threatening life on earth. But that critique would come long after Smith's time, and in any case shows no signs, correct as it may be, of revolutionizing the capitalist world.

22.

James Boswell

⬚⬚⬚

Around the time that Adam Smith began tutoring a duke in France, James Boswell played host to a dinner for six at the Mitre Tavern in London on July 6, 1763. As a wealthy, twenty-three-year-old Scot who had recently finished law school, and who would inherit both an extensive Ayrshire estate and the title Lord Auchinleck, Boswell had recently moved to the metropolis to further his education in the ways of the world. This summer evening, his pre-eminent guest at the Mitre was Dr. Samuel Johnson, then fifty-three, whom he admired unconditionally.

Boswell's guests included the author Oliver Goldsmith, who would soon become known for *The Vicar of Wakefield*, and a Scottish Presbyterian minister, John Ogilvie, who had recently published a book of poems, and who "was very desirous of being in company with my illustrious friend." Later, in *The Life of Samuel Johnson*, the sharp-eyed Boswell would write that Ogilvie "proved unlucky in speaking ardently of his native Scotland." Challenged by the Anglo-Irish Goldsmith, he insisted that Scotland "had a great many noble wild prospects."

A Literary Party at Sir Joshua Reynolds' *finds (left to right) James Boswell, Samuel Johnson, and Joshua Reynolds, among other luminaries.*

"I believe, Sir, you have a great many," Johnson responded. "But, Sir, let me tell you, the noblest prospect which a Scotchman ever sees, is the high road that leads him to England!"

This now-famous sally, Boswell tells us in *The Life*, "produced a roar of applause." Here, we see both the wit of Johnson and, in its vivid evocation, the observational genius of Boswell. But more than that, between the lines, we read the temper of the times. Johnson's jest won approval not just for its wit, but because everyone at the table, whether English, Anglo-Irish, or Scottish, understood, accepted, and even shared the assumptions that informed it: the Scots were perennial figures of fun, and could safely be targeted in any gentleman's jest.

What we do not see in this moment, because it would not emerge for years, is the resolve and determination that, coupled with his powers of observation, enabled Boswell to become one of the great literary figures of the age. By making himself and his questing part of the story, and by incorporating documentary reportage (from his journals) and novelistic scene-making, he invented, or at least revolutionized, a literary genre: biography. Canadian authors who have written significant biographies must count Boswell as one of their most notable ancestors. That list would include, to name just a few, Donald Creighton, Richard Gwyn, Maggie Siggins, David A. Wilson, Peter C. Newman, Elspeth Cameron, Charlotte Gray, John English, Rosemary Sullivan, and Charles Foran.

▨▨▨

The Boswells had owned land in Scotland since the mid-1400s, long before John Knox introduced Calvinism to their environs. James Boswell was born in 1740 near St. Giles' Cathedral in Edinburgh, where, in the 1560s, Knox had regularly railed against Roman Catholicism and its idolatries. His parents were both strict Calvinistic Presbyterians, and his father, a judge, was the dour Scot of stereotype: austere, strict, and given to duty, hard work, and self-possession.

As a child, Boswell began attending James Mundell's Academy, where he was anxious and unhappy. From age eight, after his father inherited the family estate at Auchinleck, seventy miles southwest of Edinburgh, young Boswell began studying with private tutors.

At thirteen, shy and awkward, given to a "melancholy temperament" and "terrified by everything [he] did not understand," Boswell enrolled in the arts course at Edinburgh University. He suffered a nervous breakdown, but on recovering, almost overnight, he changed. He turned into a gregarious young buck about town. His father got wind of the transformation and sent him off at nineteen to Glasgow University, there to study with such serious figures as Adam Smith.

Boswell judged this no substitute for the conviviality of Edinburgh. He informed his parents that he intended to convert to

Roman Catholicism and become a monk. His parents summoned him home to Edinburgh, but the young rebel ran away to London. There, immediately after becoming nominally a Roman Catholic, he hired a prostitute and savoured the "melting and transporting rights of love."

Boswell spent three months enjoying the fleshpots of London. Then his father fetched him back to Edinburgh and the university where, according to the terms of a familial truce, the young man began studying law. Boswell passed his oral law exam, and in July 1762, his father permitted him to return to London with an allowance suitable to a gentleman.

The young man had published poems in the *Scots Magazine* and reviewed plays for the *Edinburgh Chronicle*, though he expressed no ambition to become a man of letters. Yet now he began to keep a journal—one that, compulsively maintained for two decades, and extraordinary for its honesty, acuity, and vividness, would prove invaluable when it came time to write *The Life of Samuel Johnson*.

Young Boswell was irrepressible, and notable for his lack of inhibition and his reckless unconcern for reputation. At the theatre one night, while waiting for the show to begin, he entertained the audience by mooing like a cow. On another occasion, when rowdies in the cheap seats hurled abuse at two Highland officers, his "Scotch blood boiled with indignation," and he leapt onto a bench and swore at the offenders.

Given his family background, Boswell was not a social climber in the ordinary sense. But, while drinking, gambling, and whoring— bedding any woman who would have him, and paying for sex when he would otherwise go without—the young man also searched out intellectuals and writers with the enthusiasm of a puppy.

Johnson was the only one who inspired a two-decades-long obsession that culminated in a biography. But at various times Boswell also sought the company of the actor David Garrick, the painter Joshua Reynolds, the Irish statesman and political theorist Edmund Burke, and the philosophers Voltaire and Jean-Jacques Rousseau. He called on these Frenchmen in France, essentially inviting himself. He plagued them with questions about Christian faith and the afterlife—they were both avowed atheists—and then wrote sketches of them. More than that: after visiting Rousseau in February 1766, he offered to accompany the Frenchman's mistress to London. While en route in a horse-drawn carriage, he enjoyed a tryst with her.

Boswell's chutzpah went beyond literary innovation. Let one more example suffice. In July 1776, when he heard that David Hume was dying of abdominal cancer, Boswell hurried to Edinburgh to visit the philosopher. Born in 1711, Hume was the most famous skeptic to emerge from the rationalist Scottish Enlightenment. A pioneer of the essay form, an avowed atheist, Hume had influenced Voltaire, Rousseau, and Adam Smith. He welcomed Boswell, whom he had entertained previously, into his Edinburgh home.

The biographer-to-be, nominally a Christian, was worried that his own riotous behaviour might lead, after death, to severe judgment and banishment to the nether regions. Boswell's great hero, Dr. Samuel Johnson, was haunted by nightmare fears of death and damnation. Johnson had denounced Hume as a dangerous heretic and a threat to order and society. But Boswell believed that Hume, his brilliant fellow Scot, would repent and embrace a Christian belief in the afterlife. He hurried to Edinburgh in the hope of recording a deathbed repentance.

The ailing Hume, reclining on a couch in his drawing room, said that while he had been religious as a boy, he had studied himself out of it. "Now, when I hear a man is religious," he said, "I conclude that he is a rascal—though I have heard instances of some very good men being religious." The irrepressible Boswell asked Hume directly, as he later related, if he "persisted in disbelieving in a future state when he had death before his eyes." Hume answered that his imminent death made no difference: "It is a most unreasonable fancy that we should live forever."

Eight years later, after the death of Johnson, James Boswell began his great biography. And it is on this work, his full-scale portrait of the Great Cham, that his reputation stands. By the time he sat down to write, he had been married fifteen years. He had produced several children and was practising law in Edinburgh, decidedly without distinction. His father, Lord Auchinleck, had died two years before Johnson. Boswell had tried and failed to get into Parliament. He had indulged in unlucky speculations, got "not drunk, but intoxicated," as he insisted, and in 1788, with his great work under way, moved to London to pursue it.

▨▨

Boswell's youth, charm, and resilience had got him through many a bruising encounter with Dr. Johnson. Only his thick skin had enabled him to endure, over two decades, many a Johnsonian thrust regarding his nationality and native land. Johnson, widely recognized as the most articulate Englishman of his era, was known as the Great Cham of Literature—the word "cham," a form of "khan," suggesting that he ruled the world of letters like an oriental despot.

With his jibes, he gave voice to the prejudices of eighteenth-century England. In conveying this, obliquely and subtly, in *The Life of Samuel Johnson*, Boswell created a portrait of the age, while demonstrating that, as a literary artist, he was at least Johnson's equal. By recreating Dr. Johnson as the archetypal Englishman, Boswell elucidates centuries of tension between the Scots and the English.

One night at dinner, he tells us, when a well-to-do woman friend expressed a desire to visit Scotland, Johnson told her: "Seeing Scotland, Madam, is only seeing a worse England. It is seeing the flower gradually fade away to the naked stalk." On another evening, an American visitor wondered why Scottish colonists had taken possession of certain barren lands in his native country. Johnson declared: "Why, Sir, all barrenness is comparative. The Scotch would not know it to be barren."

By this time, a more mature Boswell had taken Johnson travelling around mainland Scotland and the Hebrides. "Come, come," he said. "You have now been in Scotland, Sir, and say if you did not see meat and drink enough there." Johnson replied: "Why yes, Sir; meat and drink enough to give the inhabitants sufficient strength to run away from home."

This litany is far from exhaustive. The point is not that Dr. Johnson was insensitive and overbearing, though that might be true, but rather that he gave voice to prevailing attitudes. And those attitudes leave the Scots playing the role of patsies, chumps, and favourite victims. The irony is that the literary achievement of Boswell far exceeds that of the subject he made famous.

Before he wrote his great biography, Boswell had achieved some literary success with *Journal of a Tour of the Hebrides*, an account of a three-month trip he had taken with Johnson to the Highlands and islands of Scotland. But at best, he was regarded as a charming ne'er-do-well. His fecklessness made him an easy target—and so he would remain for decades.

The most scathing word-portrait comes from the pen of Thomas Babington Macaulay. In 1831, he described Boswell as "servile and impertinent, shallow and pedantic, a bigot and a sot, bloated with family pride, and eternally blustering about the dignity of a born gentleman, yet stooping to be a talebearer, an eavesdropper, a common butt in the taverns of London . . . Every thing which another man would have hidden, every thing the publication of which would have made another man hang himself, was matter of gay and clamorous exultation to his weak and diseased mind."

The Boswell Arms in Auchinleck, Ayrshire, dates from the 1760s, when James Boswell himself would frequently pass this way from the family estate.

In that same essay, however, Macaulay also acknowledged Boswell's *Life of Samuel Johnson* to be the greatest biography ever written: "Homer is not more decidedly the first of heroic poets, Shakespeare is not more decidedly the first of dramatists, Demosthenes is not more decidedly the first of orators, than Boswell is the first of biographers. He has no second. He has distanced all his competitors so decidedly that it is not worthwhile to place them. Eclipse is first, and the rest nowhere." The heavyweight intellectual Thomas Carlyle seconded this opinion, declaring *The Life of Samuel Johnson* "beyond any other product of the eighteenth century."

Anyone seeking a Canadian perspective on the biographer's significance can look to literary critic Northrop Frye. Writing late in the twentieth century, Frye hailed Boswell as "a writer of genius." He noted the patience and skill with which Boswell drew out his subject, and also his powerful grasp of "the organic consistency" of Johnson's character. "We may feel," he wrote, "that Boswell had no right to be a great artist; that biographies should be factual and works of art fictional, and that they should keep apart. But there it is. Without using a single faked or illegitimate device as a biographer, Boswell has given us a real person who is also a great fictional character."

James Boswell published his *Life of Samuel Johnson* in 1791. Four years later, said to be worn out by his earlier lifestyle, he died in London at age fifty. More than a century afterwards, in the 1920s, a great cache of Boswell's private papers, including his journals, turned up in Ireland at Malahide Castle, north of Dublin. These provided new insights into his life and creative process. They spawned a new edition of his *Journal of a Tour to the Hebrides*, and also a *London Journal 1762–63* and *The Great Biographer, 1789–1795*.

The Malahide papers revealed a Boswell whose commitment and industry rivalled any in English-language literature. They showed how a shameless roustabout could create a literary masterpiece that stands alongside the greatest novels of the age. They threw open a window into the mind, the heart, and the art of one of Canada's new ancestors. And as for greatest novels . . .

23.

Maria Edgeworth

⌗⌗⌗

Irish novelist Maria Edgeworth, born five years after Boswell
met Johnson, is a stellar example of a writer shamefully
neglected. In the mid-twentieth century, critic P. H. Newby
took a stab at according her rightful recognition when he remarked
that "whereas Jane Austen was so much the better novelist, Maria
Edgeworth may be the more important. For whereas Jane Austen
surveyed with the eye of a realist ground that had already been
tilled, and brought it to perfection, Maria struck out and subdued
stretches of new territory, the psychology of children, the dignified
and humorous mind of the peasant, the resolute mind of a woman
of affairs, and she supplied an impetus for the writing of all regional
fiction."

As a description of literary pioneering, this passage would be
hard to beat. Nor was Newby without precursors. The leading literary critic of the Victorian era, John Ruskin (1819–1900), declared
that he read the tales of Maria Edgeworth and her novel *Patronage*
"oftener than any other books in the world, except the Bible . . .
They are it seems to me the most re-readable books in existence."

And Ivan Turgenev (1818–1883) wrote that his sketches of Russian peasants were inspired by Edgeworth.

Several twentieth-century critics have argued that Edgeworth made Jane Austen possible. Certainly, by introducing a new naturalism into the still-emergent genre of the novel, the Anglo-Irish author prepared the way for Austen. And that novelist herself, who began publishing when Edgeworth was already famous, sent the older author a copy of *Emma* when it appeared in 1816. Initially lukewarm, according to biographer Marilyn Butler, Edgeworth came around and would remark in 1833 that an admiration for Jane Austen was a "sign of good taste."

Admired as well by Lord Byron and Stendhal, Maria Edgeworth would become friends with only one other great literary figure: Sir Walter Scott—a friendship that illustrates the continuing cross-pollination that arose between Irish and Scottish writers. In a postscript to his novel *Waverley* (1814), which he observed "should have been a preface," Scott revealed that he had tried to invent distinctively Scottish characters "not by a caricatured and exaggerated use of the national dialect, but by their habits, manners and feelings; so as in some distant degree to emulate the admirable Irish portraits drawn by Miss Edgeworth."

In the 1820s, Maria Edgeworth and Walter Scott exchanged many letters and even entertained each other in their respective houses. Scott's first biographer, his son-in-law John Lockhart, described Edgeworth's two-week sojourn at Scott's home in the Scottish Borders as an extraordinarily happy period: "Never did I see a brighter day at Abbotsford than that on which Miss Edgeworth first arrived there—never can I forget her look and accent when she was received by him at his archway, and exclaimed, 'Everything about you is exactly what one ought to have had wit enough to dream.'"

Edgeworth thrilled to explore Abbotsford House, which by 1823, when she visited, Scott had transformed into a castle-like abode that remains one of Scotland's premier tourist destinations. Today, one can imagine her at fifty-five, delighting in the same sights available to a contemporary visitor—not just the baronial mansion of Abbotsford, with its impressive library and collections of ancient furniture, arms, and relics, but also Sandyknowe farm and Smailholm Tower, about twenty kilometres west, where Scott spent his boyhood. When Sheena and I visited these locations, we paused beside a sign that said "Scott's View," and as we looked out over the Tweed Valley, I felt as if Edgeworth and Scott were standing there with us, gazing out over this same pastoral vista.

▨▨▨

Born in 1768, Maria Edgeworth was the second child of Richard Edgeworth, a prominent Anglo-Irish politician, writer, and inventor. He owned an estate—Edgeworthstown, 120 kilometres northwest of Dublin—and eventually engendered twenty-two children with four wives. Maria's mother died when she was five, and she moved from Oxfordshire to that estate with her father and his second wife. At age fourteen, she settled there, and her father tutored her in economics, politics, law, science, and literature. She assisted that gentleman in managing the estate, which included family, servants, and tenants, and remained there for the rest of her life.

Audacity comes in many guises. In 1795, the year James Boswell died, Maria Edgeworth published *Letters for Literary Ladies*, which included a humorous essay arguing that women should use their special gift for self-justification to challenge men with wit and intelligence. The following year, she published *The Parent's Assistant*, the first of numerous children's books. It articulated many of her father's ideas on children's education, and so began a pattern. Years later, she would write that "it was to please my Father I first exerted myself to write, to please him I continued."

Until his death in 1817, her father served as Maria's developmental editor—one who insisted on approving her stories before she read them to her younger siblings. But she continued writing for decades after his death, breaking new literary ground in those territories mentioned above, and showing a dedication that went far beyond any sense of filial obligation. As a woman, Edgeworth soon realized that writing was one of the few fields in which she could show her mettle. Eventually, she produced thirty-five titles, many comprising several volumes.

In 1798, still laying the groundwork for a major career, she published *Practical Education*, combining the ideas of Locke and Rousseau to argue that for young people, the discipline of education is more important than the acquisition of knowledge. Then, in 1800, without her father's knowledge—here we see her backbone—Edgeworth submitted for publication a short, satirical novel called *Castle Rackrent*. She informed her father only after she received acceptance.

An immediate success, the book tells the story of four generations of an Irish landholding family, the Rackrents. William Butler Yeats would call it "one of the most inspired chronicles written in English." And in his 2014 book *The Novel: A Biography*, Michael Schmidt summarized neatly: "The fiction of the new century owed a substantial debt to *Castle Rackrent*." Writers have hailed the work as the first historical novel, the first "Big House" novel, and the first regional novel in English.

This last innovation would take root and blossom in Canada, where some of our finest writers of fiction have specialized in finding the universal in the regional. Think of Nobel Prize winner Alice Munro (Southern Ontario Gothic), or of L. M. Montgomery (Prince Edward Island), Alistair Macleod (Nova Scotia), Margaret Laurence (Manitoba), W. O. Mitchell (Saskatchewan), Robert Kroetsch (Alberta), and Jack Hodgins (Vancouver Island).

Technically, *Castle Rackrent* is the first novel to use an unreliable narrator as observer rather than protagonist. That narrator is an irrepressible Irish Catholic worker, Thady Quirk, who has a colourful way of expressing himself—a distinctive voice. All this was so groundbreaking that her father, then serving as an MP in Henry Grattan's Parliament, urged Maria to add an introduction in the voice of an English narrator. This she did before publication, with a view to ensuring that her radical literary work did not undermine English support for the 1801 Act of Union—an act that most Irish would soon regret as reprehensible.

Over the next two decades, Maria Edgeworth published so many notable works—tales for young people, novels for adults, books of essays on politics and education (some in collaboration with her father)—that she became the most highly regarded female writer of the early nineteenth century. Her first three-volume novel, called *Belinda* (1801), encompassed an interracial marriage between an African servant and an English farm girl, though later editions removed this too-daring depiction.

With *Tales of Fashionable Life*, two series of short stories focusing on women, Edgeworth became the most commercially successful writer of the era. In 1813, at the height of her fame, Edgeworth went to London with her father and stepmother. Schmidt reports that more than a century later, Virginia Woolf marvelled at what she read of Edgeworth's popularity: "The town ran mad to see her; at parties the crowd turned and twisted to discover her, and, as she was very small, almost closed above her head."

When after *The Absentee* (1815), Edgeworth received a letter from an American Jewish woman complaining that the novel was anti-Semitic, she responded by publishing *Harrington,* a book-length narrative about overcoming anti-Semitism. By corresponding with such figures as Scott and political economist David Ricardo, she kept herself informed.

Maria Edgeworth was building on the success of Castle Rackrent *when, in 1807, John Downman painted this portrait. She became the most famous female writer of her day.*

After the death of her father in 1817—he who had also been her editor—she sometimes used Walter Scott as a sounding board for ideas. In 1830, she showed her awareness of and sensitivity to the Highland Clearances when she wrote Scott seeking "a bit of advice" about possibly including a Scottish character in a novel she was writing. She had heard "an account of a Scotch chieftain . . . who had been smitten on a visit to London with a wish to figure in high company, and who had been led on to extravagance of all sorts—to get or keep in the circles of fashionables—and in short ended by cutting down his woods and I believe *selling* his Scotch property."

Edgeworth wanted to know from her fellow writer whether such a character would be believable and representative, and "whether it would be a national offence to Scotch friends of whom I have many that I would not for a world of novels lose, to draw such a character." No reply from Scott has survived. But Edgeworth biographer Marilyn Butler notes that the extravagant absentee landlord who turns up in the published novel is a "run-of-the-mill wealthy young Englishman."

The early 1830s proved a challenging time for Maria Edgeworth, as during elections, the legendary Daniel O'Connell rallied Catholic tenants throughout the land to vote against their landlords. Maria and her father had always been in favour of Catholic emancipation, or allowing Catholics to vote without property restrictions. And "sympathy for the lower orders," as Butler observes, "had previously been one of her motives for writing about Ireland."

Edgeworth was hurt and disillusioned when, in 1832, some of her tenants voted in opposition to her own declared wishes. She decided against writing a novel about such events: "We are in too perilous a case to laugh, humour would be out of season, worse than bad taste . . . Sir Walter Scott once said to me, 'Do explain why Pat [the typical Irishman], who gets forward so well in other countries, is so miserable in his own.' A very difficult question; I fear above my power. But I shall think of it continually, and listen, and look, and read."

Two years later, at age sixty-four, Edgeworth published *Helen,* a comedy of manners that explores the different ways women

responded to and coped within a patriarchal society. In an introduction to a 1987 edition, Maggie Gee suggests that the novel is
one of Edgeworth's most interesting "because old age seems to have
set her free to be, and write about, herself."

Around this time, Butler tells us, Edgeworth was caught up "in
the classic position of a moderate liberal in times of revolution." In
1835, when local tenants were asked to choose between her family's
known wishes and the priest's instructions, three long-standing tenants voted with the opposition repealers. Maria would have looked
the other way. But the politically active husband of one of her step-
sisters demanded that the three pay a traditional instalment of rent
called a "hanging gale," which had originally arisen as a grace period
on rent, payable after crops were harvested and sold.

In a letter to one of her stepbrothers, Maria described how one
of the men, "old Dermod," called at the house to pay these arrears,
"hobbling and bent . . . and followed by his young son, who pres-
ently fell to crying." A chastened Dermod sorrowfully voiced his
repentance, and the son "went on sobbing and I counting and mis-
counting . . . The thoughts of the number of years I had received
rent from that old good tenant in my father's time all worked upon
me. I am ashamed to tell you my finale—that tears began flow, and
though I twinkled and rubbed them out and off they did come . . .
and it was all shameful."

In a final manifestation of resolution, Maria Edgeworth was
well into her seventies when, in the mid-to-late 1840s, the Irish
Potato Famine began devastating the population. She sought to
raise funds, writing desperate and vivid letters to the Quaker Relief
Committee. She struggled to organize famine relief for the people
of Edgeworthstown, and succeeded in securing some gifts from
America. Having thought herself retired from writing, she sat down
and produced one last work to raise money for famine relief—a
children's novel entitled *Orlandino*, about a young boy who joins a

travelling theatre troupe and falls on hard times. A tale of redemption, it highlights the need for courage and determination in facing hardship. The book appeared in 1848 and the author died a year later at the age of eighty-one.

Twenty-first-century critics have focused on *Castle Rackrent* as possibly her greatest literary achievement, and have demonstrated that, more broadly, Edgeworth used her fiction to explore what it meant to be "Anglo-Irish." She saw education as central to creating a broader, transnational awareness while retaining local attachments. And she showed that national identity is rooted in education and culture rather than ethnicity, a position that would one day inform Canadian perspectives, though first it would set the stage for the emergence of James Joyce, surely the most audacious writer who ever wielded a pen.

24.

James Joyce

❈❈❈

As we two usual suspects rambled around Dublin in mid-afternoon, cultivating our transnational awareness, we encountered revellers tricked out in Edwardian gear, many of them red-faced and merry and given to impromptu shenanigans. They were playing characters from the novel *Ulysses*—most often Stephen Dedalus, Leopold Bloom, or the yea-saying Molly—or else James Joyce himself in middle age, when he wrote that masterpiece. Today was June 16, 2014, and all of Dublin was celebrating the 110th anniversary of Bloomsday—the day on which the entire action of *Ulysses* unfolds in what the author called "dear, dirty Dublin."

The James Joyce Centre had been partying all week, offering walking tours and talks and even (surprise) a Joycean pub crawl. On the sacred day itself, the main photo on the front page of the *Irish Times* featured two young women participating in an egg-and-spoon race as part of the Bizarre Bloomsday Brunch. And on page 7, we found a second, above-the-fold colour photo from the Joycean festivities, this one deriving from a street event mounted by the Here Comes Everybody Players of Boston.

The novel Ulysses *opens at what is now the James Joyce Tower and Museum at Sandycove Point, Dublin. Here we see the room in which, briefly, the author stayed.*

But at that point, as any Joycean knows, you're leaving *Ulysses* and edging into *Finnegans Wake*, which chants a refrain of "here comes everybody" that is beginning to look prophetic. Certainly Marshall McLuhan regarded it as such. The Canadian thinker who, back in the 1960s, anticipated the arrival of today's "global village" insisted that nobody could understand his work "who is not completely familiar with all the works of James Joyce." McLuhan spoke of his communications theory as "applied Joyce," and his working title for both *The Gutenberg Galaxy* and *Understanding Media* was *The Road to Finnegans Wake*.

So while contemporary fiction writers owe Joyce for stream-of-consciousness technique, Canadians generally are in his debt for "the ways we speak and think about communication." Theorists Donald and Joan Theall explain that "McLuhan borrowed, though he also changed and adapted, many of his insights from Joyce." In the *Canadian Journal of Communication*, they write that McLuhan was dazzled by the Irish writer's boldness: "No one before Joyce had set about to explore our universe of signs with the encyclopedic thoroughness that he did."

⬚⬚⬚

In the twentieth century, Ireland produced an astonishing array of winners of the Nobel Prize for Literature. William Butler Yeats, George Bernard Shaw, Samuel Beckett, Seamus Heaney: these four emerged from an Irish literary tradition that can be traced back to at least the sixth century. An Irish missionary, Saint Columba (521–597), helped launch that literary history when he founded a now-famous monastic site on the Scottish island of Iona.

The longevity of the tradition helps to explain why literary genius is so at home in Ireland: Maria Edgeworth, John Millington Synge, Flann O'Brien, Oliver Goldsmith, Brendan Behan, Sean O'Casey, Elizabeth Bowen, Bram Stoker. In recent decades, the Irish have added another multitude: John Banville, Edna O'Brien, Frank McCourt, Colm Tóibín, Roddy Doyle.

Yet, in all this distinguished company, Joyce remains the towering figure. He is alone in having been honoured by *Time* magazine as one of the one hundred most important people of the twentieth century. Born in Dublin on February 2, 1882, Joyce was the oldest of ten surviving children whose parents soon began a long, slow slide down the social scale. Through most of his childhood, his father, a heavy drinker, worked as a collector of property taxes.

Joyce was nearing the age of nine when, in November 1890, Charles Stewart Parnell was found guilty of adultery and hounded from political office, only to die the following year. Joyce's father, an ardent Parnellite, denounced his own Roman Catholic Church for betraying the politician. As an adult, Joyce drew the same conclusion: he writes of Parnell in every one of his books. And at thirty, he published an essay, *The Shade of Parnell*, detailing what he regarded as the betrayal of that statesman, who remained, according to biographer Gordon Bowker, "an enduring passion and defining part of his identity."

As a boy, Joyce spent four years at Clongowes Wood College, a Jesuit boarding school founded by Daniel O'Connell and one of Parnell's grandfathers. He had to leave when his father, about to lose his job, could no longer afford the fees. At sixteen, after finishing his secondary education in Dublin at Belvedere College, another Jesuit school, Joyce enrolled at University College. While a student, he attracted attention by publishing reviews and articles, and by publicly abandoning the Catholic Church.

At twenty, when he sat down with William Butler Yeats over coffee in a downtown restaurant, he told the older writer, with the arrogance of youth and the bravado of genius: "We have met too late. You are too old for me to have any effect on you." Joyce got accepted into the medical faculty at the University of Paris, but soon after arriving in the City of Light, he abandoned medicine, obtained a "ticket," or library card, for the Bibliothèque Nationale, and, while living hand to mouth, resumed his literary pursuits. According to Bowker, Joyce had "discovered that hunger and privation were preferable to the constraints of religion and the demands of nationalism."

Back in Ireland in 1904, Joyce began *Stephen Hero*, a novel that would evolve into *A Portrait of the Artist as a Young Man*. On June 16, he spent his first evening with his future wife, Nora Barnacle. Later, he marked that turning point in his life by setting the action of *Ulysses* on that date. Now the young writer yearned again for continental Europe. From the long-suffering Yeats in London, with whom he had left a sheaf of poems and prose "epiphanies,"

he received an encouraging letter. He consulted Lady Gregory—
the playwright, theatre patron, and friend of Yeats—who promised
some financial assistance should he line up a teaching job in Paris.
He managed that, then convinced Nora Barnacle to join him and,
in October 1904, left Ireland for the continent.

In *A Portrait of the Artist as a Young Man*, his alter ego, Stephen
Dedalus, sets out "to forge in the smithy of my soul the uncreated
conscience of my race." In real life, Joyce spent the next decade
shuttling around Europe. He had an extraordinary facility with languages, spoke several fluently, and claimed to understand eleven.
For a while he worked in a bank in Rome, but mainly he taught
English in Trieste, Italy. He fathered a son and a daughter and, with
the help of his brother, Stan, managed to keep the household afloat
while devoting his best energies to writing.

Joyce struggled to find a publisher for *Dubliners,* a classic story
collection which Irish printers perceived as dangerously subversive. During the nine years leading to 1914, when *Dubliners* finally
appeared, Joyce submitted the book to fifteen publishers. Two
years later, when *A Portrait of the Artist as a Young Man* surfaced,
it drew raves on the continent but mixed reviews in Ireland. The
novel's audacity extended into the political realm. It communicated
a transnational perspective (almost Canadian) and, as the Thealls
write, explored "the disinheriting of Irish culture by England."
Marshall McLuhan, having converted to Roman Catholicism as an
adult, "interprets Joyce while evading Joyce's overt commitment to
socialism and anarchism, as well as his critique of the Church and
the politics of contemporary Europe."

In 1915, with the First World War escalating, Joyce had moved
from Italy to Zurich in neutral Switzerland, and there spent the next
four years. By now he was deeply engaged in writing *Ulysses*. With
Portrait, he had pushed stream-of-consciousness writing as far as it
could go. Now he moved beyond that groundbreaking technique,

running "the stream" through a multitude of narrative voices or points of view. The work presents such a detailed evocation of Dublin in 1904 that Joyce claimed the city could be rebuilt from his novel.

As he focused on writing this wildly ambitious work, Joyce never ceased obsessing over Ireland. The uprising of 1916 shocked him with its violence. He was stunned by the execution of Patrick Pearse, one of the ringleaders—a man who had taught him Irish (Gaelic). Then an old friend, Francis Sheehy-Skeffington, was shot dead while leading a pacifist demonstration. None of this fostered any desire to return to the land of his birth.

The American Sylvia Beach published *Ulysses* through her Paris-based bookstore, Shakespeare and Company, in 1922. Joyce's most sophisticated contemporaries recognized it as a work of genius. The poet T. S. Eliot described it as "the most important expression which the present age has found; it is a book to which we are all indebted, and from which none of us can escape." A French critic pronounced Joyce the greatest living English-language writer, and added: "With this book, Ireland is making a sensational re-entrance into high European literature."

The most audacious novel of the twentieth century, *Ulysses* dazzled Ernest Hemingway, Thomas Wolfe, William Faulkner, and Anthony Burgess. The work opened up entire lines of influence into Canada—not just into the stream-of-consciousness fiction of Nobel Prize winner Alice Munro, but also, through Edna O'Brien, to Irish-Canadian Emma Donoghue, and, through Thomas Wolfe and Jack Kerouac, to Ray Robertson and others.

After writing *Ulysses,* and while struggling with ulcers, failing eyesight, and a troubled daughter, Joyce produced one more major work, *Finnegans Wake.* Here, pushing stream of consciousness to its limits, he abandoned conventional narrative and character development for wordplay, allusions, and free association. Defiantly Irish, the book rummages through Joyce's personal past while revisiting

Irish figures from the mythical Finn MacCool to Oscar Wilde and, of course, Charles Stewart Parnell.

The musical *Wake* entranced Marshall McLuhan. In this work, Joyce plays with the tension between oral and written expression, between writing and print. He does this, the Thealls observe, "in his own practice of writing as well as writing about it. The oral and the written became both medium and message, so that quite literally in the *Wake* the medium is the message." McLuhan's philosophical ancestry—and that of his many followers—would appear to be established beyond doubt.

When James Joyce died in 1941, he was buried in Zurich without religious ceremony. Around the world, his death elicited literary paeans. Ireland was slow to embrace this most iconoclastic of native sons, but came eventually to lead the world in celebrating Bloomsday every June 16—the date on which James Joyce first walked out with Nora Barnacle, the woman he would marry.

This larger-than-life bronze of James Joyce, created by Marjorie FitzGibbon, stands near O'Connell Street in Dublin. For Joyce, the artist remained "above his handiwork, invisible, refined out of existence, indifferent, paring his fingernails."

PART FIVE

PERSEVERANCE

Whewn we consider perseverance, we Canadians often forget the beaver. But we shouldn't. Except for a small minority of humans, beavers are the most industrious mammals the world has ever known. When they move into an area, attracted by running water, they cut down trees to build a dam, and they work day and night until they are done. Using their big front teeth, they sever six-inch tree trunks. They trim and cut rough trees into short logs and drag these into position. Using mud and rock to wedge the logs in place, they build dams that reach a hundred metres in length. And they don't quit until they are done. That is why, despite a righteous campaign to honour the polar bear, the beaver deserves to remain our national animal.

More than most peoples, thanks to our Celtic (Norse-Gaelic) heritage, we Canadians value determination, persistence, industriousness, tenacity, resolution, and grit—all present in our favourite buck-toothed rodent. Yet when we hear the word "perseverance," we forget the workaholic beaver. The higher-minded among us think of Vimy Ridge. We think of how, during the First World War, Canadian soldiers achieved an impossible victory at Vimy in France, taking the heavily fortified position by forcing their way across a killing field where the Allied nations had already lost more than one hundred thousand troops to withering fire.

Younger, less history-oriented Canadians might think, alternatively, of Silken Laumann, and remember how, in May 1992, while training for the Summer Olympics, the twenty-seven-year-old athlete battled back after suffering an accident that would have devastated most people. The Canadian rower, who had won a gold medal in single sculls at the previous year's world championships, shattered her right leg in a collision with another boat. "I looked at the leg for a few seconds," she said later, in a widely reported interview, "and knew it was serious when my muscle was hanging at my ankle and I could see the bone."

Doctors told her she might never row again. Obviously, they had never encountered the courage, drive, and tenacity that this Mississauga-born athlete now found within herself. Of the ten weeks that remained before the Olympics, Laumann spent three in hospital, undergoing five operations. She resumed training and, by late June, was back on the water. On August 2, 1992, Silken Laumann accomplished what has been called "the greatest comeback in Canadian sports history." Competing against the foremost athletes in the world, she won a bronze medal, and was chosen to carry the Canadian flag at the closing ceremonies of the Olympics.

Laumann would win more medals on the international stage, including a silver in single sculls at the 1996 Summer Olympics. She would be inducted into the Canadian Sports Hall of Fame, and win the Thomas Keller Medal for her outstanding career as a rower. But what we Canadians find inspirational, even today, is the grit and determination she showed in coming back from that horrific injury: her resolute refusal to be crushed. Her perseverance.

To certain slightly older Canadians, no use denying it, that word evokes memories of the original Hockey Summit between Canada and Russia. This was an eight-game series between two national teams, both claiming to be the best in the world. Represented by National Hockey League stars, and with the first four games slated to be played in Canada, Canadians expected a cakewalk. Incredibly, the Russians took home a one-game lead. Then, in Moscow, they won game five. Could this really be happening?

Down by two games, and with their backs to the wall, the NHL players tapped into the resolve and determination, the perseverance that is a hallmark of the Canadian psyche. Our team won the next two games, each more physical and fierce than the last. Going into the final game, the series was tied. Not only that. Strange as it seems, the Hockey Summit had become emblematic of the decades-long struggle between two ways of organizing economic life: communism versus capitalism.

Game eight arrived: September 28, 1972. Across Canada, people gathered around television sets in their workplaces. Schools suspended classes and held assemblies so students (and teachers) could watch the contest. Ryerson Polytechnic Institute in Toronto, where I was studying journalism, mounted television sets here and there in the hallways. I remember the final moments of the third period, standing in Jorgenson Hall, watching with an excited throng of fellow students. Canada had just scored to tie the game five-all. We all knew that this was not good enough. The Russians had outscored Team Canada overall, thirty-two to thirty, and if the game ended in a tie, they would claim victory. Seven minutes remained in the series. Six minutes, five.

Back and forth the players went, up and down the ice. Then came what Canadian hockey fans call the Goal of the Century. Deep in the Russian end zone, Phil Esposito corralled a loose puck and, off-balance, fired a weak shot at the net. The Russian goalie, Vladislav Tretiak, gave up a rebound and Paul Henderson banged at the puck. Tretiak kicked out that shot . . . but Henderson kept banging away, there was no quit in him, and, suddenly, the puck bounced into the Russian net. "He scores!" Foster Hewitt shouted what, though scarcely believing, we could see for ourselves: "Henderson has scored for Canada!"

With thirty-four seconds remaining, Canada had won the series. Of course, we went nuts, yelling and jumping up and down. Today, you can watch a YouTube video of the endgame in which a narrator suggests that the Henderson goal defined "the heart and character of Canadian hockey." Arriving at the end of a twenty-seven-day tournament, during which the Canadian team battled back from an overwhelming deficit, winning the last three games in a row, that turnaround illustrates the fifth bedrock value we Canadians have inherited from our Celtic ancestors.

One more example? We need only recall April 12, 1980, when in St. John's, Newfoundland, a young western Canadian man dipped his artificial leg in the Atlantic Ocean. Then he faced west and set out to run to Vancouver, 7,500 kilometres away, using a distinctive hopping motion that Canadians who saw him would never forget. Bent on raising money for cancer research, Terry Fox had begun his Marathon of Hope. That marathon, and the courage Fox displayed, would inspire hundreds of thousands of people around the world.

Born in Winnipeg on July 28, 1958, Fox grew up mostly in Port Coquitlam, British Columbia, where dogged persistence enabled him to excel as both an athlete and a student. But in March 1977, soon after learning he had a cancerous tumour, he had his right leg amputated six inches above the knee. Just before undergoing the operation, he read a magazine article about an amputee runner, Dick Traum, who had participated in the New York Marathon. "I was lying in bed looking at this magazine," he said later, "thinking if he can do it, I can do it, too."

In a biography entitled *Terry Fox: His Story*, Leslie Scrivener describes how, at the hospital, during treatment, Terry heard doctors telling children they had a 15 per cent chance of living. He heard youngsters crying in pain, and saw lives cut short. And when, after sixteen months of rehabilitation, he finally went home, he began training for what he called his "Marathon of Hope."

Using what today experts would regard as a rudimentary prosthesis, the young man whipped himself into shape by running more than five thousand kilometres. He pushed his wheelchair along the seawall at Vancouver's Stanley Park and tackled steep trails and rough logging roads, pushing himself until his hands bled. "I'm not a dreamer," he told the Canadian Cancer Society when he sought its backing. "And I'm not saying this will initiate any kind of definitive answer or cure to cancer, but I believe in miracles. I have to."

On April 12, 1980, accompanied by a few friends and family members, Terry Fox started running west out of St. John's. Initially, media coverage was light. But as weeks passed and, along the Trans-Canada Highway, Terry put distance behind him, news of his quixotic undertaking began to spread.

By the time he reached Ontario, Canadians were lining the road to see him pass, pounding forward with his fists clenched, eyes fixed on the road ahead, his gait distinctive, unforgettable. Often, people wept. Terry would set out each morning before dawn, running in shorts and a T-shirt printed with a map of Canada. "Some people can't figure out what I'm doing," he said at one point. "It's not a walk-hop, it's not a trot, it's running, or as close as I can get to running, and it's harder than doing it on two legs. It makes me mad when people call this a walk. If I was walking it wouldn't be anything."

Donations began pouring in. One day in southern Ontario, his friends and family collected twenty thousand dollars on the highway. In Gravenhurst, population eight thousand, locals raised more than fourteen thousand dollars. Terry Fox kept running. He refused to pause even to go for a checkup. "If I ran to a doctor every time I got a little cyst or abrasion," he said, "I'd still be in Nova Scotia. Or else I'd never have started. I've seen people in so much pain. The little bit of pain I'm going through is nothing. They can't shut it off, and I can't shut down every time I feel a little sore."

But on September 1, outside Thunder Bay, Terry Fox collapsed. "The day before I'd run twenty-six miles," he said later. "Now I couldn't even walk across the street." Doctors confirmed that the cancer had spread to his lungs. At a press conference, he said that he had to go home and "have some more X-rays or maybe an operation that will involve opening up my chest or more drugs. I'll do everything I can. I'm going to do my very best. I'll fight. I promise I won't give up."

His father, Rolly Fox, sitting beside him at a table, said, "I think it's unfair. Very unfair."

"I don't feel this is unfair," Terry said. "That's the thing about cancer. I'm not the only one. It happens all the time, to other people. I'm not special. This just intensifies what I did. It gives it more meaning. It'll inspire more people. I could have sat on my rear end, I could have forgotten what I'd seen in the hospital, but I didn't."

Over 143 days, pausing only to give short, inspirational speeches, Terry Fox had run a distance of 5,373 kilometres, covering the equivalent of almost one twenty-six-mile marathon each day. On June 28, 1981, one month shy of his twenty-third birthday, and with his family around him, Terry Fox succumbed to cancer. By that time, he had become a Companion of the Order of Canada, the youngest ever. He had also received the American Cancer Society's Sword of Hope.

After his death, the honours multiplied. Terry Fox was inducted into the Canadian Sports Hall of Fame and, in 1999, was voted Canada's Greatest Hero. Statues were erected in his honour across the country, and buildings, roads, and parks were named after him, as well as an 2,640-metre peak in the Rocky Mountains. In Ontario, an eighty-five-kilometre stretch of the Trans-Canada Highway between Nipigon and Thunder Bay is called the Terry Fox Courage Highway.

The annual Terry Fox Run, first held in 1981, has become the world's largest one-day fundraiser for cancer. It flourishes in more than fifty countries. The Terry Fox Foundation, inspired by the young man's courage and dedicated to preserving his ideals, has raised more than $650 million for cancer research. It inspires hope and, indeed, action around the globe. But for Canadians, Terry Fox himself remains the principal focus and inspiration. He personifies tenacity, grit, and perseverance. Together with Vimy Ridge, Silken Laumann, and the Goal of the Century, Terry Fox shows why we keep forgetting the beaver. We have too many human examples.

That leaves one question unanswered. Where, among our newly recognized Celtic ancestors, should we look to find those figures who carried forward the perseverance meme, transmitting it through time and, eventually, across the Atlantic? The obvious place to begin searching is among those Scottish and Irish figures who made a habit of testing their human limitations against nature at its most ferocious. Less obviously, we might soon find ourselves in London's Westminster Abbey.

25.

Letitia Mactavish Hargrave

❈❈❈

To call the residence "a castle" would set up false expectations, even though a corbelled parapet rings the top of the attached round tower. That was our assessment anyway, when in 2011, having turned off the highway (B842) in Kintyre, Sheena and I followed the private drive through the woods to what is essentially a splendid country mansion. When Letitia Mactavish was growing up here in the 1830s, she called it Kilchrist House. And Letitia was the reason we had come.

Today, according to its website, Kilchrist Castle offers "glorious self-catering accommodation" within easy reach of both Campbeltown and the Mull of Kintyre. It combines contemporary conveniences with a high-ceilinged dining room and many restored features and furniture. The place was being renovated when we passed that way, or we would have stayed there ourselves, if only to imagine coming of age there more fully.

In autumn 1837, Letitia would have been twenty-three or twenty-four when, at the urging of her brother, William Mactavish, James Hargrave visited Kilchrist House. She must have gone walking in the woods with Hargrave, who was fifteen years older, and probably sat quietly with him in the charming garden beside the house. Then Hargrave was summoned on urgent business to return to York Fort on Hudson Bay, where he was in charge as chief trader.

Letitia Mactavish was in her early twenties when James Hargrave visited Kilchrist House, three miles south of Campbeltown. Her father built the residence in 1834.

And so he proposed by mail, with as florid a letter as any Victorian Scottish gentleman could concoct. "Rash you thought me," he wrote of what must have been some unexpected declaration. "Ah, little did you know how beat my heart as I willingly yielded my affections and offering to love,—or how reason applauded & still applauds the offering."

Letitia accepted, also by letter, and remained at Kilchrist House for two more years. Then Hargrave again turned up. He married her in January 1840 and whisked her away for an extended honeymoon in London. There, thinking of entertaining herself in the wilds, the well-educated, sharp-witted Letitia purchased what she described as "a 1st-rate square piano, seasoned for any extremes of climate."

In June, she and her husband sailed from Gravesend, near London, on a Hudson's Bay Company cargo ship called the *Prince Rupert*. After calling in at Stromness, Orkney, they crossed the Atlantic in cramped quarters. Of arriving at York Fort in August, she wrote, "I can give you very little idea of my feelings as for some days or weeks I had been so wretched that Hargrave thought if I went on shore at all it would have been rolled and carried in a blanket."

When the rising tide enabled her to make for shore, she wrote that "my first exploit on being lowered into the yawl, was to turn my back to the company and cry myself sick." But then, looking about, she pulled herself together: "I had no sooner got out of the yawl than I felt better and have ever since got stronger."

In 1840, Letitia Mactavish Hargrave arrived at York Fort (depicted here in 1853). "My first exploit," she wrote, "was to turn my back to the company and cry myself sick."

In *Canadian Exploration Literature*, anthologist Germaine Warkentin writes that Letitia Hargrave was different from the few other British women who ventured to western Canada during the fur-trade era. Her earliest letters to her mother, which she wrote from London during her honeymoon, "show her lively and impetuous temperament," Warkentin notes, "and her ability to adapt rapidly to new scenes; she was quick to judge and just as quick to withdraw her judgement, sharp of tongue yet as ready to laugh at herself as at others."

Unlike other ladylike immigrants, Letitia Hargrave adjusted to living at the back of beyond. Her evolution is reflected in her letters, which extend over more than a decade. Warkentin observes that "she matures from a gawking, seasick provincial into a shrewd and experienced reporter on the fur trade and all that went on amidst the lively scene of York Fort." Some latter-day scholars have described Letitia as a snob, and in her early days, especially, she upheld class and educational differences.

Yet alone among her peers and contemporaries, Letitia Hargrave endured. She persevered. Between 1840 and 1854, this astute, articulate woman sent home a steady stream of vivid, insightful letters. Collected in *The Letters of Letitia Hargrave* (1947), they constitute a work of singular importance to Canadian history. Vivid, unselfconscious, addressed mostly to her family back home at Kilchrist House, Hargrave's letters constitute the only extended portrayal we have of life in the fur trade from a woman's point of view.

※※

Born in Edinburgh in 1813, Letitia Mactavish belonged to one of the most powerful families in the fur trade. Granddaughter to the Mactavish Clan chieftain, she was also the oldest child of lawyer Dugald Mactavish, a prominent "sheriff," or judge, in Argyllshire. While still young, she moved with her family to Kilchrist House, five kilometres south of Campbeltown, and eight kilometres from the Mull of Kintyre. She was educated by tutors and then at a finishing school.

When Letitia Mactavish was twenty-one, her brother William joined the Hudson's Bay Company and was posted to York Fort on the western shores of Hudson Bay. Like other HBC posts, the fort would become a "factory" when a "factor" took charge, a land agent who acted on behalf of an absentee owner. Thus we have Moose Factory, Albany Factory, York Factory, and so forth. On being made a chief factor, an HBC man ceased to be a salaried employee and became a partner who received a share of company profits.

At York Fort, the senior figure was James Hargrave. He was still a chief trader, one giant step below chief factor, but governor George Simpson had described him as "a Scotchman . . . of good education and of highly correct conduct and character and very useful." Hargrave had a good business head and was "better qualified for a seat in council than 9 out of 10 of our present Chief Factors." To this man, his boss, young William Mactavish spoke glowingly of his older sister, and urged him to visit Kilchrist House.

At roughly the same time, he wrote to Letitia that "very few women would have strength of mind enough to encounter the severe winter of an inland post, where she will not see more than one or two people and probably she cannot speak so as to be understood to any but her husband."

Rupert's Land in the 1840s was decidedly no place for a lady. In *Many Tender Ties*, Sylvia Van Kirk writes that life there "required considerable physical and psychological adaptation, and the British lady was likely to lack (and would not be encouraged to develop) the bodily strength and mental attitude necessary to make a successful transition." Some young women, she notes, sickened so rapidly that "they soon had to be removed from Indian Country."

For the HBC men, Van Kirk writes, Rupert's Land involved hard work but also camaraderie. "For white women, however, it meant moving to a strange and physically inferior environment" and severing social and family ties. Fur trader James Douglas, who married a local woman and later became known as the father of British Columbia, looked askance at the "strange revolution in the manners of the country: Indian wives were at one time the vogue; the half-breed supplanted these, and now we have the lovely tender exotic, torn from its parent bed, to pine and languish in the desert."

Frances Simpson, wife of HBC governor George Simpson and friend of Letitia Hargrave, "suffered intensely" while living in Red River Settlement and decamped to England, resuming married life only after her husband relocated to Montreal. Yet Red River, harsh as it could be, was a haven of civilized congeniality compared with bleakly isolated York Fort.

True, Letitia Hargrave lived in relative comfort: she had a well-furnished house complete with a piano, and a personal maid as well as an HBC cook and butler. "I was much surprised at the 'great swell' the Factory is," Letitia wrote. "It looks beautiful . . . Our house is a good size, one bedroom off each sitting room and men servants' rooms off the kitchen, a very large closet off the dining room." And her husband, writing to a friend at Red River, registered no discontent: "Mrs. H. is perfectly contented amid these frozen regions—and what with music, cards, or conversation our winter evenings are now a heavenly contrast to those you and I have known here."

❂

Over the next decade, starting in April 1841, Letitia Hargrave gave birth to five children. When she was pregnant with her second child (who died almost immediately), she had a nursery added to the side of the house. Despite her relative comfort, during the summer, when her husband put in endless hours, often she dined alone. As the only white woman in the area, she proved an object of curiosity, and drew people to her. She writes of "the wee'est girls" coming to visit, wearing their shawls. "Hargrave bought two pounds of peppermint drops at Stromness and they laugh aloud when I give them some. They don't know a word of English or French. When I want flowers or berries I show them a specimen and give them a shove and off they go. It never happens that they fail."

Letitia caused a stir at York Fort with her fashionable gowns, but she added "leggins" and moccasins to her wardrobe, and wrapped herself in furs whenever she went walking or driving in her well-appointed dog carriole. If at times Letitia Hargrave expressed the snobbishness of her class, yet she also empathized across barriers. She castigated a minister at Red River, for example, for keeping Metis children away from mothers who had not been married in a church: "This may be all very right," she wrote, "but it is fearfully cruel, for the poor unfortunate mothers did not know that there was any distinction & it is only within the last few years that any one was so married."

While she expected deference, she became friendly with Metis women such as Harriet Vincent, wife of another chief trader and godmother of her first child. And she expressed shock at the way fur-trade society divided families. "Some people educate and make gentlemen of part of their family and leave the others savages." She cited one young man "who had not been educated and while his father and brothers are nobility at the Colony, he is a voyageur and sat at table with the house servants here. Dr. MacLoughlin, one of our grandees, at a great expense gave two of his sons a regular education in England and keeps the third a common Indian."

At one point a visiting doctor, John Sebastian Helmcken, described Letitia Hargrave as "one of those nice ladies, one occasionally meets with, kind and affable. Altho not handsome she had a decidedly nice face—and a very pleasing expression with a very good figure." Letitia herself, after three years in Rupert's Land, thinking of visiting Kilchrist House, wrote to her parents: "I have a feeling that I would not like to see anyone but yourselves and poor Mary Hamilton. I am so changed within that I daresay I am much so externally and I would shrink from exposing myself to the cool criticism of Mrs. Worsley, who delights in telling me how old people are looking, saying nothing of herself, however."

In her next sentence, she changed subject abruptly to write of a murder at faraway Fort Stikine (now Wrangell, Alaska). John McLoughlin Jr., son of the "grandee" mentioned above, had been killed by men under his command. "There has been nothing further of John MacLoughlin's murder," Letitia wrote, "except that master and men were all drunk, firing at each other till John who was in the condition of a maniac fell dead." Letitia didn't yet have all the facts, and the victim's father later turned up evidence of premeditation. Yet she drew some telling conclusions: "The gentlemen here are too apt to thrash and indeed point their guns at their men, and Mr. Anderson who came across from Vancouver last year was so detested that they confessed that if he had fallen into the River, not one would have held out a stick to him. One gentleman actually was drowned, when he might easily have been saved without a man wetting his foot."

Because her stream-of-consciousness writing is so honest, it evokes her own conflicted feelings: "The truth of the matter is that it is a hideous country for man to live in and that it is yearly getting worse . . . I pity every gentleman in it. Hargrave likes this place and is perfectly contented. I am sure there is not a man in it who would not rejoice to leave it if he could. I am as well pleased with York as at first, I only am so from never thinking. You may believe that the eternal barrenness of white water and black pines are not very enlivening to the spirits. The sky is always beautiful night and day."

Late in the autumn of 1845, explorer John Rae spent the winter at York in preparation for his first Arctic expedition. Letitia

Hargrave, born in precisely the same year as Rae, wrote that her fellow Scot had earned his doctor's diploma unusually early "and has not been home since, nor, he says, opened a medical book for seven years. He is very good-looking, and can walk one hundred miles easily in two days."

Letitia Hargrave believed that "there is not a man in [York Fort] who would not rejoice to leave it if he could." She remained and created a unique portrait of the fur trade.

The editor of Letitia's letters, Margaret Arnett MacLeod, observed that the explorer "must have been a welcome addition to York society, as he was a man of great talents and charming personality. It was said of him that he was as much at home at Court or in a London drawing room as he was in an Indian tent or an Eskimo snow house. He and the Hargraves found many tastes in common."

In 1846, her husband was granted a leave. With him, Letitia and her children visited Scotland and Kilchrist House. They left their eldest son, now six years old, at school in St. Andrews, before returning to York Fort. In March 1849, with the search for Sir John Franklin under way, she noted, "Dr. Rae and Sir John Richardson have come from the 'Sea' and did not see nor hear anything of Captain Franklin. The Gentlemen in the Country all looked very polite and as if Sir John's expedition was a very feasible exploit, but among themselves they either laughed at the whole turn out or seemed astonished that rational beings should undertake such a useless search."

That September, Letitia noted that Richardson had recently started for home: "No one now expect that poor Franklin or his party are alive but Dr. Rae is to go again to the shores of the Arctic Sea this summer with one boat and six men." To this missive, she added: "We have now made up our minds to remain at York during the time it may be necessary for Hargrave to remain in the service." Then, in 1851, Hargrave finally received a promotion to chief factor, and a transfer to Sault Ste. Marie.

Rather than try to travel overland to join him, Letitia sailed once more to Scotland. This time, she left her eldest daughter at school with her son. In 1852, with her two youngest children, she returned to North America by sailing to New York. Her husband met her and travelled with them to the new family home. Letitia had scarcely settled in when, in 1854, a cholera epidemic swept through the Sault. This most persevering of women took sick, quickly grew worse, and suddenly, at age forty-three, passed away.

Even as she lay on her deathbed, unaware that her letters home constituted a singular legacy—a warts-and-all portrait of the fur trade from a female perspective—a near contemporary from Dublin, a man four years younger, was organizing an expedition that would take him through the Sault within three years of her passing. Having got himself elected a fellow of the Royal Geographical Society, John Palliser submitted a plan to explore the southern prairies of British North America and to look for passes through the Rocky Mountains. In June 1857, he canoed westward out of Sault Ste. Marie. His work would be memorialized in Calgary with a five-star hotel.

26.

John Rae

The "ledger stone," as they call it, is brilliantly placed in Westminster Abbey, directly beneath a grandiose bust of Sir John Franklin. The inscription on the memorial could not be more modest and understated: "John Rae / 1813–1893 / Arctic Explorer." The effect is one of completion. In 2014, invited to offer "a reflection" at the dedication ceremony, I spoke of how, thanks to his grit and determination, Rae had completed the work of discovering the Northwest Passage. And, because so many Orcadian Scots had travelled south to attend, I found myself remembering the previous year.

On September 30, 2013, as darkness fell across northern Scotland, several hundred people had gathered on the pier at Stromness, Orkney. We had come to witness the unveiling of a bronze statue of Rae, born on the outskirts of town on this date two hundred years before. The statue, donated by a Stromness businessman, recognized Rae as "the discoverer of the final link in the first navigable Northwest Passage."

John Rae was one of the many Orcadian Scots who, while

working for the Hudson's Bay Company, played a major role in exploring western and northern Canada. A couple of days before the unveiling, Sheena and I had revisited Rae's boyhood home, the Hall of Clestrain, a once-grand mansion now desperately in need of restoration. In my mind's eye, while standing out front, I watched young Rae emerge from the house with a bag on his back and a musket on his shoulder, setting out on his life's adventure.

John Rae's boyhood home, the Hall of Clestrain, cries out for restoration. It is easy to imagine young Rae emerging from the house with a musket on his shoulder.

This young man would become one of the great explorers of the nineteenth century, with several stunning triumphs to his credit. Yet he is best understood as belonging to a long line of Celtic (Norse-Gaelic) adventurers notable for their determination and relentlessness. The written tradition begins with the Voyage of Saint Brendan, which tells the story of an Irish monastic saint who in the sixth century went sailing in search of the Isle of the Blessed.

In the 1970s, the modern Irish explorer Tim Severin replicated that voyage when he spent thirteen months sailing a two-masted wood-and-leather currach from Ireland to Newfoundland.

In the late eighteenth century, Scottish fur trader Alexander Mackenzie became the first explorer to cross North America from the Atlantic to the Pacific Ocean, travelling most of the way by canoe. And then Irish navigator William Brown, born in County Mayo, led Argentine naval forces to so many major victories that he is still celebrated as "the father of the Argentine Navy." In the 1850s, David Livingstone, a hardy, resourceful Scot born the same year as Rae, pioneered the investigation of Africa. He traced the Zambezi River to "the smoke that thunders," a dramatic waterfall that he named after Britain's Queen Victoria. Not long afterwards, Robert O'Hara Burke, an Irish soldier and police officer, led the first expedition across Australia from south to north, losing his life to that undertaking.

In the Arctic, John Rae was not the only shining Scot. John Richardson, a naturalist, saved the life of John Franklin on his initial expedition, and James Clark Ross became the first explorer to reach the North Magnetic Pole. At the far end of earth, working slightly later, the Anglo-Irishman Ernest Shackleton led an epochal trans-Antarctic expedition that even today supports a small industry of celebration. One of the men with him was Tom Crean, the "Irish giant" from County Kerry, who went three times to the Antarctic. During the Terra Nova Expedition of Robert Falcon Scott, Crean completed a stunning, fifty-six-kilometre solo walk across the Ross Ice Shelf to save the life of one of his fellows.

The evident perseverance of these Scottish and Irish explorers illustrates the emergence of a foundational value. By solving the two great mysteries of nineteenth-century exploration, John Rae provided an outstanding example. Rae discovered both the fate of the 1845 expedition led by Sir John Franklin and the final link in the first navigable Northwest Passage. These accomplishments capped a career during which, between 1846 and 1854, drawing on his extraordinary physicality, and methods and techniques gleaned from the native peoples, the persevering Rae led four major Arctic expeditions. He merits special attention as well because in 2014 a Canadian search expedition discovered the *Erebus*, one of the two ships that in 1845 Franklin sailed into the Arctic, and Rae is a key figure in the controversy that is evolving out of that finding.

Born in that lonely Stromness mansion in 1813, the son of a Hudson's Bay Company agent, or "factor," John Rae grew up hunting, fishing, and sailing. As a young man, he began studying medicine in Edinburgh. At nineteen, having qualified as a surgeon, he took a summer job aboard an HBC ship, expecting to return home in the autumn. But ice prevented the *Prince of Wales* from returning. During the ensuing winter, Rae felt drawn to "the wild sort of life to be found in the Hudson's Bay Company service."

Over the next fourteen years, while based at Moose Factory near the bottom of Hudson Bay, Rae apprenticed himself to the native peoples who lived in the area. He learned how to maintain snowshoes, handle a canoe, hunt and cache caribou—basically, how to live off the land. By the mid-1840s, his contemporaries were hailing him not as the greatest rough-country traveller and snowshoe walker employed by the HBC, but as "the greatest of the age." They respected his resourcefulness, his stamina, his visionary intelligence. Above all, they respected his dogged perseverance.

In 1846–47, Rae became the first European explorer to spend a winter above the Arctic Circle while living off the land. With two small boats and a dozen men, he sailed north from York Factory on Hudson Bay. While wintering at Repulse Bay, Rae mapped 655 miles of coastline, so demonstrating that Boothia Peninsula was not an island, as widely supposed, and proving that no northwest passage flowed through it.

John Rae, portrayed in 1854 in the Illustrated London News. *The Arctic explorer had just returned with news of the tragic fate of the 1845 expedition of Sir John Franklin.*

Eventually, on his four Arctic expeditions, Rae would survey 1,765 miles of uncharted territory while travelling 6,555 miles on snowshoes and sailing 6,700 miles in small boats. On this first expedition, as on every one he later led, Rae served as chief hunter and supplier of food. Here, too, he stood alone among his contemporaries. Rae kept a journal, of course, and it was first published in 1850.

Within that narrative, and as an outdoorsman, Rae presents numerous entertaining moments. On one occasion, out hunting deer before daybreak, he spots a group of animals moving rapidly towards him. These turn out to be seventeen wolves. They race to within forty yards of him, when they break off into a semicircle. Rae drops to one knee, takes aim at the leader, and fires. In the grey light he merely grazes the wolf, cutting off a line of hair and skin. "They apparently did not expect to meet with such a reception," he tells us, "for after looking at me a second or two they trotted off, no doubt as much disappointed at not making a breakfast of me as I was at missing my aim. Had they come to close quarters (which they sometimes do when pressed for food), I had a large and strong knife which would have proved a very efficient weapon."

In November 1847, Rae returned to London on leave from the HBC and published a summary of his expedition in the London *Times*. The Admiralty had dispatched Franklin more than two years before, expecting that he would quickly solve the riddle of the Northwest Passage and emerge into the Pacific Ocean trailing clouds of glory. Now, concerned that he and his men might run out of supplies, those in charge had begun organizing search expeditions, mostly by sea.

But an overland search would be led by Sir John Richardson, a Scot born in Dumfries, and educated with one of the sons of Robert Burns. Now fifty-nine years of age and serving as a hospital administrator, Richardson—a leading naturalist, but no great traveller—had not set foot in the north for twenty years. He was seeking a second-in-command who would compensate for his deficiencies. When he read Rae's brief report about his 1846 expedition in the *Times*, he jumped to his feet and cried out to his wife, "I have found my companion, if I can get him."

Energetic, resourceful, and an avid practitioner of Inuit travel methods, the thirty-four-year-old Rae had thrived for months in one of the most extreme environments on the planet. Richardson had instantly recognized what Alan Cooke, curator at the Scott Polar Research Institute (SPRI), later described as Rae's practicality, incisive foresight, and "contempt for orthodox opinion and incompetence." He recognized that Rae was an inspirational leader of almost superhuman endurance.

The wilderness expert jumped at the chance to join the legendary naturalist in seeking Franklin. The two Scots left England in 1848, made their way into the north mostly by canoe, and spent a cold dark winter at Fort Confidence. Come spring, Richardson tacitly acknowledged that he was superfluous and retreated to England. The determined Rae continued the quest, and explored the Arctic coast from the Mackenzie River to the Coppermine.

Then, in 1850–51, he conducted one of the most remarkable sledge-and-boat expeditions in Arctic exploration history. First, he slogged across an ice-covered strait in late winter, and then, as the ice melted, he continued exploring in two small sailboats. During this outing, he charted most of the southern and eastern coast of Victoria Island. When his boats got blocked by ice, he took to trekking along the coast, which was so rough and rocky that "in two hours, a pair of new moccasins, with thick undressed Buffalo skin soles, and stout duffle socks were completely worn out, and before the day's journey was half done every step I took was marked with blood."

Before he was done searching and surveying, Rae charted more than 1,750 miles of territory, including 1,538 miles of Arctic coastline (much of Boothia Peninsula and Victoria Island).

In 1854, the peerless Rae was surveying the western coastline of Boothia Peninsula when he chanced upon some Inuit hunters. This meeting would turn his life upside down, giving rise to suspicion, speculation, and outright denunciation. Rae's handwritten, nine-hundred-page autobiography ends abruptly in mid-sentence, just as the explorer is about to glean the first inkling of the disaster that had engulfed the 1845 expedition of Sir John Franklin.

The work describes how, in April 1854, at age forty-one, Rae was slogging across Boothia Peninsula in the High Arctic, beating his way through heavy snow. "It was impossible to keep a straight course," he writes, "and we had to turn to the northward out of our course, so as to select the . . ."

There ends the manuscript, with Rae about to meet the Inuit hunters and hear allegations that would excite Victorian England to frenzy. But what had happened to the rest of the work? Scholars wondered about that for years. In 1968, Alan Cooke, curator at the SPRI in Cambridge, England, expressed both pride at acquiring the manuscript and "intense disappointment" at the way it ended. "What became of the rest of the manuscript?" Cooke asked. "Certainly once there was more. After recounting in full flow the events of so many years, Rae would not have found it possible to stop just short of the greatest discovery of his career."

Some readers suggested that Rae might have suppressed the remainder of the manuscript because it revealed some dark secret he had decided to bury. The mystery remained unsolved until 1998, when I spent three months in Cambridge, scouring the files at SPRI for what would become *Fatal Passage: The Untold Story of John Rae, the Arctic Adventurer Who Discovered the Fate of Franklin.* While researching, I discovered that Rae had sent the long-lost final pages of his journal to an editor, D. Murray Smith, for inclusion in a comprehensive survey entitled *Arctic Expeditions from British and Foreign Shores / From the Earliest Times to the Expedition of 1875–76.*

John Rae was buried behind St. Magnus Cathedral in Kirkwall, Orkney, in 1893. Two years later, this Portland stone memorial was unveiled inside the cathedral.

And those pages changed nothing of what Rae had reported. The Inuit hunters informed him that the Franklin expedition had ended in disaster, with the final survivors resorting to cannibalism. Saddened but not shocked—he had spent most of his adult life in the Arctic and knew its rigours—Rae collected relics from the hunters and other Inuit. The melting ice made it impossible for Rae to cross the channel to visit the location where the tragedy had unfolded. He returned to England with what he had learned. On arriving, he sent a brief, upbeat letter to the *Times*.

To the Admiralty, as to his superiors in the HBC, he sent a more detailed report. This latter report, which he had not intended for publication, ended up on the front page of the *Times*. Lady Franklin, the widow of Sir John, was shocked and devastated, and then outraged. Victorian England responded the same way. Cannibalism? Among the men of the Royal Navy? Impossible!

The Inuit testimony Rae delivered undermined the campaign, orchestrated by Lady Franklin, to glorify her dead husband as discoverer of the Northwest Passage. To repudiate Rae, that resourceful woman enlisted the aid of Charles Dickens, the most influential writer of the age, and also the publisher of a weekly journal, *Household Words*. Not surprisingly, Dickens produced an eloquent tour de force, arguing from historical precedent.

He denigrated the explorer's Inuit sources. As I wrote in *Fatal Passage*, his two-part essay was "a masterpiece of obfuscation, self-deception, and almost wilful blindness." More than that, some sections of the two-part screed reveal such a profound racism that they must be read to be believed. Consider the passage that begins: "The word of a savage is not to be taken for it [cannibalism]; firstly because he is a liar; secondly because he is a boaster; thirdly because he talks figuratively . . ."

That is not the worst of it. By the end, Dickens stands revealed in such an unflattering light that, in the docudrama *Passage*, which is based on *Fatal Passage*, one of the author's twenty-first-century descendants (Gerald Dickens) offers a public apology to the Inuit. As for the dispute over cannibalism, and the refusal by some to believe that it occurred, contemporary forensic researchers have vindicated Rae and his Inuit informants in every particular.

In his own time, despite the tempest of insult and negativity, John Rae recanted nothing. He defended the integrity of his Inuit informants and the truth of his report. Thanks mainly to the machinations of Lady Franklin, however, historians and mapmakers ignored many of his achievements and only grudgingly acknowledged those they could not disregard.

To his credit, Charles Dickens concluded his exchange with the explorer by publishing Rae's original, 1854 report to the Hudson's

Bay Company. In it, Rae describes eventually travelling north along the west coast of Boothia Peninsula with just two men, an Inuk and an Ojibwa. He discovers that King William Land is "clearly an island"—one separated from Boothia Peninsula by a previously unknown strait. Shortly after coming to this realization, he writes, "having taken possession of our discoveries in the usual form, and built a cairn, we commenced our return."

By finding a strait between Boothia and King William Island, John Rae had discovered the final link in the only Northwest Passage navigable by ships of that era. Yet he would remain the one towering explorer never to receive a knighthood. Nor would he be recognized in Westminster Abbey until September 2014, when on what would have been his 201st birthday, officials placed that ledger stone in his honour.

Accorded the privilege of saying a few words, I spoke of how Rae had completed the work begun by Franklin. In 1846, after sailing south down Peel Sound from Parry Channel, the good Sir John got trapped in the pack ice at the northwest corner of King William Island. Eight years later, John Rae discovered not just the most salient features of the tragic fate of the Franklin expedition, but a channel to the east of King William Island—Rae Strait—that would prove to be the final link in the first navigable Northwest Passage.

Half a century later, when Roald Amundsen became the first explorer to sail through the passage from beginning to end, he explicitly credited Rae with having shown him the secret of how to sail beyond King William Island. Nobody would pass through Victoria Strait, where Franklin's ships got trapped, until 1967, when a Canadian icebreaker pounded through.

At Westminster Abbey, in the Chapel of St. John the Evangelist, I outlined all this to an enthusiastic audience which included many Orcadians. After evensong in the splendiferous abbey, we adjourned to a reception at the government's Scottish Office. This was home base for Alistair Carmichael, the politician who, backed by countless Orcadians and the John Rae Society, had spearheaded the final, successful drive to get Rae recognized in the abbey. As one woman put it, looking around at the reception, "This is an occasion we will never forget."

One year after a statue in Stromness recognized John Rae as "the discoverer of the final link in the first navigable Northwest Passage," a simple ledger stone was installed at Westminster Abbey: "John Rae / 1813–1893 / Arctic Explorer."

27.

Sir Ernest Shackleton

⌘

Westminster Abbey, the heart of history-rich London, will be the site of yet another polar commemoration in May 2016. People will gather to celebrate the centenary of a stunning Antarctic voyage by Sir Ernest Shackleton, a man who *almost* joined the ranks of those who explored the Canadian Arctic. "Now my eyes are turned from the South to the North," Shackleton wrote in 1920, "and I want to lead one more expedition. This will be the last . . . to the North Pole."

Shackleton visited Canada and drummed up financial support among Canadians. He also gleaned promises from the Canadian government, which then, inexplicably, withdrew them. The explorer eventually secured funding from a wealthy school friend, but too late in the season. He cancelled the northern voyage and looked again to the south.

Shackleton never did explore Canadian territory. And it would be easy enough to write of persevering Irish adventurers who did, among them Francis Leopold McClintock, who elaborated on John Rae's discovery of the fate of the Franklin expedition, and

Francis Crozier, who lost his life on Franklin's ill-fated voyage. But Shackleton's achievements in the Antarctic were such that Canadians who begin by getting interested in the Arctic often study them as models of perseverance and survival in the polar regions. They add a global dimension to our Celtic heritage.

Born in Ireland, Shackleton himself never fit comfortably into any national box. In 1911, for example, he was living in London but, as some complained, proved himself to be no Englishman at all when news arrived that Roald Amundsen had become the first man to reach the South Pole. First he sent a cable: "Heartiest congratulations magnificent achievement." Then he wrote in the *Daily Mail* that Amundsen "is perhaps the greatest Polar explorer of today." Speaking from experience, Shackleton praised the preparedness and speed of the Antarctic crossing: "The outstanding feature is that Amundsen made for himself an entirely new route." Meanwhile, the *Times* of London harrumphed that the reason Amundsen had outraced the Englishman "probably lies in the much more favourable route which the Norwegian chanced to take." Besides, he succeeded thanks to "British forerunners, Captain Scott himself among them."

In the *Daily Chronicle*, Shackleton insisted that "the same endurance, the same skill and the same meed of endeavour must be granted to Amundsen, as the Norwegian people would grant to [Robert Falcon] Scott if the positions were reversed" and Scott had been the first to reach the South Pole.

Scott's wife, Kathleen, complained to a friend, "Shackleton is behaving in a thoroughly Shackletonian fashion. I think he is delighted at the turn things have taken—I would willingly assist at that man's assassination."

Shackleton was out of step with English public opinion because he was Irish, as Roland Huntford demonstrated in his award-winning biography, *Shackleton*. In the first sentence of that authoritative work, he declares: "Ernest Henry Shackleton was an

Anglo-Irishman." He then explains that the Anglo-Irish were "an extraordinary breed," at once hereditary rulers of Ireland and an embattled Protestant minority with English roots often centuries old: "They identified so passionately with the country they ruled that they considered themselves Irish, and English hardly at all."

Ernest Shackleton was always out of step with English public opinion because he was essentially Irish. His father was Anglo-Irish and his mother Irish Catholic.

Even so, Shackleton managed "to break the mould of mediocrity that bedevilled British polar exploration." He brought "character and humour" to the adventure, showed what leadership can achieve, and "created in England the image of the polar explorer as hero." In 1916, Shackleton also set a new benchmark for perseverance, especially with his extraordinary open-boat journey of 1,400 kilometres, which set the stage for a legendary rescue.

Ernest Henry Shackleton was born in February 1874 in a country house near Athy in County Kildare, seventy-five kilometres southwest of Dublin. Later that year, Oscar Wilde would arrive at Oxford, William Butler Yeats would turn nine, and Charles Stewart Parnell would run for election for the first time (and lose). In Canada, James Douglas was still basking in having led British Columbia into Confederation three years before. In June, Sir John A. Macdonald would send members of the newly created North West Mounted Police westward to root out American whisky traders. And in July, while visiting his parents near Brantford, Ontario, Alexander Graham Bell would tell his father that he was on the verge of inventing the telephone.

Shackleton's paternal ancestors had arrived in Ireland in the early 1700s from Yorkshire, while his mother's Irish Catholic family had roots in Cork and Kerry. Ernest was the oldest of ten children. When he was six, his father took up medicine at Trinity College and moved the family into Dublin. According to Huntford, young Shackleton was "an ordinarily troublesome boy, and very much the Irishman." Boyhood tales "illustrate persuasiveness, plausibility, and a capacity to hide shrewd calculation under onion skins of charm." When Ernest was ten, his father moved the family again, this time to Sydenham in suburban London, where he began practising medicine.

The boy attended the nearby Fir Lodge Preparatory School, where he internalized what Huntford describes as "the most pervasive Anglo-Irish quality . . . a kind of ambivalence or ambiguity of outlook, arising from the need to be at once Irish and English." On one St. Patrick's Day, he and a fellow Irish pupil were forced to fight each other in honour of the sacred memory of St. Patrick. Huntford summarizes the end result: "An Irishman in England Shackleton remained for the rest of his days."

The young man spoke with an Irish accent. It marked him out when in 1887 he entered Dulwich College, where he was called Mick and "the fighting Shackleton." One of his fellow students reported that he was "rather an odd boy who, in spite of an adventurous nature and the spirit of romance that was in him, loved a book better than a bat, solitude better than a crowd."

He read voraciously, devouring issues of *The Boy's Own Paper*. He especially loved nautical adventures such as Jules Verne's *20,000 Leagues under the Sea*, which celebrates the heroic Captain Nemo. Shackleton took to calling himself Nemo, and used that nickname even as an adult. By age sixteen, he was clamouring to go to sea. His father wanted him to become a doctor, but relented under pressure and allowed him to begin an apprenticeship "before the mast."

Shackleton spent the next four years learning his trade. From ages twenty to twenty-six, he increased his qualifications: second mate, first mate, master mariner. In 1898, with the Union-Castle Line, he carried mail and passengers between Southampton and Cape Town, South Africa. In 1900, while serving in the Boer War aboard a troop ship, he met an army lieutenant whose father was sponsoring the National Antarctic Expedition then being organized—the first such expedition in six decades.

Shackleton seized this opportunity. He voiced his enthusiasm in interviews, and got himself appointed to the expedition as third officer on the ship *Discovery*, so also becoming a sub-lieutenant in the Royal Navy. The expedition leader was Robert Falcon Scott, six years older and recently promoted to commander. Scott ran the ship along Royal Navy lines, and Shackleton was in charge of seawater analysis, plus stores, provisions, and entertainments.

After sailing in July 1901, the ship reached the Antarctic coast the following January. Shackleton took part in an experimental balloon flight and in the expedition's first sledging trip. With the ship iced in through the ensuing winter, Shackleton edited a shipboard magazine, the *South Polar Times*, and, among the crew, became the most popular officer.

In November, Shackleton joined Scott and one other officer in a southward march towards the Pole. These three established a record "farthest south" latitude of 82 degrees, 17 minutes, but Scott described the venture as "a combination of success and failure." All twenty-two of the dogs died as a result of tainted food. And the three men suffered from snow-blindness, frostbite, scurvy, and much else, with Shackleton hit hardest of all. During the trek back to the ship, he could no longer do his share of the work. Travelling companion Edward Wilson wrote in his diary that Shackleton was "very short winded and coughing constantly, with more serious symptoms that need not be detailed here but which are of no small consequence one hundred and sixty miles from the ship."

Back on the *Discovery* in early February, Scott decided to send Shackleton home on a relief ship that had arrived during their southward trek. Some accounts, notably that of the second-in-command, suggest that tensions had already arisen between the two, possibly because of Shackleton's popularity. Back in England the men remained cordial until Scott published *The Voyage of the Discovery* (1904). That narrative cast Shackleton in an unflattering light, and fired his fighting-Irish spirit.

Since returning from the Antarctic, he had helped to outfit two relief ships, including one for the *Discovery*, and worked for a while as a journalist. Early in 1904, he became secretary of the Royal

Scottish Geographical Society. He dabbled in stocks and in 1906 ran unsuccessfully for election in Dundee, Scotland, where as a Liberal Unionist he opposed Irish Home Rule.

Meanwhile, he had begun seeking a chance to lead his own expedition to the Antarctic. He found a primary sponsor in the Anglo-Scottish industrialist William Beardmore, and in February 1907 presented his plans for a British Antarctic expedition to the Royal Geographical Society. Shackleton proposed to reach both the geographical South Pole and the South Magnetic Pole, and managed to raise just enough funds.

Originally, he had intended to use the *Discovery*'s old base in McMurdo Sound. But Scott had claimed that location as a field site, and when, on January 1, 1908, Shackleton sailed the *Nimrod* south from New Zealand, he was seeking to establish a different base of operations. He tried one area and then another, but could find no safe anchorage and set sail for McMurdo Sound. Ice conditions dictated that Shackleton establish a base at Cape Royds, about forty kilometres from the *Discovery* base at Hut Point.

In October, Shackleton and three companions trekked south to within 180 kilometres of the Pole, and so established a new "farthest south" latitude of 88 degrees, 23 minutes. The return journey became a desperate race against starvation, and his companion Frank Wild later described how Shackleton had given him his day's rations: "All the money that was ever minted would not have bought that biscuit and the remembrance of that sacrifice will never leave me."

On a second sortie, three other expedition members pinpointed the location of the South Magnetic Pole. Back in England, feted as a hero, Shackleton published an account of his voyage called *The Heart of the Antarctic* (1909). King Edward VII made him a knight (Sir Ernest Shackleton), and the Royal Geographical Society awarded him a gold medal. An English lord hailed Shackleton for

giving the lie to "the supposed degeneration of the British race," and
the Irish claimed him as well, with the Dublin *Express* attributing
his success to the "qualities that were his heritage as an Irishman."

The government awarded him a grant to clear off debts incurred
by the expedition, and Shackleton undertook a series of lectures.
He promoted several money-making enterprises that failed, and
began contemplating another expedition—notably one involving
a continental Antarctic crossing, which had been announced but
then abandoned by Scottish explorer William Speirs Bruce. After
Amundsen reached the South Pole in 1911, and Scott died in the
attempt, Shackleton described the continental crossing as the "one
great object of Antarctic journeyings" that remained.

Early in 1914, Shackleton published his plan for an Imperial
trans-Antarctic expedition. He would use two ships, the *Endurance*
and the *Aurora,* and establish bases on opposite sides of Antarctica.
Thanks to his iconic status, he raised the necessary funds and
then published one of the most famous advertisements in exploration history: "Men wanted for hazardous journey. Low wages, bit-
ter cold, long hours of complete darkness. Safe return doubtful.
Honour and recognition in event of success." Shackleton had to
sift through more than five thousand applications from those who
wished to join him. He selected men unconventionally, for temperament as much as technical ability, and eventually chose fifty-six
men, assigning twenty-eight to each ship.

In July 1914, with preparations nearing completion, the First
World War erupted. Winston Churchill, the First Lord of the
Admiralty, had been skeptical of the voyage, arguing that the South
Pole had already been discovered: "What is the point of another
expedition?" But in August, despite the war, he wired his approval:
"Proceed." And the two ships sailed from England on what would
one day be regarded as the last great expedition of the Heroic Age
of Polar Exploration.

Shackleton delayed his own departure and caught up with the *Endurance* in Argentina. From there, thanks to the example of Roald Amundsen, who had learned from the Inuit, the ship sailed with sixty-nine Canadian sled dogs. Nine or ten of these, hitched into a team, could haul a thousand pounds. Early in December, having sailed to South Georgia Island, Shackleton continued south but encountered heavy ice. The *Aurora*, torn from its moorings in a storm, and unable to re-enter the ice, struggled back to New Zealand.

Ernest Shackleton left twenty-two men on Elephant Island and set out with five others on an eight-hundred-mile rescue mission to South Georgia Island. Frank Hurley took the photo.

By January, the *Endurance* was frozen fast. And on February 24, Shackleton converted the trapped ship into a winter station. In September, as the southern spring brought warmer temperatures, the breakup of the ice put pressure on the ship's hull. Late in October, water began pouring into the *Endurance*. Shackleton gave the order to abandon ship and transferred men, dogs, and provisions onto the ice. On November 21, 1915, the wreck slipped beneath the surface. "At 5 p.m. she went down," he noted. "I cannot write about it."

Now began the great test of Shackleton's perseverance. For more than four months, in freezing-cold temperatures, he and his men camped out on a massive, drifting ice floe. When in April 1916 it began breaking up, he ordered his men into the three remaining lifeboats. After five days in difficult seas, they landed on barren Elephant Island, having travelled a total of 560 kilometres from the wreck of the *Endurance*. This isolated spot, far from shipping lanes, offered subsistence living on seals and birds but no hope of rescue.

Having failed in his original objective, Shackleton vowed to bring all his men home safely. He decided to undertake an open-boat journey through notoriously stormy seas to the whaling stations of South Georgia, eight hundred nautical miles away. On April 24, 1916, with five companions, he set out in a seven-metre lifeboat with a makeshift deck and canvas. The boat nearly capsized several times. But two weeks later, thanks to an extraordinary feat of navigation and despite a fog, the sailors could discern the cliffs of South Georgia. Hurricane-force winds prevented a landing until the following day, May 9.

The rocky beach where finally Shackleton went ashore was bleak and empty. But rather than risk further voyaging, the hardy explorer decided to make for the whaling stations on the other side of the island. This meant hiking and climbing fifty kilometres across unknown, glaciated mountains. He set out with two men, one of them that Irish giant, Tom Crean, who had piloted the lifeboats to Elephant Island. Incredibly, after a thirty-six-hour march through icy, rocky, and mountainous terrain, the trio reached the whaling station named Stromness on May 20.

Shackleton sent a boat to collect the three men on the other side of South Georgia, and set to work planning the rescue of the twenty-two still waiting on Elephant Island. After trying and failing to depart three times, Shackleton gained control, thanks to the Chilean government, of a small tug. On August 30, 1916, with a whaler behind him, Shackleton reached Elephant Island and rescued his remaining men, all still alive. Before leaving the south, Shackleton also rescued the Ross Sea party, those who had got stranded in McMurdo Sound after the *Aurora* was driven out to sea. This group had lost three men.

Such was the expedition that turned Shackleton from merely famous to legendary. Back in England, with the First World War still raging, he volunteered for the army but was rejected because of a heart condition. He tried his hand at diplomacy and participated in an economic expedition to Murmansk. In 1919, he published *South,* an account of the *Endurance* expedition. The following year, he began proposing yet another expedition—this one into the Beaufort Sea area of the western Canadian Arctic. He acquired a 125-ton whaler and renamed it the *Quest,* but then changed his destination: he would voyage once more to the Antarctic, and there attempt a circumnavigation of that continent.

In September 1921, joined by many former crew members, he sailed from England. In Rio de Janeiro, Shackleton suffered a suspected heart attack. But he refused treatment, resumed voyaging, and reached South Georgia on January 4, 1922. In the early hours of the next morning, Shackleton suffered a fatal heart attack. He was buried, at the request of his wife, on his beloved South Georgia Island.

For the next several decades, the British celebrated Robert Falcon Scott as the pre-eminent polar hero. That began to change in 1959, when Alfred Lansing published *Endurance: Shackleton's Incredible Voyage.* Changing attitudes led to further analysis and criticism of Scott. By the early 2000s, Shackleton began featuring in books about leadership—works that, in Canada, not only proved successful, but became staples of seminars and courses on leadership. His *Endurance* expedition also gave rise to several documentaries and a hit TV series starring Kenneth Branagh.

At the request of his wife, Ernest Shackleton was buried on South Georgia Island. In 2014, Canadian photographer Michelle Valberg captured this image of his grave.

The Irish town of Athy, where Shackleton was born, began mounting an annual Shackleton Conference in the year 2000. As if to illustrate the cross-pollination and integration of polar exploration, north and south, the conference has featured Canadian lecturers and numerous presentations about explorers of the Canadian Arctic. Canada's exploration history is thriving in Shackleton country, and Shackleton himself deserves recognition in this northern land because, by example, he reminded so many Canadians of the value of never-say-die perseverance.

28.

John Palliser

▨▨▨

The original itinerary for the "VIA Rail, Cross-Canada, Ocean-to-Ocean, Book Tour Extravaganza" was almost perfect. The only problem was that our westbound train, the Canadian, did not run through the Rocky Mountain town of Banff, which is rich in Canadian history and personal memory. Sheena and I wanted to spend time in Banff National Park, once our hiking-and-skiing playground, and then drive north through the Rockies to reboard the train in Jasper. The drive would take us past Mount Sarbach, where in our early twenties, as fire lookouts, we had spent one magnificent summer in the heart of the Rockies. We would sit in the sun at 7,300 feet gazing out over Howse Pass, which provided a way through the mountains for native peoples, and then for a stream of explorers from David Thompson to Joseph Howse and James Hector.

Also, we wanted to visit Calgary, and to stay at the Palliser Hotel. I had contracted to write a few articles about this trip, including one about Canada's railway hotels, and could see no way to omit the Palliser. In the end, we did detrain in Saskatoon and fly to Calgary. I have already mentioned interviewing Mordecai Richler in the Oak Room at the Palliser. During the 1980s and '90s, while working as the books editor at the *Calgary Herald*, I attended all kinds of splashy events in that hotel. My favourite was the annual Bob Edwards Award Luncheon, so named for a Scottish-immigrant newspaperman.

Not only that, but for Calgarians, and indeed western Canadians, the Palliser Hotel commemorates one of the most important expeditions in exploration history. When it opened in 1914, the hotel took its name from a determined Irishman who had led a pivotal investigation into the geography and climate of western Canada. No westerner or even ex-westerner could omit the Palliser Expedition from a book like this one.

Flash back to 1857, decades before Calgary was incorporated. Seven hundred kilometres east of the present-day city, Captain John Palliser waited with his men near Moose Jaw Creek in what is now Saskatchewan. By now, two dozen Cree were accompanying the main body of this expedition. As leader, the Irishman worried that he had lost touch with the second wing of his party, led by the Scot James Hector and a Metis guide. But at last that contingent arrived with yet another group of Cree.

Hector brought stories of wars between the Cree and the Blackfoot, and the dangers Palliser and his men faced in charting these western lands. The previous night, according to historian Irene Spry, Hector had slept in a tent where a Blackfoot scalp hung. "The women danced around it," she reported, "forcing the captured wife of the dead brave to join them in the dance." Until recently, the Cree and the Blackfoot had been at peace, and would often camp together. But two dozen young Cree hotheads had recently made off with valuable Blackfoot horses, using previously built rafts to ferry the animals across a fast-flowing branch of the South Saskatchewan River.

The Blackfoot tracked them to the river's edge, then made a show of turning around and departing as if abandoning the chase. In fact, they proceeded upriver beyond a bend, then swam their remaining horses across the river and ambushed the young Cree. They killed seventeen before darkness enabled three or four to escape—including one man who had just arrived in camp. Palliser, though concerned, insisted on going forward: he would not be frightened into quitting.

He came of a prominent Anglo-Irish family whose ancestors had moved from England to Ireland in the 1600s. Born in Dublin in 1817, he had been educated partly on the European continent and spoke not only English but also French, German, and Italian. He had attended Trinity College, Dublin, for four years, but left in 1838 without taking a degree.

The following year, he became a captain in his father's regiment, the Waterford Artillery Militia, but he had seen little active service. He had served as a High Sheriff for a year, but with his brothers and friends, devoted himself mainly to travelling "in search of adventure and heavy game," as he wrote later. One of his friends had gone buffalo hunting in the American plains around the Missouri River, and in 1847, Palliser had set out to do the same in "the regions still inhabited by America's aboriginal people . . . that ocean of prairies extending to the foot of the great Rocky Mountains."

Palliser spent eleven months hunting buffalo, antelope, and grizzly in the American west, and returned home via New Orleans and Panama. Setting up in London, he drew on his extensive journals to produce a book entitled *Solitary Rambles and Adventures of a Hunter in the Prairies.* Published in 1853, it proved hugely popular. Of course, ranging around the prairies as a gentleman-hunter is one thing, and venturing into unexplored wilderness is another. But after getting himself elected a fellow of the Royal Geographical Society (RGS), Palliser submitted a plan to explore the southern prairies of British North America and to look for passes through the Rocky Mountains. He had a dream.

The RGS, aware that American expeditions were seeking railway routes to the Pacific Ocean, not only supported Palliser's plan, but proposed to add scientific assistants. The society requested a Colonial Office grant of five thousand pounds to finance the project (the equivalent today of more than fifteen million Canadian dollars). That office encouraged the project, but wanted to know additionally whether a train route might cross the plains through British territory, perhaps along the old fur-trade route of the North West Company. It also wanted an impartial perspective on whether the prairies could support agriculture and settlement.

Captain John Palliser (left) and geologist James Hector, an Irish-Scottish combination, made an outstanding contribution to the geography of western Canada.

In London, Palliser worked out detailed plans with the help of such figures as George Simpson, governor of the Hudson's Bay Company, and 'Edward Sabine, who was spearheading a British investigation into the shifting magnetic poles. At departure, Palliser's technical team included James Hector, an Edinburgh-born geologist and physician who would become his right-hand man. With these two figures at its head, this expedition presents an early instance of the Irish-Scottish alliance that would flower in Canada.

Palliser sailed for New York in May 1857. He crossed Lake Superior by steamship, then proceeded by canoe, relying on voyageur paddlers, to Lower Fort Garry and the Red River Settlement. Late in July, with horses and carts supplied by the HBC, he set out. He travelled south across the American border, then northwest and back into British territory, taking on the Metis guide James McKay at Fort Ellice. The expedition proceeded north and west, and Palliser listened when McKay warned that proceeding deeper into Blackfoot territory might prove dangerous. Early in October, Palliser established a winter camp on the North Saskatchewan River north of Saskatoon at the HBC's Fort Carlton.

Palliser now knew that these western lands were far more extensive than planners had imagined, and that he would need to stay out at least two summers more. Certainly, he had no intention of quitting. He needed to settle accounts with George Simpson of the HBC, and to have specialists repair certain magnetic instruments, and so he travelled east to Montreal and New York—a distance, return, of more than seven thousand kilometres.

Eventually, he would receive permission by telegraph to stay an extra summer. Meanwhile, after revisiting Simpson near Montreal, Palliser stopped in Hamilton to consult John Rae, who was then building a boat to undertake a private expedition into the Arctic. Later, in the Kananaskis range of the Rockies, Palliser would name Mount Rae after that explorer.

In the spring of 1858, from Fort Carlton, John Palliser resumed leading his expedition westward. Before entering the Rockies, he split it into two to explore mountain passes. He led one group south through the North Kananaskis and North Kootenay Passes, and rejoined the others to winter over at Fort Edmonton. James Hector had crossed the mountains through Vermilion Pass, and returned via Kicking Horse Pass, which got its name from an incident in which he was kicked unconscious by one of his horses.

At Fort Edmonton, Palliser and Hector got to know chief factor William Joseph Christie, who spoke several languages, enjoyed the confidence of the native peoples, and would later serve on the Temporary North-West Council, the first government for the Northwest Territories. In 1862, as if to illustrate a point made earlier in this book about the prevalence of Scottish Metis in the fur trade, a priest visiting from Quebec would quote Christie as declaring in perfect French: "I am myself a Métis By George! We are almost all Métis in the Company. Among the chief factors there is not a single Englishman, and maybe not ten Scots with pure blood."

During the winter of 1858, with Christie's encouragement, the indefatigable Palliser travelled two hundred kilometres southwest to Rocky Mountain House to meet Blackfoot and Northern Peigan natives. In 1859, he put what he had learned to use. After mapping the Cypress Hills, the expedition pushed west through the eastern Rockies, with Palliser using the North Kootenay Pass. Hector crossed through Howse Pass, which wended into the mountains beneath the as-yet-unnamed Sarbach Mountain, on which, more than a century later, from just above the treeline, Sheena and I would sit in the sun envisaging his progress.

Neither Palliser nor Hector could find a way through the Selkirk Range, which blocked their way farther west. Rogers Pass would not be discovered for two decades. Now the explorers canoed south to Fort Colville, just below the American border. From there, they paddled 965 kilometres down the Columbia River to Fort Vancouver on the Pacific Coast. After calling in at Fort Victoria, then commanded by James Douglas, the Scotch West Indian, Palliser and Hector travelled home by ship via San Francisco, Panama, Montreal, and Liverpool.

Palliser was awarded the Patron's Gold Medal of the Royal Geographical Society for his survey work. He presented his report to the British Parliament in 1863. He noted the existence of an extensive "fertile belt" bordering what became known as the Palliser Triangle in the southern prairies. That lower region, he reported, was too dry for agriculture. This finding was disregarded, much to the detriment and dismay of those who later tried to settle there.

Palliser warned that settlement would lead to the disappearance of the buffalo, and highlighted the need to provide for the future of the plains peoples who relied on that animal. His great map of his adventure, published in 1865, would prove an invaluable resource for later surveyors. With that map, his enduring work was done, his legacy created. John Palliser later travelled to the West Indies on a semi-official mission. And in 1869, with one of his brothers, he ventured north to Novaya Zemlya in the eastern Arctic, sailing in his own specially reinforced ship. But his importance rests on the pioneering work he did in western Canada.

When he died in 1887, Palliser was buried near the family estate in southwest Ireland at Kilmacthomas, Waterford—a village less than fifty kilometres from New Ross. That same year, a Scottish writer who embodied a different kind of perseverance would tell a reporter that the book which made his reputation had come to him in a dream.

29.

Robert Louis Stevenson

▨▨▨

In autumn 1885, by which time John Palliser had retired to his Irish country house, Robert Louis Stevenson was honing his writerly craft in Bournemouth, a resort town in the south of England. "I had long been trying to write a story on this subject," he later wrote, "to find a body, a vehicle, for that strong sense of man's double being which must at times come in upon and overwhelm the mind of every thinking creature." Two years before, according to biographer Claire Harman, Stevenson had been shocked by the death of a brilliant alcoholic friend, thirty-two-year-old Walter Ferrier. What he called the "awful smash and humiliation" of Ferrier's descent contrasted sharply with other memories. When he was drunk, Stevenson wrote, Ferrier was the "lunatic brother" of the "good, true Ferrier."

After his friend's death, Stevenson resumed working on a story, a "shocker" called "The Travelling Companion," which treated the divided self, but which he would destroy after the 1886 publication of *The Strange Case of Dr. Jekyll and Mr. Hyde.* The author's wife, Fanny Osbourne Stevenson, would describe being awakened early one morning in 1885 by her husband's "cries of horror." Thinking he was having a nightmare, and not knowing he was dreaming "a fine boguey tale," she had woken him at the first transformation scene.

The author himself, interviewed in New York City in 1887, told a reporter, "At night I dreamed the story, not precisely as it is written, for of course there are always stupidities in dreams, but practically it came to me as a gift." In this case, he dreamed "that one man was being pressed into a cabinet, when he swallowed a drug and changed into another being. I awoke and said at once that I had found the missing link for which I had been looking so long, and before I again went to sleep almost every detail of the story, as it stands, was clear to me."

▩▩

Before going further, a word about literary Scots. We have already introduced three outstanding eighteenth-century figures: Robert Burns, Walter Scott, and James Boswell. Robert Louis Stevenson (1850–1894) belongs to the next century, when a number of Scottish writers forged international reputations. Sir Arthur Conan Doyle (1859–1930), a Scot of Irish descent, helped shape the detective novel by inventing Sherlock Holmes. And in 1911, the Scotland-born J. M. Barrie (1860–1937) gave the world Peter Pan.

Early in the twentieth century, during a "Scottish Renaissance," Hugh MacDiarmid (1892–1978) led a push to revive the Scots language as a medium for serious poetic works. Late that century, another Scottish literary revival arose in reaction to the neoconservative initiatives of British prime minister Margaret Thatcher. The response showed up in works by James Kelman, Alasdair Gray, Liz Lochhead, James Robertson, and Irvine Welsh.

Robert Louis Stevenson, with his almost contemporary sensibility, stands near the beginning of this modernist tradition. At one point, after his wife, Fanny, criticized the first draft of *The Strange Case of Dr. Jekyll and Mr. Hyde*, Stevenson flung the manuscript into the fireplace. He then sat down and rewrote the work, producing sixty-four thousand words, according to his stepson, in six days. The author himself wrote: "Jekyll was conceived, written, rewritten, re-rewritten, and printed inside ten weeks." His publisher, Longman's, suspected that the book would be a hit, and decided to bring it out as a small book rather than a serial in its magazine. Stevenson, already celebrated for *Treasure Island*, had no idea that he had written an instant classic.

▨▨

Born in Edinburgh in November 1850, Robert Lewis Balfour Stevenson sprang from a long line of eminent engineers and builders of lighthouses. His grandfather had conducted no less a figure than Sir Walter Scott on a tour of Scottish lighthouses. His mother's family were landholding gentry, and from them he inherited a frail constitution. All his life he suffered from a debilitating lung condition, thought then to be tuberculosis but now believed to have been bronchiectasis, which involves obstructed airways.

His live-in nanny, Alison Cunningham (Cummy), was a fervent Free Church Calvinist whose tales of religious persecution gave the child nightmares, though she also cared for him lovingly. An only child, frequently ill, he did not learn to read until age seven or eight, but in his teens he took to writing obsessively. His father wanted him to become an engineer, and urged him to "give up such nonsense."

But then he financed the printing of his son's first story, an account of a Protestant Covenanters' rebellion. Already, at sixteen, Stevenson could write with panache: "Those who kept together—a miserable few—often halted to rest themselves, and to allow their lagging comrades to overtake them. Then onward they went again, still hoping for assistance, reinforcement, and supplies; onward again, through the wind, and the rain, and the darkness—onward to their defeat at Pentland, and their scaffold at Edinburgh."

When he was eighteen, Stevenson changed the spelling "Lewis" to "Louis" while retaining the original pronunciation, the most plausible reason being that his father had taken a fierce dislike to a political radical called David Lewis. Meanwhile, he honed his craft, and whenever he came across a passage showing "either some conspicuous force or some happy distinction in the style," he would sit down and try to emulate that success, and so "played the sedulous ape" to any number of notable stylists.

At the University of Edinburgh, Stevenson enrolled to study engineering, but gravitated to a debating club, the Speculative Society, and made his friends there. He used to go and write, he said later, at an old pub frequented by sailors, criminals, and "the lowest order of prostitutes—threepenny whores." He insisted that the girls were "singularly decent creatures, not a bit worse than anybody else."

Stevenson wore a black velvet smoking jacket and smoked a pipe, affecting a bohemian appearance. At twenty, he joined three literary law students in editing a new periodical called the *Edinburgh University Magazine*. His father rejected his notions of setting out on "the devious and barren paths of literature," but allowed him to shift from engineering to law. His best friend was his older cousin Robert (Bob) Stevenson, who was bent on becoming an artist, and with whom he mounted elaborate practical jokes.

Early in 1873, challenged by his father, he revealed that he no longer believed in Christianity, and that he had become an atheist. "If I had foreseen the real Hell of everything since," he wrote to a friend, "I think I should have lied as I have done so often before." The revelation opened an emotional gulf, but his father, though shocked, never ceased to support the young rebel. When illness laid Stevenson low, and doctors urged a change of climate, the engineer sent his only son to the south of France.

Late in 1873, while visiting his cousin Bob in England, Stevenson became friends with two figures well-connected in literary circles: Fanny Sitwell and Sidney Colvin. Colvin placed Stevenson's essay "Roads" in a paying magazine and introduced him to influential writers and editors. In 1875, he did qualify for the Scottish bar, though he went to court only once. He undertook a canoe trip with a friend, and in 1878 published a travel book about that adventure: *An Inland Voyage*.

Stevenson had begun a protean career as a writer who produced fiction, non-fiction, and poetry. He projected a book on "four great Scotsmen"—John Knox, David Hume, Robert Burns, and Walter Scott—but reduced it to essays on Knox and Burns. Thanks to his cousin Bob, he began visiting an artists' colony at Grez-sur-Loing in Belgium, just across the Channel, and there he fell in love with the melodramatic, unhappily married and separated American Fanny Osbourne. For a while, he lived with her and her children in France. She returned to California, and in August 1879, without informing his parents, and against the advice of his friends, Stevenson went after her.

He sailed to New York on a second-class ticket, and then took trains across the country. At one point, when a conductor put a drunk off the train, and the man reached for a gun, only Stevenson took him seriously. "They were speaking English all about me," he wrote later, "but I knew I was in a foreign land." Stevenson grew especially upset when his fellow passengers made fun of displaced native Americans: "I was ashamed for the thing we call civilisation."

The journey took a severe toll on his health: "I had no idea how easy it was to commit suicide," he wrote. "There seems nothing left of me; I died a while ago; I do not know who it is that is travelling." He reached California, but was soon flat on his back. Here we discover yet another kind of perseverance—a lifelong struggle that would pit debilitating and recurring illness against a writer's determination to live a life that would allow him to communicate his distinctive vision—a life devoted to literary creation.

By mid-October, he had convinced Fanny to divorce her estranged husband. Later, he credited her with nursing him back to health, and in May 1880, he married her in a civil ceremony. Then came a difficult sojourn in the hills south of San Francisco, an interlude Stevenson would turn into a book called *The Silverado Squatters*. By July, thanks to the generosity of his father, he and his wife were travelling back to Scotland, first class all the way. His American adventure had taught Stevenson that "I have been a Scotchman all my life, and denied my native land." This realization led him to write such Scottish-themed works as *Kidnapped*, *The Master of Ballantrae*, *Catriona*, and *Weir of Hermiston* (an unfinished masterpiece).

But first came *Treasure Island*, which features the unforgettable Long John Silver. This pirate tale, published in 1883 after serialization in a children's magazine, made Stevenson's name. With its treasure maps, tropical islands, talking parrots, and one-legged pirates, it would become iconic. Interestingly, given that modernism had yet to be born, *Treasure Island* gave rise, in Stevenson's hands, to a postmodern experiment—an astonishingly prescient development. In a story called "The Persons of the Tale," two main characters from *Treasure Island*, Long John Silver and Captain Smollett, take a break between chapters to smoke a pipe "not far from the story" and debate their relative importance to the author.

The cold, damp climate of Scotland urged Stevenson southwards, and again his father came through, providing a house in Bournemouth. Working from there, the author published two notable works in 1886: *Dr. Jekyll and Mr. Hyde* and *Kidnapped*, a historical novel which draws on the Jacobite history of Scotland. It explores historical differences between Lowland and Highland Scots, and stands comparison with the classic *Waverley* by Walter Scott.

No less a literary theorist than Henry James would insist that *Kidnapped* was no mere adventure story for boys, and hail "the author's talent for seeing the actual in the marvelous, and reducing the extravagant to plausible detail." He praised the creation of the Highland hero Alan Breck Stewart as "a masterpiece," and declared a quarrel in the mountains "a real stroke of genius [that] has the very logic and rhythm of life."

While battling debilitating illness, Robert Louis Stevenson managed to create such literary classics as Treasure Island, Kidnapped, *and* The Strange Case of Dr. Jekyll and Mr. Hyde.

In 1887, following the death of his father, and driven by his sick man's yearning for a more salubrious climate, Stevenson accepted an invitation from an American millionaire to revisit the United States. He sailed from England on "a tramp ship," an experience that dispelled his "cares and labors" and proved one of the happiest of his life. With this sailing, according to his stepson, Stevenson moved from one epoch of his life to another, as from then on he was "one of the most conspicuous figures in contemporary literature." According to the *Reader's Digest*, the very tugboats that escorted his ship into New York were nicknamed the *Jekyll* and the *Hyde*.

So began a westward push that would carry Stevenson, writing all the way, and backed by magazine and book publishers, to the South Sea Islands. He was still in New York when his widowed mother—wealthy, not yet sixty years old, and freed from domesticity—suggested sharing a voyage around the islands of the Pacific. Already in California on personal business, Fanny located a suitable yacht. And in June 1888, with his extended family, Stevenson sailed for the South Seas.

He never returned to Scotland. After six months in Hawaii, he explored the Pacific islands further. In 1890, he built a singular hillside estate in Samoa. He embroiled himself in local politics. His near contemporary Oscar Wilde did not approve: "In Gower Street [London]," Wilde opined, "Stevenson could have written a new *Trois Mousquetaires*. In Samoa he wrote letters to the *Times* about Germans."

But Wilde was not privy to the details of Stevenson's battle with illness, and so did not grasp that this relocation represented a creative solution to unique challenges. From Samoa, Stevenson wrote to a friend: "In the South Seas, I have health, strength, I can walk and ride and be out of doors, and do my work without distress . . . My feeling for my friends has pulled me hard; but can you wonder if the hope of . . . some snatch of the man's life after all these years of the sickroom tempted me extremely?"

Even so, Stevenson could extend his life only so long. On December 3, 1894, while in mid-conversation, he collapsed and died of a brain hemorrhage. Incredibly, given what he had accomplished, Robert Louis Stevenson was only forty-four years old. In *Rapt in Plaid: Canadian Literature and Scottish Tradition,* Canadian literary critic Elizabeth Waterston writes that "Stevenson's tales of adventures and escapes, of hardy travel and daring encounters, were closer to Canadian reality and Canadian dreams than were the spidery finenesses of a Henry James or the depressing naturalism" of many another writer.

Waterston sees his influence in the fiction of such early writers as Ralph Connor and L. M. Montgomery, and also in the poetry of Dennis Lee. The divided self (*Dr. Jekyll and Mr. Hyde*) turns up in Margaret Atwood's *Alias Grace,* where we encounter Grace Marks and Mary Whitney—two women in one. In Canadian non-fiction, Stevenson's work has given rise to numerous books. The best known would have to be that blockbuster by Flora Rheta Schreiber entitled *Sybil: The Classic True Story of a Woman Possessed by Sixteen Personalities.* Worth noting, as well, is Adam Crabtree's *Multiple Man: Explorations in Possession and Multiple Personality.*

For Canadians who discover it, Stevenson's story is inspirational. What lingers most vividly is the way he persevered. Chronic illness could not stop him. The man wrote through it. Joy and sadness, triumph or tragedy, Stevenson persevered. Nothing could stop him. In that respect, his life was like music . . . traditional Celtic music. Robert Louis Stevenson played on.

30.

The Chieftains

⬛⬛⬛

A wheeler-dealer American music promoter named Jo Lustig announced in Dublin that he had booked a semi-profes-sional band to play a St. Patrick's Day concert. The year was 1975. The projected venue: London's prestigious Royal Albert Hall, which holds six thousand seats. Band leader Paddy Moloney told the promoter he was barking mad. Outside of a festival situation, in which a number of musicians take turns onstage, the Chieftains had never performed in a club that held more than two hundred. Moloney said, "Jo, we're not ready for such a big concert."

Lustig pressed on. If he sold out that massive venue, he wanted the Chieftains to go full-time, with himself as manager. According to John Glatt, author of *The Chieftains: An Authorized Biography*, Moloney worried that the concert would be a disaster: "I knew that after 15 years hard work this could destroy the band if it flopped."

The other band members felt the same way. Even Lustig began to worry. But within two weeks, he had sold out the Royal Albert Hall. The day before the concert, on March 16, 1975, *Melody Maker* magazine ran a full-page preview headlined: "Chieftains on

Trial." Next night, when the seven Chieftains walked out onstage, the audience erupted into prolonged applause. Later, Moloney would liken it to "going into a football stadium and listening to the crowd roaring as the teams come onto the pitch." The band played for two and a half hours. No singing. No dancing. Just Irish traditional music.

At the end of their second set, after a single encore, the audience was still hollering for more. Bandmates hugged each other with tears in their eyes. And then they went back down the ramp to play on. "It was a great breakthrough for Irish music," Moloney said later. And bandmate Sean Keane put it this way: "We all knew that there was something different going on. There was a change. We were turning a corner and we were onto a new road."

The Dublin-based band had taken the name Chieftains a dozen years before. The musicians originally involved—Moloney, Sean Potts, Michael Tubridy, Michael Fay—had all been playing traditional Irish music since boyhood. Some of the instruments they played had endured for centuries. The timpan, for example, a form of hammer dulcimer, dates back to the fourth century, when troops of timpan players would lead armies into battle. The music lived on, and those who excelled at playing it were those who had earned the privilege of carrying it forward.

The Chieftains did not invent Celtic music. Neither does the band illustrate or exemplify perseverance. But Celtic music itself? That has shown remarkable staying power, travelling through time and across space. Anyone seeking an enduring meme, to use the term coined by Richard Dawkins, need look no further than this music. That is what Jo Lustig realized. Traditional Irish music had already established a presence when the Chieftains emerged onto the scene. But that band did serve as a remarkably effective conduit. It popularized the music in North America and elsewhere. The Chieftains represent those thousands of musicians who, most important, from the perspective of this book, helped install Celtic music in concert halls and pubs across Canada.

▨▨▨

Paddy Moloney, the bandleader-to-be, was born in a north Dublin suburb in 1938. He grew up in a musical family and at age four began playing his mother's single-row melodeon, a type of accordion. He turned to the tin whistle and then, four years later, discovered the uillean pipes. Developed in the eighteenth century as a more complex, indoor version of Irish or Scottish bagpipes, these instruments have a smaller bag filled not by blowing through the mouth but by a bellows held under the arm.

As a boy, Moloney immersed himself in traditional music, playing with older musicians at informal ceilidhs and in underground clubs. He made music as a hobby, in his free time, like virtually every other traditional musician in Ireland. At sixteen, to put bread on the table, he began working as an accountant trainee for Baxendales, a large Dublin-based supplier of building materials.

By the mid-1950s, Moloney was playing regularly with Michael Tubridy and Sean Potts, who were also holding down full-time jobs. In his early twenties, he joined Sean O'Riada's Ceoltoiri Chualann, a band which took traditional Irish songs and arranged them with a variety of instruments. "I was never happy with the thump, thump, thump," Moloney said later, "and all the instruments playing together in what I called 'thrash the beetle.' I always felt that there had to be something extra put in it."

In 1959, while still working at Baxendales, Moloney helped Garech Browne, heir to the Guinness fortune, create Claddagh Records. Two years later, when he attended a Celtic music festival in Brittany, France, Moloney realized that traditional Irish music belonged to a broad Celtic tradition: "The Breton music punched me completely with its incredibly melodic form that fitted in perfectly with traditional Irish music. I've never lost hold of it since."

When Garech Browne invited Moloney to form a group with a view to making records, the composer-arranger jumped at the chance: "I knew exactly what I wanted to achieve." He wanted to go beyond "just reels, jigs and hornpipes," he said later. "I wanted to create a different flavour of music with songs and airs." Moloney had thought to call the band the Quare 'Fellows after a play by Brendan Behan. But writer friend John Montague, later to occupy the Ireland Chair of Poetry, was working on a book of stories called *Death of a Chieftain*, and suggested a better name.

The self-titled album surfaced in 1963. It garnered radio play and led to a first public appearance, following a harp competition, at Dublin's Gresham Hotel on downtown O'Connell Street. At the urging of Garech Browne, Moloney left his job at Baxendales, where he had risen to become an executive, to focus full-time on making music.

In 1968, the Chieftains played for a week at the Edinburgh Festival on the same bill as the Scottish duo the Corries. By now, Moloney had become the main record producer for Claddagh, and had supervised the recording of forty-five albums. He made fans of rock stars Mick Jagger and Marianne Faithfull, who said Moloney "used to tell Mick and me about his mission to spread traditional music through the world and we thought he was wonderful."

On the band's second album, *The Chieftains 2*, Moloney—the band's main arranger—recorded a work composed by the blind harpist Turlough O'Carolan, who lived in the mid-1600s. He also composed a track called "The Fox Hunt," which recreates the sounds of hunting horns, galloping horses, and barking dogs, and pointed the way to future orchestrated works. By the early 1970s, the Chieftains were receiving offers to go professional—all but Moloney were still holding down day jobs—and produce an electric album of Celtic rock. Moloney said no: "I wanted to follow the lines of the true tradition."

The Chieftains did a first American tour in 1972 and drew raves in the New York Irish press. "It was ridiculous," according to Sean Keane, one of the slowly changing roster of band members. "I was up a telegraph pole hanging lines the day after I got back from New York but my head was in another place."

After a visit to western Ireland, Moloney composed "The Battle of Aughrim," his most ambitious work yet. It evokes the climactic 1691 battle between the Irish Jacobites and the forces of King William III, an epic struggle that, as he walked near the historical site, evolved in his mind like a vision. He put "Aughrim" on *Chieftains 4,* and later told Glatt, the biographer, that he often felt he belonged in that distant past, where things happened at a slower pace. "Things that happened were talked about for a whole year. So you know it meant something. And that's why there was better music composed in those days."

After the 1975 concert at the Royal Albert Hall in London, despite the enthusiastic reception and the promises of the new manager, Moloney had a tough time convincing the other band members to leave their jobs. Including children, the current group of Chieftains had twenty-seven mouths to feed, so it was a big decision. Finally, Moloney persuaded the others to go full-time for three years, as an experiment.

The rest, of course, is musical history. A second appearance at the Royal Albert Hall prompted a writer from *Melody Maker* to hail the Chieftains as having more real power than any dozen electric bands: "It was my first exposure to the traditional Irish music that is their forte, and it was like being confronted with a life source, a purity that has not been allowed to degenerate, nor has been robbed or made sterile like many other ethnic music forms."

Filmmaker Stanley Kubrick convinced the Chieftains to provide much of the soundtrack for *Barry Lyndon*, a movie that won four Oscars. That soundtrack led to a full-scale tour of North America, which included a wildly enthusiastic reception in Toronto. In New York, journalist Geoffrey Stokes criticized the Chieftains for refusing to comment on the Troubles between the north and the south of Ireland. "The Chieftains not only ignore that conflict," he wrote, "they negate it, participating in it only as anthropologists rather than believers."

Later, to the Chieftains' biographer, Moloney defended the band's apolitical stance. Sounding more like a postmodern Canadian than a nineteenth-century Fenian, he pointed out that Irish traditional music goes back far beyond ideological differences: "One great thing is that at our concerts we do have Protestants and Catholics. There's no religious or political barrier."

Over the years and indeed decades, with Moloney and three other musicians providing a core group, the Chieftains evolved slowly, subtracting some members and adding others while remaining true to the music. They have played with everyone from Van Morrison to Sinéad O'Connor and the Dubliners, from Luciano Pavarotti to the Rolling Stones, Madonna, Tom Jones, Jackson Browne, Ricky Skaggs, and Willie Nelson. For one gala production, Moloney brought in step-dancer Michael Flatley, who later created *Riverdance*, to lead a group of dancers in a grand finale. The Chieftains also pointed up the universality of the ancient music by collaborating with musicians in France, Spain, Mexico, South America, and even China and Japan.

Among Canadian musicians, the Chieftains have played with Ashley MacIsaac, Sarah McLachlan, and Joni Mitchell. In Japan, as part of a Great Music Experience broadcast to over thirty countries, they played with Mitchell on her elaborate protest song "The Magdalene Laundries," which depicts the shameful treatment accorded unwed mothers by the Catholic Church in Ireland. Fellow musician Ry Cooder described that "bone-chilling" performance as the zenith of the whole concert.

For Moloney, tellingly, the concert highlight was meeting Japanese musicians and discovering how much, musically, he shared with them. "I remember we went into a room with the Okinawans and we just started playing and they joined in. It was totally incredible. You wouldn't believe how we all jelled together." Cooder, a celebrated American guitarist and musical theorist, claims that Moloney has a special talent "for spotting connections in music from different countries and then bridging the gap . . . If you are looking at diatonic music, which probably half the world is into historically, Irish music is as deep as any of it, and it fits. Somehow it will link up with just about everything because of the scales and melodies."

For the past half century, the Chieftains have been channelling traditional Irish music. Here in Canada, that music is everywhere: ubiquitous, pervasive. This country's larger cities all have numerous Irish pubs that regularly feature traditional music. And the smaller centres? Fredericton has the James Joyce, Windsor has the Kilt and Fiddle, Kelowna has O'Flannigan's, and the list goes on. Paddy Moloney has often said that he had "a dream to spread the gospel about Irish music and what it really is."

Here in Canada, at least, we can only say: mission accomplished. For contemporary Canadians, the music of the Chieftains, and of all those who keep the tradition alive, constitutes a direct pipeline to our ancestral past. Yes, we say when musicians strike up a tune in a pub. Yes, we say to the sounds of our ancestors. Yes, we can hear you. Yes.

The Day Lightning Struck

⌘

While visiting Ottawa not long ago, strolling along the Sparks Street Mall, I stopped at the plaque dedicated to Thomas D'Arcy McGee. It rightly identifies him as a "journalist, poet, Irish patriot, Canadian statesman, and father of Confederation." And it mentions several dates: 1848, fled to the United States; 1857, settled in Montreal; 1858, elected to the legislature; April 7,1868, "felled near this site by an assassin's bullet." But what I noticed was that the plaque omits what I have come to regard as the most significant date of all: October 2, 1863. That was the day Thomas D'Arcy McGee, a Roman Catholic Irishman, crossed the floor of the Canadian House of Commons to join forces with John A. Macdonald, a Protestant Scot.

I was researching this book, and I reflected that this Irish-Scottish alliance, which gave rise to Confederation, has ancient antecedents. Later, I would detail what raced through my mind: the intertwined saga that has wound through this book. Once upon a time, the Irish and the Scots were essentially one Celtic people. In the 500s, the Irish missionary Saint Columba built an abbey on the Scottish island of Iona and, from there, promulgated a Celtic-Christian culture that united most of those who lived in Ireland and Scotland. That culture became more complex while absorbing an influx of Scandinavians that started in the 800s. It became Norse-Gaelic. As late as 1094, the Gaelic-speaking, Scotland-born Norseman Godred Crovan ruled a kingdom comprising the Scottish Hebrides, Dublin, the Isle of Man, and key parts of Ireland.

Centrifugal forces then became dominant. In 1164, Somerled of Argyll tried and failed to recreate Crovan's unified sea world of Gaelic-speakers. In the early 1300s, Robert the Bruce of Scotland sought to create a pan-Gaelic alliance. He found an Irish ally in Donal O'Neil, Earl of Tyrone. With the Anglo-Normans expanding their influence, he argued that the Scots and the Irish shared the same ancestry, as well as a common language and customs. But in southern Ireland, clan chieftains regarded the Scots as no different from the Anglo-Normans, and the initiative failed.

From the political agenda, reunification vanished. As distinct nations, the Scots and the Irish created separate traditions of heroes and heroines. Separately, they developed ideals which they passed on from one generation to the next. Separately, they learned to value independence, democracy, pluralism, audacity, and perseverance. Individually, they never lost contact. In the 1560s, when the Irish Pirate Queen set out to reassert her primacy at sea, she sailed with some two hundred sailors, among them scores of elite Norse-Gaelic warriors from Scotland. Later that century, when the Great O'Neill began openly resisting English encroachment, he ignored orders to stop communicating with the Scots and hired hundreds of those same Scottish troops, with whom he shared a language and culture.

Flash forward two centuries. With the landscape transformed, and the English language pre-eminent, Walter Scott and Maria Edgeworth forged a Scottish-Irish literary friendship that made a difference to both. In the mid-1800s, when Irish explorer John Palliser set out to map western Canada, he brought the Scottish James Hector as his right-hand man. Later that century, William Butler Yeats wrote to an Edinburgh-based Scot about mounting plays, arguing that they might do more than anything else "to make the Irish, Scots, and other Celts recognize their solidarity."

The Irish Catholic poet Seamus Heaney, a winner of the Nobel Prize for Literature, wrote a paean to Robert Burns, Scotland's national poet. And while still based in Ireland, Thomas D'Arcy McGee hailed Scottish intellectual David Urquhart as "one of the most remarkable men of the age." From Urquhart, McGee gleaned an appreciation both of federalism and of the British crown as a symbol of liberty.

None of these personal relationships changed the world. But then Thomas D'Arcy McGee met John A. Macdonald. Having settled in Canada in the late 1850s, McGee had already begun calling for the creation of "a new nationality." In his biography of Macdonald, Richard Gwyn acknowledges McGee as "Canada's first nationalist," and the first to articulate a vision "of Canada as something larger than the sum of its parts."

Conventional Canadian history tells us that Confederation became almost inevitable after three influential politicians became allies: John A. Macdonald, George Brown, and George-Étienne Cartier—two Scottish Protestants and a French Roman Catholic. But this narrative discounts the aversion to Confederation then prevalent in New Brunswick, Prince Edward Island, and Nova Scotia. The man who single-handedly overcame this opposition was Thomas D'Arcy McGee.

In the drive to Confederation, the "irreplaceable man" is said to be John A. Macdonald. But Macdonald was only half of the irreplaceable element. He would have failed without McGee, who brought vision, audacity, and eloquence to the creation of Canada, eliminating deep-rooted maritime opposition to the project before the Charlottetown Conference began. McGee's passion and eloquence brought Nova Scotia and New Brunswick into Confederation with Ontario and Quebec. As historian Owen Dudley Edwards, based for years at the University of Edinburgh, has observed: "If there was one man from whom all Celts and all Canadians have everything to learn today, it is Thomas D'Arcy McGee."

Richard Gwyn tell us that Macdonald responded to the romantic visionary in McGee. For his part, McGee saw in Macdonald someone who could get things done. The gesture of mutual recognition came in Ottawa on October 2, 1863, during a stormy debate about the projected intercolonial railway. As I stood there on the Sparks Street Mall, that is what came to me. Biographer David A. Wilson describes how, sitting as an independent, McGee accused the Reform government of behaving like "a pack of tricksters" towards the maritime colonies.

He was one of the few Canadians who had visited Nova Scotia and New Brunswick. He answered an attack by praising Macdonald as a statesman "of large and liberal views." And he contrasted Macdonald with Reform government leaders, "whose religious prejudices and narrow-minded views" rendered their party "obnoxious to a large class of the community." Then, following what a journalist described as "one of the most eloquent, witty, and caustic speeches" he ever delivered, McGee crossed the floor to the "loud and prolonged cheers" of Macdonald's Conservatives, who were temporarily in opposition.

Contemporary Canada became feasible when Thomas D'Arcy McGee threw in his lot with John A. Macdonald. Working together, these two, the Irish Catholic and the Scottish Protestant, launched the political process that led to Confederation and beyond. Their alliance marks a reunification of a Celtic people divided for centuries, and a collaboration that sealed those bedrock values elaborated in this book. October 2, 1863: that was the day McGee crossed the floor of the House of Commons to join Macdonald. In the creation of Canada, that is the day when two charged traditions came together. That is the day lightning struck.

Top: On the Isle of Man, Snaefell Mountain offers a view of seven kingdoms, usually identified as those of England, Scotland, Ireland, Wales, Man, Heaven, and the Sea. The mountain takes its name from the Old Norse for "snow mountain." Bottom: We visited Dunnottar Castle, a ruined medieval fortress on the northeast coast of Scotland, while voyaging with Adventure Canada. Dunnottar was the hiding place of the Honours of Scotland during the seventeenth-century invasion of Oliver Cromwell.

Acknowledgements

※※

A s a long-time professional writer, I am no stranger to rejection. So when I received word from the Canada Council that I had been awarded a juried grant to develop this book, I whooped and did a happy dance. That grant made a difference. I am also grateful to Adventure Canada (and Matthew Swan) for inviting me to sail around Scotland and Ireland while researching this book, and to Tourism Ireland for providing travel assistance. The Royal Society of Edinburgh brought me to Scotland for a speaking engagement, and the Stromness Museum to Orkney to spend a week as writer-in-residence. These votes of confidence, too, were much appreciated.

Sections of this work have appeared, in different form, in *Celtic Life International*, *Canada's History*, *Destinations*, the *Globe and Mail*, the *National Post*, and *The Arctic Journals of John Rae*. To a glaring omission, I much prefer a slight overlap, so I have revisited a few figures from *How the Scots Invented Canada*.

This is my seventh book with the team at HarperCollins Canada, who are probably the best in the business. I want to give a shout-out to Rob Firing, Leo MacDonald, Colleen Simpson, Alan Jones, Noelle Zitzer, Michael Guy-Haddock, Cory Beatty, and Maria Golikova. Copy editor Chandra Wohleber also did a superb job. This is my first time publishing with Patrick Crean, and I can tell you that his stellar reputation as a substantive editor is well deserved. He made a big difference to this book. Thanks for that! My agent, Beverley Slopen, was involved from the get-go, and showed yet once more why she is renowned throughout the book industry. On the home front, I owe thanks to the usual suspects: Keriann, Carlin, Sylwia, Travis, James, and Veronica. Last but not least, check out the photo credits. Without Sheena Fraser McGoogan, my photographer, life partner, and fellow traveller, this book would not exist—and that is the truth. Long may we run.

Select References

Angel, Barbara, and Michael Angel. *Letitia Hargrave and Life in the Fur Trade.* Agincourt, ON: Book Society of Canada, 1981.

Bentman, Raymond. *Robert Burns.* Boston: Twane Publishers, 1987.

Bermingham, Ann, and John Brewer. *The Consumption of Culture 1600–1800: Image, Object, Text.* London: Routledge, 1997.

Bew, Paul. *Enigma: A New Life of Charles Stewart Parnell.* Dublin: Gill & Macmillan, 2011.

Boswell, James. *The Life of Samuel Johnson.* Hertfordshire: Wordsworth Editions, 1999.

Bowker, Gordon. *James Joyce: A Biography.* London: Weidenfeld & Nicolson, 2011.

Buchan, John. *Sir Walter Scott.* New York: Coward-McCann, 1932.

Butler, Marilyn. *Maria Edgeworth: A Literary Biography.* Oxford, UK: Oxford University Press, 1972.

Campey, Lucille H. *An Unstoppable Force: The Scottish Exodus to Canada.* Toronto: Dundurn, 2008.

Chambers, Anne. *Ireland's Pirate Queen: The True Story of Grace O'Malley.* New York: MJF Books, 1998, 2003.

Coogan, Tim Pat. *Michael Collins: A Biography.* London: Hutchinson, 1990.

Cook, Judith. *Pirate Queen: The Life of Grace O'Malley, 1530–1603*. Polmont, Stirlingshire: Mercier Press, 2004.

Creighton, Donald. *John A. Macdonald: The Old Chieftain*. Toronto: Macmillan, 1955.

———. *John A. Macdonald: The Young Lion*. Toronto: Macmillan, 1952.

Daiches, David. *James Boswell and His World*. London: Thames & Hudson, 1976.

Damrosch, Leo. *Jonathan Swift: His Life and His World*. London and New Haven: Yale University Press, 2013.

Dawkins, Richard. *The Selfish Gene*. Oxford, UK: Oxford University Press, 2006.

Douglas, Hugh. *Flora MacDonald: The Most Loyal Rebel*. Gloucestershire: Sutton Publishing, 1993.

Edwards, Owen Dudley. "Ireland and Nationalism in Scotland and Wales." In *The Celtic Consciousness*. Edited by Robert O'Driscoll. New York: George Braziller, 1981.

Elliott, Marianne. *Wolfe Tone: Prophet of Irish Independence*. New Haven and London: Yale University Press, 1989.

Ellmann, Richard. *Four Dubliners: Wilde, Yeats, Joyce, and Beckett*. New York: George Braziller, 1987.

———. *James Joyce*. New York, Oxford, Toronto: Oxford University Press, 1982.

———. *Oscar Wilde*. London: Penguin, 1987, 1988.

———. *Yeats: The Man and the Masks*. New York: Macmillan, 1948; Norton, 1978.

Fisher, Andrew. *William Wallace*. Edinburgh: John Donald/Berlinn, 2002.

Foster, R. F. *W. B. Yeats: A Life*. Vol. I, *The Apprentice Mage*. Oxford, New York: Oxford University Press, 1998.

Geoghegan, Patrick M. *King Dan: The Rise of Daniel O'Connell, 1775–1829*. Dublin: Gill & Macmillan, 2008.

Girard, Charlotte S. M. "Sir James Douglas' Mother and Grandmother." *B.C. Studies*, no. 44 (Winter 1978–79).

Glatt, John. *The Chieftains: The Authorized Biography*. New York: St. Martin's Press, 1997.

Goring, Rosemary. *Scotland: The Autobiography*. London: Viking, 2007.

Gwyn, Richard. *John A. The Man Who Made Us: The Life and Times of John A. Macdonald*. Vol. 1, *1815–1867*. Toronto: Random House, 2007.

———. *Nation Maker. Sir John A. Macdonald: His Life, Our Times*. Vol. 2, *1867–1891*. Toronto: Random House, 2011.

Harman, Claire. *Robert Louis Stevenson: A Biography*. London: HarperCollins, 2005.

Harper, Marjory. *Adventures & Exiles: The Great Scottish Exodus*. London: Profile Books, 2004.

Hayes, Derek. *First Crossing: Alexander Mackenzie, His Expedition across North America, and the Opening of the Continent*. Vancouver: Douglas & McIntyre, 2001.

Heilbroner, Robert L. *The Essential Adam Smith*. New York and London: W. W. Norton, 1986.

Huntford, Roland. *Shackleton*. London: Hodder & Stoughton, 1985.

Jeffares, Norman A. *W. B. Yeats: A New Biography*. London: Hutchinson, 1988.

Joyce, James. *Dubliners*. Corrected text. London: Jonathan Cape, 1967.

———. *A Portrait of the Artist as a Young Man*. London: Jonathan Cape, 1924.

Kee, Robert. *The Laurel and the Ivy: The Story of Charles Stewart Parnell and Irish Nationalism*. London: Penguin Books, 1994.

Kelly, James. "'No Dumb Ireland': Robert Burns and Irish Cultural Nationalism in the Nineteenth Century." *Eire-Ireland* 47 (Fall/Winter 2012): 251–268.

Kenneally, Christine. *The Invisible History of the Human Race: How DNA and History Shape Our Identities and Our Futures*. New York: Viking, 2014.

MacDermot, Frank. *Theobald Wolfe Tone*. London: Macmillan, 1939.

MacDiarmid, Hugh. *John Knox*. Edinburgh: Ramsay Head Press, 1976.

Mackey, James A. *Robert Bruce: King of Scots*. London: Robert Hale, 1974.

MacPhee, Kathleen. *Somerled: Hammer of the Norse*. Glasgow: Neil Wilson Publishing, 2004.

Marsden, John. *Somerled and the Emergence of Gaelic Scotland*. East Lothian: Tuckwell Press, 2000.

Marshall, Rosalind K. *John Knox*. Edinburgh: Birlinn, 2008.

Martin, Peter. *A Life of James Boswell*. London: Weidenfeld & Nicolson, 1999.

McCavitt, John. *The Flight of the Earls*. Dublin: Gill & Macmillan, 2002.

McDonald, R. Andrew. *The Kingdom of the Isles: Scotland's Western Seaboard c. 1100–c. 1336*. Edinburgh: Tuckwell Press, 1997.

McGee, Thomas D'Arcy. *Popular History of Ireland from the Earliest Period to the Emancipation of the Catholics*. Vol. I. Glasgow: Cameron & Ferguson, 1863.

Moffat, Alistair. *The Sea Kingdoms: The Story of Celtic Britain & Ireland*. London: HarperCollins Publishers, 2001.

Moore, Christopher. *1867: How the Fathers Made a Deal*. Toronto: McClelland & Stewart, 1997.

Moore, David W. *The Other British Isles: A History of Shetland, Orkney, the Hebrides, Isle of Man, Anglesey, Scilly, Isle of Wight and the Channel Islands*. Jefferson, NC: McFarland & Co., 2005.

New, William H. "McGill Movement." In *Encyclopedia of Literature in Canada*. Edited by W. H. New. Toronto: University of Toronto Press, 2002.

O'Connor, Frank. *The Big Fellow*. New York: Picador, 1937, 1998.

O'Faolain, Sean. *The Great O'Neill: A Biography of Hugh O'Neill, Earl of Tyrone, 1550–1616*. New York: Duell, Sloan and Pearce, 1941.

O'Hagan, Andrew. *A Night Out with Robert Burns: The Greatest Poems*. Toronto: McClelland & Stewart, 2009.

Phelan, Josephine. *Ardent Exile: The Life and Times of D'Arcy McGee*. Toronto: Macmillan, 1951.

Prebble, John. *The King's Jaunt: George IV in Scotland, 1822*. London: Collins, 1988.

Reid, W. Stanford. *Trumpeter of God: A Biography of John Knox*. New York: Charles Scribner's Sons, 1974.

Ridley, Jasper. *John Knox*. New York and Oxford: Oxford University Press, 1968.

Ross, Ian Simpson. *The Life of Adam Smith*. Oxford: Clarendon Press, 1995.

Schmidt, Michael. *The Novel: A Biography*. Cambridge, MA: Harvard University Press, 2014.

Scott, Ronald McNair. *Robert the Bruce: King of Scots*. New York: Peter Bedrick Books, 1989.

Sisman, Adam. *Boswell's Presumptuous Task: Writing the Life of Dr. Johnson*. London: Penguin, 2000.

Sjoholm, Barbara. *The Pirate Queen: In Search of Grace O'Malley and Other Legendary Women of the Sea*. Berkeley: Seal Press, 2004.

Spry, Irene M. *The Palliser Expedition*. Toronto: Macmillan, 1963.

Stanley, Michael. *Famous Dubliners*. Dublin: Wolfhound Press, 1996.

Sykes, Brian. *Saxons, Vikings, and Celts: The Genetic Roots of Britain and Ireland.* New York: Norton, 2006.

Theall, Donald, and Joan Theall. "Marshall McLuhan and James Joyce: Beyond Media." *Canadian Journal of Communications* (Simon Fraser University) 14, no. 4 (1989): 46–66.

Tranter, Nigel. *Lord of the Isles.* London: Hodder & Stoughton, 1983.

Trench, Charles Chenevix. *The Great Dan: A Biography of Daniel O'Connell.* London: Jonathan Cape, 1984.

Tytler, Patrick Fraser. *Lives of Scottish Worthies.* London: John Murray, 1831.

Waite, P. B. *The Life and Times of Confederation, 1864–1867: Politics, Newspapers and the Union of British North America.* Toronto: Robin Brass Studio,1962, 2001.

Warkentin, Germaine. *Canadian Exploration Literature: An Anthology.* Don Mills, ON: Oxford University Press, 1993.

Wilson, David A. *Thomas D'Arcy McGee.* 2 vols. Montreal: McGill-Queen's University Press, 2008, 2011.

Yanofsky, Joel. "Mordecai's Version." *Quill and Quire*, no. 12 (1997).

ILLUSTRATION CREDITS

※※

Celtic Lightning features sixty-five images. Sheena Fraser McGoogan contributed the vast majority (forty-three) of these: frontispiece (2), and pages 29, 30, 34, 36, 41, 52, 69, 83, 92, 121, 125, 131, 132, 138, 142, 147, 149, 163, 164, 175, 187 (2), 190, 194, 199, 203, 230, 241, 244, 249, 253, 255, 280, 292, 297, 309, 316, 319, 334, 372 (2).

p. 116: Photo courtesy of Stephen Morrissey.
p. 331: Photo courtesy of Michelle Valberg / Valberg Imaging.

All other pictures come courtesy of Wikimedia Commons, which makes available images in the public domain.

p. 22:   U.S. Library of Congress, cph.3b15295.
p. 61:   Project Gutenberg 13112.png.
p. 77:   nl: Gebruiker: Kansterle.
p. 98:   U.S. Library of Congress: LC-BH83-555.
p. 107: Library & Archives Canada: C-016749.
p. 143: U.S. Library of Congress: LC-DIC-pga-01586.
p. 154: Czech Academy of Sciences: HumL/31.1889/17/139.png.
p. 182: Perry-Castaneda Library, University of Texas. William Humphrey. From E.A. Duyckinck's Portrait *Gallery of Eminent Men and Women in Europe and America* (1873).
p. 203: *The International Magazine*, Dec. 1, 1850.
p. 214: Stephen Allen Spencer, d. 1911. BC Archives: sn-3B3C70C.
p. 224: Napoleon Sarony, 1882. Wikimedia Commons 151130601.
p. 262: Richard Wilson, d. 1782. Sotheby's ecatalogue 2012: L12034.
p. 274: Wellcome Library, London. ICV No. 7057. Photo: V0006842. Creative Commons License BY 4.0. Engraving by William Walker, after James E. Doyle. Published 1 July 1848.

p. 287: John Downman, 1807. www.nancycudis.com/2012/03/.

p. 310: J.H. Schofield, 1835. University of Manitoba Archives, MacLeod Fonds, PC 13 (Box 1, Fd. 1, Item 8).

p. 316: HBC Company Archives / National Archives of Canada/C-16826/A.

p. 323: Illustrated London News, Oct. 28, 1854.

p. 333: The Heart of the Antarctic, 1909. NOAA Corps Collection: corp2866.

p. 339: Frank Hurley, April 1916. South, E. Shackleton, 1919.

p. 357: Robert Louis Stevenson Knox Series, 1880 (trussel.com / rls-pc 1).

Map on endpapers by Dawn Huck.

A Celtic
Perspective

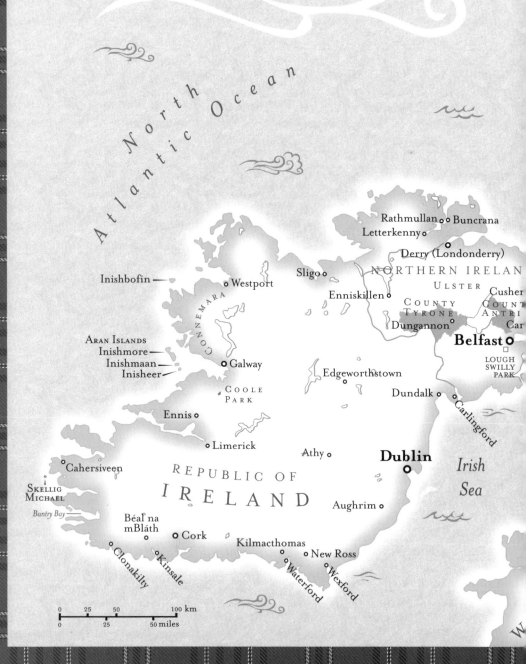

North
Atlantic Ocean

Rathmullan o o Buncrana
Letterkenny o
Derry (Londonderry) o
Inishbofin — o Westport
Sligo o NORTHERN IRELAN
ULSTER
Enniskillen o Cusher
COUNTY COUNT
TYRONE ANTRI
Dungannon o Car
ARAN ISLANDS
Inishmore — o Galway **Belfast** o
Inishmaan —
Inisheer — LOUGH
SWILLY
PARK
COOLE Edgeworthstown o
PARK
Dundalk o o
Ennis o Carlingford
Limerick o Athy o **Dublin** o
Cahersiveen o REPUBLIC OF Irish
SKELLIG Sea
MICHAEL I R E L A N D
Bantry Bay — Aughrim o
Béal na
mBláth
o Cork Kilmacthomas
Clonakilty Kinsale New Ross o
Waterford Wexford

0 25 50 100 km
0 25 50 miles